THE
CANADIAN
AUTO WORKERS

THE CANADIAN AUTO WORKERS

The Birth and Transformation of a Union

Sam Gindin

James Lorimer & Company, Publishers
Toronto, 1995

James Lorimer & Company Ltd. acknowledges with thanks the support of the Canada Council, the Ontario Arts Council and the Ontario Publishing Centre in the development of writing and publishing in Canada.

Cover design based on Clive Gardner poster.
Excerpt from "I Am the People, the Mob" in CHICAGO POEMS by Carl Sandburg, copyright 1916 by Holt, Rinehart and Winston, Inc. and renewed 1944 by Carl Sandburg, reprinted by permission of Harcourt Brace & Company.

Canadian Cataloguing in Publication Data
Gindin, Sam
    The Canadian Auto Workers: the birth and transformation of a union

Includes bibliographical references.
ISBN 1-55028-499-1 (bound) ISBN 1-55028-498-3 (pbk.)

1. CAW–Canada – History. 2. International Union, United Automobile Aerospace and Agricultural Implement Workers of America. Canadian Region – History. 3. Trade-unions – Automobile industry workers – Canada – History. I. Title.

HD6528.A82C384   1995   331.88'1292'097109
C95–932099–7

James Lorimer & Company Ltd., Publishers
35 Britain Street
Toronto, Ontario M5A 1R7
Printed and bound in Canada

Contents

To those workers and their families,
named and unnamed, past and present,
who built and sustained this union.

Preface

This book is not a history of the CAW, but an essay on that history. My goal is not to be comprehensive in the sense of documenting every strike and struggle, but to address and develop questions and themes that are relevant to the union in the present, and are likely to continue to be relevant in the future.

The Canadian section of the UAW emerged in the 1930s. The breakthrough came after the twenties, a decade when trade unionism seemed to have lost its dynamism, and during a period when capitalism itself seemed to have exhausted its potential. The birth of the union in Canada was very much inspired by the struggles of American workers, and the Americans generally continued to play a leading role in our relationship with them over the next forty-five years.

Yet in the mid-eighties, the Canadians suddenly decided to break from the Americans and establish their own union. What accounted for that Canadian change of heart and mind? Was it as sudden as it seemed? How did the Canadians develop the confidence to go off on their own, especially at a time when the economic and political élite were pushing the Canadian economy towards greater integration with the U.S.? What further changes did the creation of a new Canadian union demand? These questions cannot be addressed without considering the history of the union and its changing culture: how the union operated, how it saw itself, how it addressed its limits and goals.

This focus on the breakaway in 1985 meant a concentration on the traditional section of the union: heavy manufacturing in central Canada. But just as the Canadian UAW was transformed over time into the CAW, the union was transformed again by the mergers, new organizing, and changes it faced in the decade after 1985. I have not dealt in detail with the wide range of histories and rich experiences that came with the new groups for the obvious reason that doing them justice would have required a level of research and familiarization that wasn't possible within the time limits this book faced.

I hope that CAW members and others who open this book will find it informative and interesting, but above all that it will stimulate them to develop their own local and union histories and challenge them to think more self-consciously about their individual responsibilities in building the union and shaping history. History helps us to understand how things happened and why. But that understanding is only a base for addressing how we can participate in determining what happens next.

Like all books, this one was completed only because of the support and help of others who considered the project worth doing. Buzz Hargrove and Jimmy O'Neil not only encouraged me to start it, but kept it going by refusing to accept any arguments I made for postponing it. My friends and co-workers in research services picked up, with no complaints, the slack while I was gone. Nick Saul assisted with some of the research and was a ready sounding board. Nancy Kearnan, who works with me as a secretary, passed decisive judgement — as she's been doing on my writing for fifteen years — on the book's relevance and readability. Kathy Bennett, the CAW librarian, was always ready with useful archival advice and found things, it often seemed, before I had finished asking for them. And Ron Dickson, who just by being there shared his quiet dignity with us, also agreed to share some of his poetry in the pages of the book. The Centre for Work and Society at York University provided me with an office I could hide in, away from distractions.

A number of people read through sections of the manuscript and offered, sometimes quite detailed, suggestions: Charlotte Yates, who also generously loaned me her index file on fifty years of UAW/CAW-related articles in the *Globe and Mail*; David Sobel, who also helped with photographs and whose passion for history is infectious; Craig Heron, whose own work is a model of both working class sympathies and historical integrity; Herman Rosenfeld, whose energy and intellectual curiosity, while sometimes exhausting, is something we need more of; and Leo Panitch, with whom I long lost the ability to distinguish which ideas were mine and which were his. Eileen Koyama suffered through the often tedious work of copy-editing, and was extremely helpful.

Jonah, my older son, gave me another troubling perspective on history by surpassing me in height while I wrote this book. Lucas, my younger son, is already working on a CD-ROM of the book with animation and an original musical score. If I said that Schuster — my friend, partner, and the real writer in the family — was "admirably patient," anyone who ever called me at home would raise an eyebrow; my credibility would be gone before they got to the book itself. Schus and the kids harassed me enough to keep me in touch with the immediate world, but also understood that what I was doing was important enough to complete. They maintained my sanity and have, for so many years now, kept me going.

> *Royalties from the book will go to a CAW scholarship fund established in memory of former activists Larry Bauer and Jim Ashton.*

...The best of me is sucked out and wasted.
I forget.
Everything but Death comes to me
and makes me work and give up what I have.
And I forget.
Sometimes I growl, shake myself and sputter a few
red drops for history to remember.
Then — I forget.
When I, the People, learn to remember,
when I, the People, use the lessons of yesterday
and no longer forget who robbed me last year,
who played me for a fool —
then there will be no speaker in the world
say the name: "The People," with any fleck of sneer in
his voice
or any far-off smile of derision.
The mob — the crowd — the mass — will arrive then.
     — Carl Sandburg

Introduction

Historical information about employers is non-value-added information so we destroy it.

— A General Motors manager

When you come right down to it, history is the only teacher workers have.

— David Montgomery

This is my faith. For all these years we have advanced because we, the people, do learn.

— George Burt

Two historic events marked 1985: the fiftieth anniversary of the founding of the Congress of Industrial Organizations (CIO) and the formal breakaway of the Canadian section of the United Automobile Workers (UAW) to form its own union.

Linking Two Stories

The first event, the emergence of the CIO in the mid-1930s, was a response to the failure of the existing labour movement to deal with a critical new development within capitalism. National and international corporations, organized on a multiplant basis, had come to dominate rapidly growing and increasingly important mass production industries such as auto, rubber, electrical, and steel. These powerful corporations were revolutionizing the organization of the workplace, the economy, and society. But the main form of trade unionism at that time, craft unionism, was incapable of dealing with the new challenge.

Craft unionism had emerged in the mid-1800s, when skilled workers came together to form the first significant and lasting unions in Canada. These unions established a sense of mutual aid and pride in manual labour, and in the early 1870s, they engaged in a historically crucial fight for the nine-hour day. Although unsuccessful, this struggle established links across communities in southern Ontario and Montreal and thereby represented the first stage in the establishment of a Canadian labour movement.

This form of unionism organized workers according to their specific skills; for example, a toolmaker belonged to one union and a pipefitter to another, even if both were in the same workplace. But more important, craft unionism was exclusive. It limited itself only to skilled workers and essentially ignored the rest of the workforce — what one Teamster official of the time called "the riff-raff." Industrial unionism, by contrast, welcomed all workers in any particular workplace, across national companies, and even attempted to bring workers within entire sectors into one organization. This type of unionism was democratic and universal, reaching out beyond skill level, gender, colour, and accent.

Attempts to launch industrial unionism had been made in earlier decades, by the Knights of Labor in the last quarter of the 1800s and by the Industrial Workers of the World (IWW or "Wobblies") in the decade before the World War I, but neither group had endured. The 1930s signalled the

Toronto factory (Steel and Radiation Ltd.) c. 1905. Courtesy of City of Toronto Archives, SC416.

The Knights of Labor was a labour central established in the U.S. in 1869 and in Canada, primarily in Ontario and Quebec, in the early 1880s. The uniqueness of the Knights lay in their inclusion of the unskilled as well as the skilled, and their acceptance into the organization of women and blacks — though not Asians. By the end of the century, they had lost out to the craft-based American Federation of Labor.

The Industrial Workers of the World, known popularly as the Wobblies, emerged in the early 1900s and had their main influence in the period before World War I. Their goal was to organize all workers into One Big Union — not just to fight the boss, but to prepare workers for one day taking over and running the economy. In Canada, they were most influential in the West, especially amongst miners and forestry workers.

explosion of a new and, this time, lasting movement for industrial unionism. It was led by the CIO.

The ideology and structure of the CIO brought unity and coherence to the spontaneous worker outbursts occurring throughout industry. Suddenly, that unorganizable riff-raff in increasingly important new industries were not only joining unions, they were also leading the way. Immortalized by a wave of sit-down strikes in the American Mid-west, the spirit of the CIO inspired Canadian workers to overcome their uncertainties and initiate direct action. As Irving Abella phrased it in an article for the Canadian Historical Association, to Canadian workers, "CIO was a magic name. Whenever they heard it, they flocked; whoever used it they trusted."

Five decades later, the split of the Canadian UAW from its parent organization exposed an American failure and Canadian potential. By the early 1980s, it was clear that over the four decades since the CIO's breakthrough, American labour had failed to build a movement that could effectively respond to the new era of restructuring and corporate aggressiveness. The American leadership of the UAW chose to sell concessions, and their demoralized membership acquiesced. The Canadian section of the union rebelled, and that rebellion ultimately led to the formation of a new union — that of the CAW (Canadian Auto Workers).

In the thirties, the Canadians had welcomed, with little or no controversy, the American-based UAW to Canada. At that time, it was obvious that the UAW would be not only helpful, but also necessary. In the eighties the membership rejected the UAW with remarkably little controversy within the union. This time, the Canadian workers knew that they could no longer be defended, nor their labour movement built, from within the UAW.

At one level, the Canadian rebellion was conservative. The stubborn Canadians simply refused to change the traditional role of the union in collective bargaining. But at a more meaningful level, something radical was happening. Somewhere along the line, Canadians had developed the confidence to take on

On 5 December 1984, Bob White, alongside his two assistants, Bob Nickerson and Buzz Hargrove, left a UAW executive board meeting to announce that, since the UAW could not accommodate the Canadian demands, the Canadians would go their own way. That same day Brian Mulroney was in New York to tell the world that "Canada was open for business." For autoworkers, fighting the corporate agenda and coming of age had meant moving towards Canadian autonomy and Canadian sovereignty. For the Canadian élite, it meant dropping any pretence of a Canadian perspective and launching the free trade campaign to formalize continentalism; free trade was to be their North American constitution for corporate rights.

both their parent union, previously held in awe, and the new conventional wisdom of competitiveness and management-labour partnerships, which was sweeping the Western world.

The Past as Present

When we identify these events — the formation of the CIO and the formation of the CAW — as "historic," what do we really mean?

At the most obvious level, we mean they were important. They had a crucial impact not only on the union, but also on the establishment of a Canadian working class and on broader developments such as the emergence of the welfare state and the nature of our politics. The formation of these groups is therefore significant in terms of their relationship to the present, to the story of how we arrived where we are today.

That story may be interesting in and of itself, but it is only really alive if it is linked to the story of what we are striving to become — if it's about the future as much as the past. From this perspective, these two particular events are exceptionally important and may be termed historic. They are significant

5

stories because they reveal and symbolize the potential of workers, not only to be part of history, but also to take steps to collectively shape it.

From the early days of the emergence of a wage-earning class (stretching back roughly two hundred years), working-class families fought against the destruction of former values and methods; they opposed, resisted, rioted, went on strike, and formed unions. But these protests were always fragmented. They occurred sporadically and on a regional rather than national basis. In addition, they involved only particular sections of the working class. The protests were defeated because, while they kept certain ideas alive, they were unable to build the institutions and capacity required for a sustained response to capitalism.

Industrial unionism held out the hope of finally creating that permanence and that capacity. The movement for industrial unionism called forth a vision of a new kind of working class institution that was independent of its bosses and that had enough staying power to win immediate demands, move towards broader reforms, and possibly even transform society. This movement was distinct in its scale, scope, and breadth: it reached out to all workers, established a base in each workplace, and participated in other movements emerging in the turmoil of the times.

The 1930s witnessed an upsurge in working class politics: workers' study groups were established; co-ops formed; alternative newspapers linked themselves to a new readership; municipal elections saw independent farm and/or labour candidates step forth; and new parties, such as the Cooperative Commonwealth Federation (CCF) entered the national political arena. This upsurge awakened a new creativity amongst artists: literature, plays, street theatre, posters, and especially songs reflected popular struggles.

For a brief moment in the thirties and again immediately after the war, working people were living and breathing one of those rare and glorious historical moments when so much seemed truly possible. It was a time when, with some exaggeration, but reflecting the growing public legitimacy of unions in the United States, union posters quoted the American president as saying, "If I worked in a factory, the first thing I would do would be to join a union." It was a time when the American Senate actually passed — even if it later sidetracked — a bill to establish a thirty-hour week, and polls in the bastion of capitalism showed that forty-one per cent of the American population supported nationalizing the banks. It was a time when the working class was present not only in the sense of reacting and defending, but

6

also in the sense of actually flexing its potential and daring to think about making history.

At the beginning of the thirties, the level of unionization was actually slightly higher in Canada than in the United States. But the new mass production industries, such as auto, rubber, and electronics, had developed faster and further in the United States. In these sectors, the American labour movement was ahead in numbers, resources, legislative recognition, and momentum. Neverthe-

It is sometimes difficult for Canadians to appreciate that in the mid-1930s the United States was more socially progressive than Canada. While President F.D. Roosevelt was introducing unemployment insurance, massive job-creating public works programs, and labour legislation supporting unions, Prime Minister R.B. Bennett was setting up forced work camps which paid twenty cents per day to single young workers. While the governor of Michigan, Frank Murphy, was refusing to use the National Guard against the strikers in Flint, the premier of Ontario, Mitch Hepburn, was threatening to establish his own army if the federal government wouldn't provide troops. And it was in the United States rather than in Canada that the largest demonstrations of the unemployed and the most militant actions of those fighting for unionization took place.

less, Canadian workers directly shared in the excitement and cross-border solidarity of the times. During this period, Canada faced tough and heroic labour struggles, showing creativity in inventing effective tactics and making tangible gains.

In retrospect, the Canadians still had an additional step to take, one that would overcome the dependency on their American "older brothers." For the Canadian autoworkers, that step, tied to both the Canadians' growing self-confidence and the Americans' growing resignation, would come fifty years later. While the American-led movement for industrial unionism certainly accomplished a great deal, it eventually faded and fell far short of its promise. That failure was linked both to changes in the economy and society, and to the concerted efforts of companies and governments to weaken unions. But crucial to that story were decisions made and opportunities ignored that were internal to the trade union movement: issues of democracy and bureaucratization; attitudes towards the independent role of unions in the workplace and society; and responses to past successes and openness to charting new directions and energizing new members.

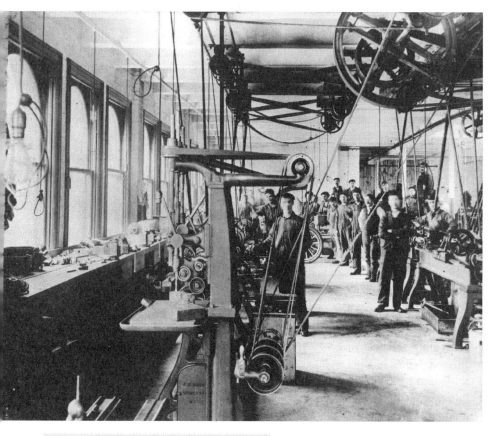

Auto machine shop, c. 1905.
Courtesy of Wayne State Archives.

These problems, it must be emphasized, are not simply the result of a trade union leader "selling the union out" (though anger at some leaders is not mis-directed). Nor did these failures suddenly emerge from nowhere in the late seventies and early eighties, when, perhaps, their existence became clearer. Their roots were laid much earlier and even included the "good times" — when the union was establishing itself and winning major benefits for its members. That's why these issues are so complex and why they currently challenge unions on both sides of the border.

The history of any union is the story of how, in spite of incredible odds, working people built their own organizations in order to have a voice. It's about overcoming bitter defeats and sharing sweet victories. It's the story of how these working class organizations responded to and effected change, thereby transforming themselves, influencing society, and touching the lives of distant others. When they are at their best, unions are in the vanguard of challenging the status quo and driving social change.

Out of such challenges grew a culture of resistance and a legacy that, while sometimes faint, still swirls around the halls, meetings, and picket lines of unions. The history of a trade union is about the creation of a vehicle through which working people can act to win immediate gains and thereby build a collective memory — a culture of struggle — to be passed on to new activists and new generations.

The history of the CAW falls naturally into four interrelated stories:

Waiting

The prehistory of the union: the crisis in the labour movement as it struggled directionless through the twenties and early thirties, and the challenge of developing a new kind of unionism to give voice to workers in the emerging mass production industries (Chapters 1–2).

The Union Arrives

The establishment of the UAW in Canada and the U.S. as a stable and permanent institution: the early breakthroughs, growth in numbers, acceptance by both employers and the state, structural changes and innovative gains, and the carving out of a permanent space within society as a progressive social union (Chapters 3–5).

Limits

The challenges to the institutionalization of the union: problems created by its successes, the demands of a new generation of workers in the sixties, and the counterattack by corporations and governments in the mid-seventies (Chapters 6–7).

Towards Movement Unionism

The breakaway from the UAW: how and why the Canadians developed in a different direction, the direct events leading to the split, and the subsequent changes and problems in the creation of a new kind of union (Chapters 8–10).

PART ONE: WAITING

Unionization wasn't established in the auto industry until three decades after the first car factories were built in Canada, and two decades after the introduction of the assembly line. Part One deals with the immediate background of the UAW's birth: the development of the auto industry and assembly line production (Chapter 1) and the social and economic context of the Great Depression (Chapter 2).

AUTO-WORKERS

In 1913–14, the Industrial Workers of the World (IWW or "Wobblies") were organizing autoworkers in Detroit. In 1913, they led what was perhaps the first major strike in auto history (at Studebaker). Courtesy of Wayne State Archives.

CHAPTER 1

MAKING CARS, REMAKING PEOPLE

Who would use it?
    — Seigfried Marcus, forgotten creator of the
    first workable car in 1875.

*The automobile industry stands for modern industry all
over the globe. It is the industry of industries.*
    — Peter Drucker

*Never had there been such a device for speeding up
labour. You simply moved a switch and a thousand men
jumped more quickly. It was [like] an invisible tax...
[and] even if the worker learns about it, it is like the tax
in that he can do nothing about it. If he is a weakling,
there are a dozen strong men outside waiting to take his
place. Shut your mouth and do what you're told!*
    — Upton Sinclair

The new mass production industries such as auto, rubber, and electronics, as well as related older industries such as farm machinery and steel, settled in southern Ontario. They concentrated there in response to earlier national policy decisions, markets and population, and dependency on the American manufacturing belt around the Great Lakes. The revival of unionism at this particular time in Canadian history would depend on the success of industrial unionism. Canadian unionism would therefore rise or fall with struggles taking place in communities such as Windsor, Sarnia, Hamilton, St. Catharines, Brantford, London, Kitchener, and Oshawa. The key industry in these southern Ontario communities was automobiles — an industry once called "capitalism's favourite child."

Capitalism's Favourite Child Comes to Canada

The auto industry stood at the centre of the new stage of capitalism by virtue of its relative size, dynamic growth, importance to other key sectors, and revolutionary role in reorganizing production. By the depression, auto comprised North America's major manufacturing sector, and General Motors (GM) was the largest manufacturing company in the world. Productivity growth far exceeded the rate of other sectors. The industry supported other key sectors, including steel, rubber, glass, and tool-and-die production, and the assembly line had come to represent, in industry circles and beyond, the ultimate in mass production techniques. After World War I, automobiles became the symbol of a prosperous materialist culture that affected our values and the structure of our lives. It was reflected in transportation systems, the development of cities and suburbs and changes in shopping habits, private versus collective space, recreation, and how we measured personal success.

The auto industry was relatively new, emerging only at the beginning of the twentieth century. Through the next two decades, almost two hundred companies attempted to become full-scale manufacturers in North America, but by the early twenties, an on-going shake-out had left only two of these firms in clearly dominant positions: GM and Ford. Chrysler joined them in 1925, and by the depression, the Big Three controlled over three-quarters of the market. One reason for the rapid shake-out was the critical importance of corporate size and product volume, especially after the introduction of the assembly line in 1913. Another reason was the move in the mid-twenties to

annual model changes and their subsequent demands for design, marketing, and financing.

Outdoor body drop, Ford Highland Park (near Detroit), c. 1913.
Courtesy of Wayne State Archives.

Canada remained a player through this period not as a result of the free market, but in spite of it. Given the American advantages of access to a large market and experience in the design and manufacturing of cars, the free market would have quickly decreed that we simply import our vehicles from the United States. But jobs and our own industrial strategy demanded otherwise. The industry remained in Canada as a result of conscious government intervention, by way of tariff policy, to change the logic of the market. A tariff of thirty-five per cent forced the manufacturers to at least assemble the vehicles and some components in Canada.

In addition to having its own market, Canada was the back door to the British Empire. Outside imports faced high tariffs in all countries of the empire, and this policy discouraged direct sales from the United States. These tariffs could, however, be circumvented by using one of the countries within the empire as a base, and that role fell to Canada. By the early twenties, Canada ranked second only to the U.S. in the production of vehicles (a position Canada lost during the depression when protectionism within

15

Europe pressured the auto companies to set up facilities overseas).

The companies exploited the tariff to keep prices high in Canada. Since the industry was concentrated in Ontario, there was, not surprisingly, pressure from the West to lower the tariff. In 1926, an innovative solution emerged that would form the core of Canadian auto policy for the next six decades: the tariffs would be lowered, with the precondition that companies had to increase the level of Canadian content.

Although initially opposed by the parts companies, this policy quickly increased the number of parts jobs in Canada. Imports of vehicles also increased as some of the smaller assembly companies, unable to meet the content requirements, closed their assembly plants and shipped from the United States. Overall, the number of auto jobs grew, doubling in the twenties to reach over 16,000 by 1929 (still only about three per cent of the more than 500,000 auto jobs in the U.S.). In the Windsor area, the overall population increased fivefold between 1904, when Ford began production there, and 1929.

An Animated Tool of Management

The auto industry had emerged out of the bicycle and carriage industry, which had been based in Michigan, Ohio, and southern Ontario. Production was in the hands of all-around mechanics who worked at fixed stations to complete a single vehicle. At first, they moved around the workplace to retrieve parts and to change tools, but soon helpers were hired to bring the tools and parts so that the skilled workers could spend "the company's time" on what they did best. From the start, some specialization was common; in a small group of workers making a car, each individual concentrated on a different set of tasks.

These skilled workers had a full conception of the car they were making; they performed a variety of tasks and used their initiative, skills, and imagination to iron out problems as they occurred. They were, of course, pressured by supervisors, but the knowledge that resided in their hands and minds limited their vulnerability to the employer. It was this knowledge that management, by way of the assembly line, systematically tried to separate from the workers and capture for the company.

The assembly line was the culmination of a series of innovations in machine tools, standardization of parts, electrification of equipment, and the

Workshop at Packard showing auto frames on horses before assembly line was developed, c. 1913. Courtesy of Wayne State Archives.

mechanical — virtually clockwork — integration and flow of components. A moving line passed in front of workers, each of whom repeatedly performed a narrowly defined task that was part of a whole conceived by others. Although the final assembly line accounted for only fifteen to twenty per cent of the workforce, it drove the process, setting the philosophy, direction, and goals of all operations.

In selling their labour, workers were selling their potential as productive "doers." In exchange for a wage, workers more or less left it to others to structure both how their skills were used and how those skills were developed. The move to assembly line production was a particularly dramatic and historically crucial extension of this system. In assembly line production management's

We are here in this world to develop ourselves by working – by doing things.

— Henry Ford,
The Toronto Star,
15 February 1937

17

Ford upholstery shop and assembly line, Windsor, 1925. Courtesy of Ford Canada.

drive to reduce labour to "one input like any other input" took a giant step. This philosophy eroded the difference between workers and nonhuman factors of production by directly attacking the inconvenient fact that, unlike other elements of production, workers could still think and protest. As this working class editorial of roughly 75 years ago reminds us, no one spelled out the implications better than the workers themselves (opposite page).

The problem for management had been that, while it could formally buy the labour power of workers, buying that living commodity was different from buying a set of tools or a machine. Workers could still limit the extent to which they passed on their knowledge, skills, experience, and ideas to the company. This capacity translated into a measure of power for workers and a barrier to the company. Breaking down this measure of worker autonomy and transferring it to machines and supervisors allowed the company to become more efficient, to plan better, and to strengthen its hand in the on-going conflict over production pace.

Editorial in *International Molders Journal*, 1918.

The one great asset of the wage worker has been his craftsmanship. We think of craftsmanship ordinarily as the ability to manipulate skilfully the tools and material of a craft or trade. But true craftsmanship is much more than this. The really essential element in it is not manual skill and dexterity but something stored up in the mind of the worker. This something is partly the intimate knowledge of the character and uses of his tools, materials, and processes of the craft ... But beyond this and above this, it is the knowledge which enables him to understand and overcome the constantly arising difficulties that grow out of variations not only in the tools and materials, but in the conditions under which work must be done ...

... the greatest blow that could be delivered against unionism and the organized worker would be the separation of craft knowledge from craft skill ... The first [way this is done] is the introduction of machinery and the standardization of tools, materials, product, and process which make production possible on a large scale, and the specialization of the workmen. Each workman under such circumstances needs and can exercise only a little craft knowledge and a little craft skill. But he is still a craftsman, though only a narrow one and subject to much competition from below.

The second, far more dangerous than the first is the gathering up of all scattered craft knowledge, systemizing it and concentrating it in the hands of the employer and then doling it out again only in the form of minute instructions, giving to each worker only the knowledge needed for the performance of a particular relatively minute task ... When [this process] is completed, the worker is no longer a craftsmen in any sense, but is an animated tool of the management.

... if we do not wish to see the American workmen reduced to a great semi-skilled and perhaps little organized mass, a new mode of protection must be found for the working conditions and standards of living which unions have secured and some means must be discovered of giving back to the worker what he is fast losing in the narrowing of his skill and theft of his craft knowledge ...

Henry Ford bragged that, in contrast to the former workplace, which was dominated by skilled mechanics and their helpers, better than two of every five workers could be trained within one day under the new system, and an equal number could be trained within a week. For Ford, the dream of replaceable autoworkers had arrived.

Pierre Chardain worked in the assembly division. He attached the rear springs. His hand held an iron shackle plate. The chassis moved. Pierre Chardain had one minute and twelve seconds. He fastened the shackle plate. He worked properly. After all, he had three children. His pay was four francs seventy-five centimes an hour. He wanted more. He wanted to buy a new bed. He even dreamt about a new apartment: his window faced a blind courtyard, and his youngest daughter, who was already four years old, still couldn't walk. He had lots of dreams ...

It now took only fifty-five seconds to attach a shackle-plate. Now seventy chassis moved past Pierre every hour. He still received the same four francs seventy-five centimes. He didn't buy a bed. His daughter still hadn't learned to walk. He would come home, dismal and mindless. He was always silent. He seemed to have forgotten how to talk. All he knew how to do was fasten a shackle-plate. In fifty-five seconds. He would die five years ahead of time. But now each automobile was six centimes cheaper.

— Ilya Ehrenburg, *The Life of the Automobile*, 1929

Eliminating Discontent

The first principle of labour relations for the major auto companies was to keep unions out and force workers to confront the company as isolated individuals. The dehumanization of the pace and content of work may have made unionization more important than ever to autoworkers, but the immediate impact of the changes in production also made unionization extremely difficult.

The trades had provided the foundations of unionism. Canada, as a latecomer to industrialization, was dependent on immigration for its workforce; it had looked to countries such as England and Scotland for its trades. These tradespeople brought with them better-developed union traditions and socialist ideas. Even within Canada, recruitment of trades from other sectors into auto often brought workers with union experience in other sectors. But once the new system of auto production had cut the number of skilled workers to a minority of the workforce (less than fifteen per cent), the issue of unionization clearly shifted to organizing the unskilled and semiskilled workers.

Amongst the semiskilled workers were skilled trades, people whose work had been deskilled. Furthermore, the assembly line arrived somewhat later in Canada than in the United States, and the deskilling of jobs had not yet

gone as far. But by the late twenties, even in Canada, the majority of workers were unskilled and the logic of the assembly line dominated the organization of production. These unskilled workers came from

Kelsey workers making wheels during the depression. Courtesy of *Windsor Star.*

rural communities that had no previous exposure to unionism (mechanization and concentration were reducing the farm population and pushing workers into industry). Or, the workers were immigrants from the British Isles and Eastern Europe. Although these immigrants included workers with socialist backgrounds and the tight ethnic communities became a base for future unionization, radical changes required a cohesive movement which, like the confidence to take on the companies, would take time to develop.

From the beginning, workers resisted the assembly line. Many individuals simply quit: after the introduction of the assembly line in 1913, Ford had to hire *ten* workers to get one who would not, very shortly, quit. By 1918, Ford still had to hire over 55,000 workers to keep a workforce of 14,000. The rate of turnover was also high for more senior workers, especially if other jobs were available. This high turnover, along with the large number of workers who viewed their employment as temporary (e.g., those who were saving for a farm), made collective action through unionization more difficult.

The auto companies, led by Ford, paid relatively high wages. The great increases in productivity as a result of assembly line production allowed for both high wages and high profits. But high wages were also a response to the extraordinary turnover of workers and early unionization drives such as those led by the IWW even before World War I. During these prosperous times, the high wages attracted a steady stream of labour to the auto towns. Henry Ford, in his autobiography, described his decision to stabilize his workforce by raising wages as "one of the finest cost-cutting moves ever made."

The high wages didn't necessarily translate into high income because of the cyclical nature of car sales and the introduction of annual model changes in the late twenties. GM and Chrysler didn't follow Ford's wage system; they continued to use payment systems based not on work-time but on output (piece rates and group bonuses). These systems required less supervision since they exerted pressure on workers to police themselves. This pressure was especially high in the group bonus structure because any group members who weren't carrying their load directly lowered the bonus for all.

Higher wages were only one tactic the companies used to keep unions out. The companies used every kind of coercion they had at their disposal — or they could create — to keep unions from establishing a foothold in the industry. The regular bouts of lay-offs, at a time when seniority was only a distant dream, provided management with an enormous weapon to wield against workers. This weapon was used to cast aside older workers, to enforce discipline and compliance, and to weed out agitators and troublemakers.

Workers did not have to be reminded of how fragile their hold on their jobs was. But many supervisors, facing the pressures of production and having the power to fire people at will, didn't hesitate to abuse, and reinforce that power with favouritism. Plant-

Every foreman had favourites; chore boys [who] would cut his lawn and paint his home ... you had to call the foreman to see if you would be called back to work ... there was no respect for seniority, years of service, or age.

— Albert C. Ward, who started at Ford in 1913 and in 1941 was a member of the first bargaining committee.

level favouritism was also linked to a network of shop-floor informers amongst the workers.

Yet even this structure of power was not enough for the companies in their anti-union crusade. Ford's crusade was supplemented by an internal "service" department of 3,000 thugs, spies, and enforcers. Chrysler employed the Corporations Auxiliary Company, a private anti-union agency. General Motors' strategy included coercion, but it also focused on the lure of welfare schemes. The company's paternalism included profit-sharing plans, sickness insurance, health benefits, dances, bands, company-financed mortgages (approximately three-quarters of Oshawa workers in the thirties had such mortgages) and, especially important, a broad range of sports clubs.

Once unionization became a possibility, GM added an externally hired spy system. In the U.S., the company employed at least fourteen private detective agencies in the mid-1930s. The Pinkerton Detective Agency, which specialized in providing spies, agent provocateurs, and private anti-union armies, had GM as its largest customer. General Motors didn't want a third party (a union) interfering with its operations, but was prepared to hire as many third parties as it could to keep things that way. One of the sub-committees of the U.S. Senate, popularly known as the La Folette Civil Rights Committee, was holding hearings in the mid-thirties on the corporate spying against the unions. It characterized the contract between GM and Pinkerton's as "... a monument to the most colossal super-system of spies yet devised in any American company."

In Canada, the role of spies is less documented, but auto companies often employed the Corporations' Auxiliary, an organization set up by employers to infiltrate and undermine union organizing drives. The spies would name union activists, and the resultant firings and suspicions about who might be a spy intimidated and demoralized workers.

During these years, the auto companies also intensified their demands on the independent parts companies. At first, the auto makers were primarily involved in the design of the vehicle and the coordination of its assembly; they bought components from independent companies. Then, the majors began to consolidate internal parts production. This move strengthened their bargaining position with the suppliers: in addition to playing one producer off against another, the auto majors could also threaten to do the work themselves. This new pressure on the parts companies led directly to intensified pressures on the wages of parts workers.

The labor spy business was a big one in the 1930's. The automobile companies were the best clients of the Pinkerton Agency and Corporations Auxiliary. Spies in the auto plants were instructed to report on every meeting and every casual conversation among workers about their grievances.

INSTRUCTIONS FOR LABOR SPIES — Samples from the National Manufacturers Syndicate, an espionage training organization:

. . . There is nothing about your relationship with your fellow workers which can be considered underhand or deceitful . . .

. . . It is very plain in order for us to be successful we must conduct our work in an invisible manner. The ordinary worker, in his ignorance, is apt to misunderstand our motives if he knows of our presence and identity in the plant . . .

. . . When assigned to inside work in mill or factory, get a rooming place the same as any other worker would do. Do not share it with others. The presence of an outsider would interfere with the writing of your confidential reports and making up of expense accounts . . .

. . . In giving conversations always give the name of the man or his number, then tell what you said to him and what he says to you. In all these conversations try to talk about the work so as to find out how each man feels about the foreman and superintendent or anyone else in authority. You want to find out when the union meets, if there is a union. Then maybe we will have you arrange to attend their meetings so that we can see just what is going on, and be able to report whether any of the men where you are at work are members of the union. Be sure to report whether any agitation is going on . . .

. . . The minds of those who are dissatisfied and disgruntled must be changed. As our representative, you must find out first of all who are the dissatisfied ones; then cultivate their friendship and win their confidence. You will then be in a position to help us eliminate discontentment . . .

Report of National Recovery Administration (NRA) on spying by companies on workers in American industry, 23 January 1935.

Stuck in Second Gear

In spite of the risks, strikes did take place in auto during this difficult period, and, on occasion, they were successful. The trades in particular, though now a minority, had not completely lost their ability to shut down production. Before World War I and in the twenties, there were a number of attempts at forming industrial unions in auto, but these attempts were consistently undermined by the craft-based Trades and Labor Congress (TLC), which refused to support these organizations, or expelled them as dual unions competing in jurisdictions where unions already existed.

Given the absence of a union base, the workers' only strength lay in tight production schedules. Militancy, when it did occur, therefore tracked upturns in the business cycle. In 1928–29, the Canadian auto industry was at a peak. As a young industry, its potential was high, and it had grown rapidly during the twenties. This growth was reinforced by a highway building program. In addition, not only was the economy and therefore Canadian demand booming, but trade policy had increased Canada's share of North American production. At the same time, however, competition for market share was intensifying. With Ford in the midst of completing a major shut-down and massive restructuring, the title of industry leader was up for grabs. The smaller assemblers desperately tried to avoid the competitive crush of the giants.

The result was that the companies were intensifying pressures on workers at the same point in time that the industry could accommodate a response by workers. A rash of strikes erupted in 1928–29: GM in Oshawa; Chrysler in Windsor; Willys-Overland in Toronto; Studebaker in Windsor; Canadian Top and Body in Tilbury; Ford in Windsor; Dodge in Toronto; and again GM in Oshawa. Most of these strikes lasted only a few hours, and although the cause was no doubt an accumulation of grievances, the dissatisfaction was expressed through a focus on wages and methods of payment.

The most significant of these strikes was the first: the one-week strike in Oshawa in March, 1928. This early strike attracted attention and excitement amongst groups trying to organize autoworkers in Detroit. It began with the walk-out of 400 trimmers — skilled workers who had experienced the steady deskilling and downgrading of their work over the past decade, and whose work allowed for some regular communication amongst themselves. General Motors had enforced cuts in piece rates in 1927 and, in spite of record profits that year, announced further cuts in 1928. The rest of the workforce (3,000

In the late 1920s Canadian labour was divided into four labour centrals:

1. The TLC, established in 1886, was based on craft unionism and was dominated by its American counterpart, the American Federation of Labor.
2. The Canadian and Catholic Confederation of Labour in Quebec, established in 1921, was closely linked to the church. It supported cooperative class relations and fiercely opposed the politics and militancy of emerging industrial unionism.
3. The All-Canadian Congress of Labour was established in 1927 by a combination of conservative unionists, nationalists, and communists. What unified these groups was their opposition to the craft-based and American-dominated unionism of the TLC.
4. The Workers Unity League (WUL) was established in 1928 after Moscow pressured communists to set up their own labour centrals to lead a more militant industrial unionism, strengthen links to unorganized and unemployed workers, and work to transform (not just reform) the capitalist system.

worked in the facility at the time) soon joined the walk-out, and the workers were militant enough to both reject the strike committee's recommendation of independent arbitration and insist on union recognition.

Through the intervention of the TLC, workers eventually accepted the company's withdrawal of the cut in pay, went to arbitration, and established a local linked to the TLC. The workers were not ready to join forces with the smaller, less established, more radical labour central that was formed the previous year — the All Canadian Congress of Labour (ACCL). The eventual arbitration ruling was a bitter disappointment, and the union was generally discredited. When 250 tool-and-die makers went on strike in March, 1929, their efforts were defeated after two-and-a-half weeks. There were some departmental strikes at GM in 1930 and 1932, but they were isolated events.

The communist-led Automobile Workers' Industrial Union (AWIU) had been formed in June, 1928, in Windsor, where the Communist Party (CP) had a base and the support of a similar auto union established earlier in Detroit. The AWIU was formed after the first GM strike and in the middle of a rash of other strikes. Labour historian John Manley has argued that "For most of the 1920s the single voice unreservedly advocating industrial unionism in Canada belonged to the Communist Party (CP)." Until 1927, the CP worked to spread this message within the craft-based TLC, with virtually no success. It was only after the TLC began to encourage member unions to expel militants endorsing industrial unionism that the CP began to develop an independent base amongst workers.

The AWIU called for an industrial unionism based on class struggle but also encompassing immediate demands in bargaining that were to resurface in the historic strike in Oshawa in 1937, and political demands that reflected the potential of unions as a social force. Amongst those demands were the eight-hour day and the forty-four-hour week; an overtime rate of time-and-a-half; regular shifts; the rejection of the bonus system (pay linked to output) in favour of pay for time worked; enforcement of safety regulations; equal pay for equal work regardless of age, sex, or race; and unemployment insurance paid for by the state and the employers. The AWIU quickly set up locals in Toronto and Oshawa, as well as in the Windsor area, but by 1930, the short life of the union was over.

The companies had become more aggressive in combining wage incentives as the carrot attached to the stick of firings and intimidation. The union had meanwhile weakened itself through splits over edicts from Moscow over direction. When the depression hit in 1929, slightly more than a year since the formation of the AWIU, the devastating collapse of the industry essentially put further unionization in cold storage for a few winters.

The early years of this century witnessed the arrival of the automobile, a product that changed how we live. The restructuring of work that accompanied the automobile's evolution, especially the development of the assembly line, radically changed the role and status of skilled workers, robbing many individuals of their knowledge and ability to use their skills, and undermining their autonomy. Along with this shift to a workforce that was predominantly semiskilled and unskilled came expanded mechanisms for controlling all workers. Those controls were rooted in the production system itself: the assembly line, tight supervision, and methods of payment. But as workers resisted and looked to unionization, more underhanded and coercive tactics — including spying on the social and union life of the workers — became common.

The first significant hopes of unionization in the automobile industry occurred in the late twenties. This development was, however, blocked by the depression. The severe economic collapse had provided the companies with an additional weapon to push unionism aside. However, the idea of an industrial union had been placed on the agenda, and experience had been gained. Whether this union could challenge the control of auto giants over their workers would depend on broader developments in society.

Poster by Clive Gardner for campaign to buy motor vehicles and other goods within the British Empire in late 1920s and early '30s. Courtesy of National Archives, C102879.

CHAPTER 2

SEARCHING FOR A
NEW DEAL

I perceive the divine patience of your people, but where is their divine anger?
  —Bertholt Brecht

The decadent international but individualistic capitalism in the hands of which we found ourselves after the war [WWI] is not a success. It is not intelligent, it is not beautiful, it is not just, it is not virtuous — and it doesn't deliver the goods. But when we wonder what to put in its place, we are perplexed.
  — John Maynard Keynes, 1933.

If there is technological advance without social advance, there is almost automatically an increase in human misery.
  — Michael Harrington

The limits and possibilities of bringing unionization to the auto industry were shaped by the broader social context of the twenties and thirties. The unsuccessful stabs at unionization of auto in the twenties were part of a more general defeat of Canadian labour in that decade. Although workers continued to struggle for union representation in the early thirties, they were confronted by the seemingly insurmountable obstacles of powerful companies, hostile governments, and an extremely unfavourable economic environment. A breakthrough would result only if unionization was part of something much bigger.

As the depression dragged on, the failure of the economic system to provide any measure of security led to a questioning of the power of the élites and sometimes of capitalism itself. The collapse of the economy, which had at first weakened the labour movement, soon led to an explosion of social protest and organization. Industrial unionism was a fundamental part of that upsurge, reviving the possibility of finally establishing permanent unions in auto and the other mass production industries.

From Silence to Protest

In 1919, the labour militancy that had been building throughout Canada during World War I culminated in a general strike in Winnipeg. That strike was defeated, and that defeat affected Canadian labour well into the thirties. Business moved quickly and with confidence to consolidate its victory. For business, with American capital playing a prominent role, it was a period of dramatic expansion and concentration of corporate power. Keenly aware of the opportunities in the new mass production industries such as auto, business planned its restructuring of markets, technology, and labour's role in production.

For unions, the twenties were a decade of falling membership, division, and disarray. Union membership declined by sixteen per cent over the decade, even though the population increased by 1.6 million. Craft-based unionism, with its fossilized central labour bodies in both Canada and the U.S., watched from the sidelines — unable, but also unwilling, to address the new challenge of organizing the unskilled and semiskilled workers in these industries-of-the-future. Although there were some political upheavals in provincial and local politics, the Roaring Twenties roared right by the Canadian working class. Industrial unionism had taken its first steps decades

Winnipeg General Strike

The Winnipeg General Strike of 1919 shut down this major city for six weeks, leaving decisions about essential services to the workers and their strike committee. It was supported by organized and unorganized workers, joined by sporadic sympathy strikes across the country, acknowledged at rallies in Europe, and even had the support of the police force (they were eventually replaced). The strike was part of an international explosion of militancy in the West after World War I, which in Europe temporarily threatened to overthrow governments and even the capitalist system.

The strike began over the issue of union recognition but, with the employers' intransigence and the workers' growing confidence, it quickly escalated into the most encompassing general strike in North America — before or since. The strike represented a peak of labour militancy, but it also revealed labour's weakness in confronting the employer-state alliance.

Those heady days, and the response of the employers and the government, left a legacy that influenced both the culture of the labour movement and the future development of working class parties. But the defeat also set the stage for labour's limited role in the twenties.

earlier in mining, rail, and the textile industries. But by 1920, its most radical sections had been savagely repressed by employers and the state, and the remaining base became marginalized.

In the twenties, employers looked for less overt and more stable ways to deal with the economic restructuring ahead. Major companies such as Massey-Harris, which manufactured agricultural machinery, introduced so-called industrial councils to take advantage of the demoralized state of labour and to circumvent the development of independent unionism. These councils were really a form of company unionism, which sometimes included profit-sharing schemes and generally restricted workers to playing an advisory role on a plant-by-plant basis. In the steel industry in Hamilton, the union was eventually able to capture the council structure in the founding of an independent union. But the more common outcome was that summarized by G.D. Robertson, the federal minister of labour, in February, 1921.

> If the industrial council plan had not been brought into existence I am very sure that today our industrial difficulties would be much greater than they are ... because of it, thousands of men in this country have had their viewpoints altered and have seen and realized the difficulties with which their employers have to contend.

These councils were common in the twenties, though rare within the young auto industry. General Motors Canada made a tentative move in this direction after the 1928 Oshawa strike, but neither GM nor the other auto majors found it necessary to follow suit elsewhere in either Canada or the U.S. until the thirties, when unionization became a more general threat. Like their present counterparts, these management-initiated union alternatives were primarily geared to workers' identification with the company's — as opposed to other workers' — problems.

A *Financial Post* survey of leading Canadian Bankers and Financiers, done three months before the Great Crash, "failed to reveal any person that is pronouncedly pessimistic as to the future." Once the crash hit, the bankers and the press responded by ignoring it:

Fundamental conditions are sound
    — Bank of Montreal

... future as promising as any time in ... history
    — Dominion Bank of Canada

... undiminished confidence in Canada's continued growth
    — Bank of Commerce

Canada stands unshaken after market collapse
    — The Ottawa Citizen

Vancouver can create in the 1930's the greatest era of activity this continent has ever known
    — Vancouver Sun

There's very little the matter with Canada!
    — Saturday Night

Source for quotations: Pierre Berton, *The Great Depression, 1929–39*

Labour's defeat in the 1920s, and the consequent growing inequality in income and power, became a factor in the coming depression. Without a strong labour movement and a progressive bloc, income lagged behind the accelerating capacity of the economy to produce goods. A crisis of under-consumption became inevitable: who would buy the goods? Without angry demands for an end to speculation and the regulation of the financiers, unsustainable fortunes imparted a superficial glow to a society about to crumble. And without a countervailing power that challenged the prevail-ing orthodoxy of free markets and fiscal restraint, the coming catastrophe was reinforced.

Four years into the Great Depression, the value of output and exports in the economy had fallen by half. Unemployment had increased tenfold (from under three per cent to over thirty per cent). Incomes across the country had fallen by forty to fifty per cent (over seventy per cent in Saskatchewan). In auto, production was down by eighty per cent and employment, by fifty per cent. In rail alone, 65,000 workers were laid off. One in eight Canadians depended on a restricted and ungenerous emergency relief system.With the single exception of the U.S., Canada was hit harder than any other country by the Great Depression.

When the depression hit, unions and other social or political groups were hardly in a position to respond effectively. But as it became clear that the economy was not going to revive itself, and the squeeze on living standards would only get worse, opposition grew amongst farmers, young unemployed workers, and those still working. People began to question the system and its incredible failure to address their needs. The business élite, which had taken the credit for the gains in the Roaring Twenties, was increasingly held accountable for the horror of the thirties, as Conrad, Finkel, and Strong-Boag note in History of the Canadian People:

> Nothing disappeared as quickly during the thirties as sup-port for laissez-faire. Suddenly unable to find work, people blamed profit-seeking capitalists for their plight and no longer found the ethos of 'free' enterprise so captivating.

Farmers lobbied and protested; tenants formed organizations to fight land-lords and eviction; families fought local officials for relief; municipal politics became the scene of popular struggles; workers confronted company goons, police, and sometimes even the militia for the most basic of rights; and the

Oh why don't you work like other men do?
How the hell can I work if there's nothin to do!

Chorus:
Hallelujah, I'm a bum,
Hallelujah, bum again!
Hallelujah, give us a hand-out
To revive us again!

Oh, I love my boss; he's a good friend of mine;
That's why I am standing out on the bread line.
[Chorus]:
Oh, why don't you save all the money you earn?
If I didn't eat, I'd have money to burn ...
[Chorus]:

— Harry McLintock,
"Hallelujah, I'm a bum"

unemployed organized themselves at the community level, joined workers on the picket line, and took to the streets in major demonstrations across the country (in 1931, 13,000 marched in Toronto; 12,000 in Winnipeg; and thousands more, in Vancouver and Montreal). Young single workers, unemployed and forced into relief camps, demanded jobs and dignity. Their increasing militancy culminated in the famous On-to-Ottawa trek. Hundreds of young men, whose average age was under twenty, rode the rails, and headed for the nation's capital before they were stopped in Regina.

Socialists and Industrial Unionism

These strikes and protests could not have happened without the active intervention of socialists — people who had a vision of society beyond capitalism and who were dedicated to building the resistance and political force that could achieve change. As the practical historians of labour, the socialists brought with them a link to past struggles. They, along with militants they influenced, provided the leadership that gave voice to frustrations and channelled anger into action.

There have always been links between trade unionism and socialism. Socialists wanted to replace capitalism, and workers who faced and challenged corporate power on a daily basis, readily lent an interested ear to their arguments. For instance, in Germany, socialist parties played a leading role in establishing the first unions, while in England, the unions built socialist or labour parties. This overlap of unionism and politics brought rich perspectives and added vital resources to trade union struggles; however, it

Young unemployed workers on the way to Ottawa (On-to-Ottawa trek). Courtesy of Wayne State Archives.

was also a source of division that profoundly affected the development of unions.

After World War I, the socialist movement was divided into two main camps: the communists and the social democrats. What differentiated them at that time was primarily their views on the process of change. The communists looked to the Russian Revolution, the upheavals taking place in Central Europe, and general strikes like those in Winnipeg and Seattle as confirmations that revolutionary change was possible. Social democrats looked to these same events to conclude the opposite. In the Canadian context, for example, social democrats argued that, given Canada's democratic traditions, the only realistic model of change was a series of gradual reforms. Over time, these disagreements about process grew into differences about ultimate goals, the role of the working class in achieving change, and the international perspective of socialists (where they stood in the cold-war conflict between the U.S. and the Soviet Union).

The Canadian CP was born in 1921. Its goal was to end capitalism and replace it with a society that was democratically controlled and planned by workers. Given the obvious reaction of those with power, the party empha-

MAKING PARTS

The worker wears torn gloves.
He stamps enigmatic parts
On a large, heavy, oily machine.
For many hours the worker stands making parts
On a large, heavy, oily machine.
The worker thinks of time, time overwhelms him
Time preoccupies his mind, time oppresses him.
The place where the worker stands is noisy
The smell of oil pervades, makes the worker nauseous.
Occasionally the worker looks up to see
What the other workers are doing.
Some workers are performing the same tasks as he, making parts.
Others, like a greying man holding a broom
Look pleased with themselves.
The worker envies the greying man holding the broom,
The way the greying man holds the broom, free
To hold the broom anyway he pleases,
The worker begins to think of what he'll do after work.
Visit his kids, perhaps. Go for a beer, perhaps.
Attempt a reconciliation with his wife, perhaps.
The worker looks at the clock on a nearby wall.
The clock never moves,
The worker wants to smash the clock.
He begins to imagine he has been here forever.
The clock never moves.
the clock drives the worker crazy.
They must be holding back the clock or keeping it still.
The worker begins to misjudge the rhythm of the machine.
The worker stares at the machine with contempt.
The worker miscalculates the rhythm of the machine
The workers hand hesitates, confused.
The worker sacrifices harmony for speed.
The worker becomes distraught.
The inexorable movement of the machine captures the worker's hand
The clock never moves.

RON DICKSON

Poem by Ron Dickson, former chairperson at Hiram Walker, Windsor and retired staff member.

sized that a strategy which depended solely or even primarily on parliament would fail. It was absolutely crucial to build a base that provided people with both a full appreciation of what was at stake and organizations through which they could defend themselves and fight for change. The working class was given the preeminent place in communist theory and practice, because of its direct participation in production, access to organizational resources, and potential leadership role in society. The main focus of communists was therefore to unify workers as a social force and develop amongst workers the understanding, confidence, and skills necessary for carrying out their potential role.

Throughout the twenties and especially in the thirties, communists played a leading role in strikes, in local protests of all kinds, and in organizing the unemployed and linking them with the employed. Few workers accepted the communist call for a revolution. But many responded to the arguments of the communists and respected their militancy, the resources and networks they brought to struggles, and their clear commitment to workers. In the thirties and forties, it was the communists who developed the deepest roots within the working class and trade unions, including those of the UAW in Canada.

Canadian social democrats coalesced into the CCF (Cooperative Commonwealth Federation) in 1932. Its founding members included a loose alliance of farmers, workers, and urban intellectuals. In those first years, with capitalism's credibility increasingly challenged by the waste of the depression and by the possible development of a new party, the CCF insisted on calling itself a "movement" rather than a "party." As a movement, the focus was on educating, organizing, and inspiring people with possibilities and a vision. Leaders distributed reading lists, formed study groups, and travelled across the country to inform and to debate the issues. Newspapers were established to disseminate information and analysis: during the thirties, the CCF's central news co-op supported six newspapers in six different provinces.

Although the CCF's Regina Manifesto (adopted in 1933) echoed with denunciations of capitalism, the views of the groups that made up the CCF alliance were very diverse. The CCF quickly evolved to an orientation geared to the reform, rather than the replacement, of the existing system. It viewed workers as an important constituency but not as the central actor in social change, and, unlike the communists, the CCF leaders chose parliament as their main arena for struggle. This development led social democrats away from the emphasis on mobilization and concern with in-depth

The ringing preamble to the CCF's Regina Manifesto tells us of the mood of the times:

We aim to replace the present capitalist system with its inherent injustice and humanity by a social order from which the domination and exploitation of one class by another will be eliminated, in which economic planning will supersede unregulated private enterprise and competition, and in which genuine self-government based upon economic equality will be possible ...

education as the requirements of radical change, and towards the pragmatic compromises that seemed to make electoral victories possible.

Many working class militants wished to avoid the emerging confrontation between the CCF and the CP. They saw grounds for cooperation around workplace struggles and relevant reforms. Between 1935 and 1937, the critical period leading to the formation of the UAW, cooperation between communists and social democrats (the latter considering themselves simply "socialists") was at a peak in both Canada and the United States. The broad left that eventually developed within the Canadian UAW emerged from this period and included communists, many CCF members, and independent militants.

But the institutional demands of the CCF and the CP (i.e. the growth and influence of the two groups within the unions), and the interaction between these demands and internal union conflicts over positions and policies, increased tensions and aggravated divisions. David Lewis, national secretary of the CCF at the time, made it clear in his autobiography (David Lewis, *The Good Fight*), that the CCF's top priority in the unions was "to wrest control from the communists" no matter how "negative and distasteful" the process nor how "lacking in idealism" were some of the trade unionists with whom the CCF consequently made alliances.

Social democrats attacked the communists as impractical extremists. More important, and with some legitimacy, they charged that the CP's centralized structure was undemocratic and that the party itself was dependent on Moscow. That dependence led to swings in policy based on Moscow's needs and dictates, rather than those of Canadian workers, and it made workable alliances impossible. Communists responded, also with some legitimacy, that the parliamentary strategy of the CCF led to a preoccupation with convincing business of the respectability of social democrats. These conflicts not only damaged work amongst the working class, but also meant that social democrats were obsessed with distancing themselves from communists.

Charlie McDonald, a Ford employee in the late twenties who eventually became a president of Windsor Local 200, remarked that in the early days, all those who fought for workers were united in that they were all labelled "communists." He added that "The alleged commies were crucial to building the union in the early days ... Nobody else back then was crazy enough to believe it was possible ..."

Enter the CIO: Stepping on the Gas

In spite of the impressive protests and developments in Canada, the most dramatic mobilizations and the most significant changes occurred in the United States. The American economy was much more developed and urbanized than Canada's. Corporations had grown the fastest in the U.S. in the twenties, and the American economy had fallen the hardest in the depression. As in Canada, business heroes who so gladly took the credit for the good times were now less happy to be held accountable for the bad. Relative to Canada, the mythic size of the American heroes and the optimism of their promises left a proportionately greater resentment towards their failures.

In 1932, with the economy in a shambles, financial markets in chaos, the economic and political élite in a daze about what to do, and the Republican Party in disrepute, Franklin D. Roosevelt was elected. Roosevelt viewed his mandate as saving capitalism by reforming it. He initiated the New Deal promising above all else to restore a sense of hope. His recovery program included bank regulation, credit to farmers, massive public works programs (especially in rural areas), a conservation program linked to jobs for young people, unemployment insurance and pensions, and labour reform that would limit the use of injunctions against workers and support the right to organize. This last right was driven less by any long-term commitment to the ideals of unionism than by Roosevelt's need to have labour as an ally and by the recognition that competition through wage cuts would drive purchasing power down, blocking any recovery.

The legislation Roosevelt introduced to promote union recognition was at this point very weak. But the impact of the public legitimacy the president gave to unionization cannot be underestimated. There was, according to the American Federation of Labor (AFL) executive, a "virtual uprising" of workers spontaneously organizing themselves to unionize. In the period

39

from 1933 to 1935, the number of union members increased by one-third in the U.S., as almost one million workers rushed to join. In contrast, over the same period in Canada, union membership declined.

American companies did not share the new enthusiasm for giving workers an independent voice. The workers' zeal for unions and a measure of democracy in the workplace was met and matched by a corporate determination to keep these allegedly radical unions out. As the confrontations escalated, workers broadened the fight to include the unemployed, to bring non-union workers into their struggles, and to introduce new and innovative tactics. In general, American socialists and communists played critical leadership roles in these struggles.

The polarization of American society, in and out of the workplace, and the failure of business to put forth any agenda that could solve both the economic crisis and growing social problems pushed the New Deal further. In 1935, Roosevelt's administration introduced, amongst other things, legislation on minimum labour standards (wages, hours of work, working age) and union recognition. The Wagner Act was designed to limit and control industrial unrest by granting workers the right to organize. The act established the freedom of workers to organize unions of their own choice without employer harassment and put in place labour boards to enforce this right, supervise elections, certify unions, and ensure that employers negotiated with the chosen union. The legislation excluded the past practice of allowing companies to establish company unions alongside a properly elected independent union.

The new protections for union activists meant that battles with employers could be fought on more equal terrain. But they also meant that the union could survive even if it lost a particular battle. Before the legislation, if a union lost a strike, it was gone. Without union recognition and with the employer free to fire activists at will, those activists still around after a defeated strike were defenseless. With the legislation, American workers seemed to be on the verge of the breakthrough to industrial unionism.

But the craft-based structure of the existing unions remained a barrier. At an AFL convention in 1935, John Lewis of the United Mineworkers challenged the leaders and the affiliates to move towards industrial unionism. He had experienced the growing militancy in his own union in which recommended contracts had been repeatedly rejected by the rank-and-file, and he knew that the radicalization of workers in the new industries would only grow: a rebellion was brewing amongst workers. Rebuffed, he joined with

American Workers Rebel

In the textile industry, 325,000 American workers used cavalcades of pickets in cars and trucks to shut down workplaces across the southeast in September, 1934. In San Francisco, a strike by longshoremen — led by a rank-and-file movement after the existing leadership refused to do so — included a series of confrontations that saw 1,700 scabs brought in, two workers killed by police, and then a general strike in July, 1934, with an estimated 130,000 workers off the job. (This included restaurant workers, taxi-drivers, cleaners and dryers.)

In Minneapolis in May, 1934, teamsters led a fight out of a strike headquarters in an old garage. Five hundred workers were ready, at any time, to join picket lines. This number included mechanics working around the clock to service the 100 trucks available to transport the picket and a kitchen which, at its peak, served 10,000 meals in one day. In the same month in Toledo, a strike at an auto parts plant (Auto-lite) was weakened by an injunction and 1,500 scabs until unemployed workers, previously organized in unemployed councils, joined the fight and eventually forced the recognition of the union and the rehiring of the strikers. Two more workers were shot and killed.

Organizations of the unemployed had been playing a major role since before Roosevelt's election. In 1930, over one million unemployed workers were, according to some estimates, involved in demonstrations across the United States. Funerals for workers killed became political demonstrations of solidarity. In New York, 50,000 marched in one funeral after a worker was killed in a demonstration of the unemployed.

In 1932, a funeral in Detroit for four workers killed in a march of the unemployed on Ford's Dearborn plant included an estimated 20,000 people. The march had called for jobs, reduced work-time, free coal for the winter, medical care for employed and unemployed workers, and union recognition. In Chicago, approximately 60,000 came out in support at a funeral for three people killed in a fight over the eviction of a widow in one of Chicago's African-American neighbourhoods.

leaders from industries including textiles, rubber, radio, printing, and auto to form the CIO. His own union supplied the majority of staff and resources to start building industrially based unions. Over 150 full-time organizers were recruited and paid by the United Mineworkers to organize steelworkers.

The American labour movement could now combine the spontaneous militancy of workers confronted with the depression; militant leaderships at the local and national levels; public support (or at least less resistance from governments, the police, and the courts); and a structure appropriate to the new challenges. The remaining details were when, where, and how the movement would make that crucial breakthrough toward complete organization of a major industrial sector.

Canada: Shifting Out of Low

In Canada, as in the U.S., the despair of the depression and the discrediting of the élites eventually led to resistance and growing militancy. This militancy led to local victories and even national advances. For example, in response to the growing unrest, some leading members of the business community accepted the need for an unemployment insurance program as a concession to the unemployed. In 1934, Charles Gordon, one of Canada's leading industrialists with close links to the banking sector, made the following argument in a letter to the prime minister, R.B. Bennett: "May I suggest ... that for our general self-preservation some such arrangement (of unemployment insurance) will have to be worked out in Canada." (In fact, however, unemployment insurance didn't come into effect until 1941).

Soon after these events and prior to an election, Bennett — as business-oriented a prime minister as Canada ever had — made an astonishing about-face arguing that "free competition and the open marketplace, as they were known in the old days, have lost their place in the system and the only substitute ... is government regulation and control." The prime minister went on to advocate, as part of his election platform, his own New Deal, which sounded very much like the American New Deal.

Bennett's conversion arrived too late to compensate for the losses in credibility he had accumulated over the preceding five years. But whether or not he was sincere, this turnaround reflected the same general factors that were also at work in the United States: the continuing bankruptcy of business and conservatives in dealing with the crisis and the growing pressures mobilized by the opposition outside of parliament. To those fighting for change, even the defeats left in their wake precious new contacts with other individuals and groups, as well as anger waiting for an outlet of expression. And the growing activism politicized thousands of formerly demoralized Canadians.

In the early thirties, militant strikes occurred across the country. They involved garment workers in Montreal, fishermen in British Columbia, chicken

Champion spark plugs (Windsor), 1935. Courtesy of the National Film Board.

pluckers in Stratford, miners at Noranda-Rouyn in Quebec, and textile and furniture workers in Toronto. The majority of these strikes were led by the Workers Unity League (WUL), the communist labour central.

In auto, the failure to organize at the assemblers had shifted the focus to the parts industry and the possibility of making inroads in smaller, more manageable confrontations. These strikes were led by the Auto Workers Union (formerly the Automobile Workers' Industrial Union), also a WUL affiliate. Although one-third of the workforce in the Windsor area was unemployed in 1933, signs of an economic upturn encouraged strike action in the auto parts sector. By early 1934, two successful strikes had taken place (at Auto Specialties and Windsor Bedding), a third was under way (at Canadian Motor Lamp), and others were waiting in the wings. At Auto

Specialties, after hearing that the company might "scab" the plant (hire temporary workers during the strike), hundreds of unemployed workers joined the picket line in solidarity.

The fight for union recognition couldn't, however, be won in the auto parts sector — the auto majors simply would not let that historic precedent be won amongst their suppliers. And so the parts companies would, when necessary, make concessions to workers in good times. When, however, circumstances moved in the companies' favour, management used the downturn to fire union activists and demoralize the rest of the workforce. Even where the movement had a foothold and made gains, it didn't yet have the capacity to sustain the fight in the workplace and build a union.

Through this period, only about fifteen per cent of Canadian workers were unionized, a figure comparable to that for the U.S., but less than half the level British unionists had achieved in an earlier period. In addition, few of these workers were in the increasingly crucial industrial sector. The mobilization that had taken place, as impressive as it was, remained local and regionally based. The workplaces and communities that engaged in struggles had few ties with each other; even strong regional movements — farmers in Saskatchewan, miners in Nova Scotia — remained isolated from one another. The missing link was the strong national political force that could bring Canada its own New Deal.

From today's perspective, it may seem that the CCF was the logical inheritor of the social democratic task of creating a more favourable political climate for unionism. But the CCF was itself regionally based (independent farmers formed its strongest core), and it was especially weak amongst industrial workers. In 1934, for example, the CCF in Ontario was virtually paralyzed after the Ontario leadership was ousted by the national office for having moved too far to the left and cooperating with communists. The CCF did not become a serious political threat to the Liberals and the Tories until almost a decade later, after the industrial unions were more firmly established and the CCF had secured roots in these unions.

In the context of the depression and given the power wielded by employers over workers desperate for a job, successful unionization called out for a measure of public legitimacy and legal-administrative support from governments and the courts. Without these elements, the task of building and sustaining organizations to take on the corporations was overwhelming. The young movement could not overcome the barriers it faced — high unemployment, corporations still powerful in spite of some loss of credibility, and the refusal of the state to acknowledge unionism as a basic democratic right. As it turned out, the missing ingredient in the thirties did not come from political developments within Canada; it came from the inspiration of the CIO victories in the United States.

Canada did not have a New Deal, but by way of the CIO, the American working class essentially shared its victory with Canadians. The CIO provided the opening that let Canadians move on to their own victories. When autoworkers in Flint and across the American Mid-west — who *were* in a position to win — took on GM, the Canadian border couldn't block the power, excitement, and implications of that victory.

PART TWO: THE UNION ARRIVES

The establishment of the UAW as a permanent institution began with its first breakthroughs in the thirties (Chapter 3), continued with the winning of recognition from both companies and the state in the forties (Chapter 4), and solidified with the development of its basic collective bargaining strategy and structure in the fifties (Chapter 5).

Meeting of Local 222 during Oshawa strike, April 1937. Courtesy of Wayne State Archives.

THE BREAKTHROUGH

...the sitdowns seemed to take place in a nightmare world where the laws of capitalism, if they operate at all, worked the way the law of gravity works in a dream.

— *Fortune*, November, 1937

... the fifteen day walkout of some four thousand (Oshawa) workers marks the birth of the Canadian labour movement as we know it today.

— Irving Abella

I'm glad that the boys and girls are ready to come back to work.

— R. S. McLaughlin (President of GM Canada)

The period between the two world wars was a time of rapid change in the economy and in society. Working people were generally marginalized in the sharing of benefits and, especially, in influencing the direction of the changes. From this perspective, the twenties and thirties were a dark period of disappointments and suffering. Yet by the mid-thirties, there was a budding and vibrant mini-revolt against the failure of the system to address the concerns of ordinary people.

The most exciting of the new movements — the movement for industrial unionism — didn't come out of the blue. It emerged out of a general climate of resistance and protest. The breakthrough occurred in the United States and, more by example than anything else, it flowed into Windsor, St. Catharines, and then Oshawa, which became the test site for the new unionism in Canada. After a long and painful lull, working people seemed ready to participate in the unfolding of history.

Flint: Standing Up by Sitting Down

The UAW was officially born in South Bend, Indiana, in April, 1936. While the AFL had chartered the union the year before, and a constitution was jointly drafted by the AFL and UAW, it was the AFL executive that appointed the president. In response, approximately 1,200 determined delegates forced the AFL to both grant them the autonomy to elect their own president, Homer Martin, and expand the UAW's jurisdiction to include *all* workers in the sector. At that point, the UAW began to make plans to take on the industry giant, GM. Autoworkers intended to show not only that the UAW had arrived, but also that it was unpacking its bags and settling in as a permanent fixture in workers' relationships with employers.

The experience and confidence for the famous test of strength in Flint, Michigan, which was the centre of GM's production empire, were the product of crucial work stoppages throughout the industry in 1935 and 1936. The protest at Flint was preceded by strikes to establish the UAW at GM in Cleveland, Atlanta, and Kansas City; at parts plants including Bendix and Kelsey; and at Chrysler's Dodge plant, where workers had already won seniority rights and overtime pay. (In the mid- to late thirties, Chrysler wasn't the "little sister" of the Big Three; it was selling as many or more vehicles than Ford.)

Key organizers, led by Roy Reuther (younger brother of the future presi-

Excerpt from the Preamble of the UAW's First Constitution
Adopted in Detroit, Michigan, August 1935
(At this conference the AFL first gave autoworkers a charter as the
"International Union, United Automobile Workers of America," though
they were not given the autonomy to elect their president until a second
convention in South Bend, Indiana, the following year. The union was
eventually expelled from the AFL and became part of the CIO.)

*... Management invests thousands of dollars in the automobile business. The
automobile worker's investment in the business is his life, his blood, his sinew.
The automobile worker seeks a place at the conference table, together with
management, when decisions are made which affect the food the automobile
worker, his wife and children shall eat; the extent of education his children may
have; the kind and amount of clothing they may wear. He asks that hours of
labour be progressively reduced in proportion as the modern machinery increases
his productivity. He asks that the savings due to the inauguration of the
machinery and changes in technical methods shall be equitably divided between
management, the investor, and the worker. The automobile worker asks that
those who may be discharged be paid adequate dismissal wages to enable them to
start afresh in another field; that society undertake to train them in new skills
and that it make provision through ameliorative social laws for the innocent and
residual sufferers from the inevitable industrial shifts which constitute progress.*

dent of the UAW, Walter Reuther) and communists Wyndham Mortimer,
UAW Vice-President, and Bob Travis, the president of the Toledo Chevrolet
local and a popular organizer, had been laying the groundwork in Flint, and
others had fanned out across the country to other key GM facilities.
Roosevelt had been reelected by a landslide in November, 1936, and the
union members waited patiently until Frank Murphy, whom they considered
supportive, became governor of Michigan before they made their move.

The actual sit-down didn't begin on a prearranged date. It started when
workers, concerned that the company was transferring dies to plants with a
weaker union base, contacted their leaders. Given the go-ahead at the end
of December, 1936, the workers took over Fisher Plants One and Two at the
Flint complex; the Flint sit-down had begun. Sit-downs and strikes followed
at other GM facilities across the country. By mid-January, three-quarters of
GM's 150,000 production workers had taken strike or sit-down actions in
support of the union.

Summer 1936

Automobile Workers Take to the Air

On Friday evening from 10:15 to 10:30 and Saturday evening from 7:15 to 7:30 over Station —

WMBC Dial 1420 Kilocycles

will be heard the Voice of United Automobile Workers of America.

These programs will be brought to you weekly at the above listed hours.

Hear Richard P. Frankensteen, former President of the Automotive Industrial Workers tell why the Independent Unions have amalgamated their forces with those of the United Automobile Workers.

Hear the set-up and organization plans of the United Automobile Workers.

Don't fail to dial WMBC tonight and tomorrow evening.

International Union
United Automobile Workers
of America

Flyer for radio show sponsored by UAW, summer 1936. Courtesy of Wayne State Archives.

The sit-down strategy was key. In contrast to a strike, in which employees vacate the workplace, a sit-down requires that a minority of workers occupy the plant. The sit-down had been successfully tested during the crucial strikes of rubberworkers in Akron, Ohio, earlier that year and, on a smaller scale, within the UAW at plants such as Kelsey Hayes Wheel in Detroit. The sit-down was designed to overcome the depression reality of high unemployment, which was creating large numbers of potential scabs, and the readiness of anti-union employers to use

There were 477 sit-downs in 1937 involving approximately 500,000 workers. The sit-downs spread madly to other sectors. There were sit-downs in heavy manufacturing, in government offices, in hotels and restaurants, in the fur industry, and at schools. One kindergarten class sat down because it seemed like fun.

Even the UAW itself was hit: UAW headquarters didn't have towels because launderers were sitting down and when the UAW tried to send out charters to the new locals mushrooming across the land, this was delayed because of a sit-down by the workers making the mailing tubes.

In France, hundreds of thousands of workers — two million by one estimate — sat down in their workplaces in 1936 to win union recognition, the right to strike, minimum wages, and the forty-hour week. But American and Canadian autoworkers did not generally seem to be aware of these incredible events.

A Detroit reporter commented that "sitting down has replaced baseball as our national past-time."

hired thugs, police, or the army to bring the scabs in. Where the union had a significant but small core of committed militants and a sympathetic but uncertain membership, a sit-down in the plant by that minority, reinforced by the presence of the rest outside the plant, made obvious sense. To Roy Reuther, the sit-downs were "the union's greatest organizers."

With the workplace as their base, employees could more effectively defend themselves, reduce violence and — with the complete shut-down of production — shorten strikes. The workplace even became a social space, democratically organized for discussions and entertainment; subcommittees watched over the equipment, distributed food and information, and planned for the defence of the plant in an attack. The logic of sit-downs is, in fact, so compelling that the real question isn't why workers once used this strategy, but why and how it so quickly disappeared from labour's arsenal.

UAW, Women's Auxiliary, Women's Emergency Brigade, ready to defend men sitting down in Chevrolet Plant #9, Flint, 1 February 1937. Courtesy of Wayne State Archives.

Amongst the factors that contributed to the victory at Flint and GM, the determined courage of the workers stands first. Not to be neglected, however, was the ongoing resourcefulness of the UAW leadership in responding to a series of crises that threatened the success of the sit-down.

For example, the union kept morale high with rallies and mass demonstrations outside the plant, aided by the support of tough women's auxiliaries. When GM tried to rally public opinion against anarchy and the illegality of the takeover of private property, the union fought back with the information from the La Follete hearings which publicized GM's high expenditures for spying on the workers and the union. When a local judge announced an injunction against the sit-down, the union exposed the fact that the judge held shares in GM; the ruling was voided on grounds of conflict of interest.

Then, two weeks into the sit-down, with food and heat cut off, the police launched an attack on the plant to dislodge what they hoped would be a demoralized and vulnerable group of workers. The union, with another Reuther brother, Victor, in the lead, rallied the workers to defend themselves. The workers stopped the police in their tracks with a barrage of the parts used to build cars and profits for GM. Icy weather showed its solidarity as the workers flushed the police away with water hoses. This action led the governor to call in the National Guard — not, as the company wished, to break the strike, but to prevent other attacks by the police or city vigilantes and to keep the peace.

When they tie the can
to a union man,
Sit Down! Sit Down!
When they give him the sack
they'll take him back,
Sit Down! Sit Down!

When the speed-up comes
just Twiddle your thumbs
Sit Down! Sit Down!

When the Boss won't talk
don't take a walk, but …
Sit Down! Sit Down!

— Maurice Sugar,
"Sit Down"

As time dragged on, the workers started to grow weary, and the company seemed to be getting the upper hand; the union astutely decided to escalate the struggle. Aware of GM spies in their midst, union members leaked information about another planned takeover, this time at Chevrolet Plant Nine in the Flint complex, and had the workers in that facility battle the police to divert them. Meanwhile, a separate core of workers took over the real target — Chevrolet Plant Four, which made the engines for all the Chevrolet assembly plants.

The ruse succeeded brilliantly. Ten days later and forty-four days into the strike, GM was feeling the economic pressure; but more important, the company realized that the union would not, at least at this point in time, be defeated. On 11 February 1937, GM recognized the union and agreed to enter into discussions on a collective agreement. At the beginning of the Flint sit-down, UAW membership stood at 88,000. Six months later, virtually all the major companies in auto, with the exception of Ford, had unions, and UAW membership stood at over 400,000. With Flint as the spark, overall union membership in the United States doubled between 1936 and 1938 from under 4 million to over 8 million. Over the same period, membership in Canadian unions increased by only 80,000.

Oshawa: Taking on the Motors

In Canada, the first UAW local — Kelsey Wheel in Windsor (a subsidiary of Kelsey Hayes Wheel in Detroit) — was chartered as Local 195 on 9 December 1936, shortly before the sit-down in Flint. The Kelsey workers won an agreement after holding one of Canada's first sit-downs and a strike, and after workers at the parent company in Detroit threatened to go on strike in support of their Canadian brothers and sisters. In spite of the settlement, the agreement did not acknowledge the UAW as the formal representative of the workers; that recognition would take Kelsey Wheel workers until 1948 to achieve. Nevertheless, the strength of the membership in Windsor meant that the company had to deal with the union whether or not there was official recognition. Nine days after the Kelsey Wheel workers in Windsor got their charter, workers at McKinnon, a wholly owned but separate subsidiary of GM, in St. Catharines, formed the second UAW local in Canada (Local 199).

> ... *without the Europeans (about one quarter of Windsor's population was then East European) we would never have been able to organize the union at Kelsey. They understood trade unionism far better than Canadians and they were better equipped at organizing due to being far more politically advanced. Many had seen workers' rebellions back home ...*
>
> — Jim Napier, the first UAW member in Canada and leader at Kelsey Wheel

> *In the early and difficult period after George Burt became the Canadian director, he warmly said of the Kelsey unit that "little need be said of Kelsey Wheel, which is always 100 per cent organized and dues paying. These men are always ready to help other plants."*
>
> — Canadian Council, 8 July 1939

As in the United States, the test of the UAW's permanence would come in a battle with the giant of the industry, GM. From its beginning, the famous Oshawa strike of 1937, which effectively brought the UAW to Canada, was intimately tied to developments in the United States.

Though Ford, rather than GM, was the dominant producer in Canada and though the union was stronger in Windsor, where Ford was located and a number of parts strikes had already occurred, the Canadian break-through came at GM — because that's where the American breakthrough emerged.

Local 199 retirees Pudge Dawson (left), who began work at McKinnon (GM) in St. Catharines in 1938 and Charlie Williamson (right) who was a charter member of the Local when it was founded in 1936. Photo by Tony Mill.

On Monday, 15 February 1937, the same day that the Flint workers returned to work, sheet-metal workers in Oshawa put down their tools as GM Canada increased the line speed from twenty-seven units to thirty-two units per hour. The order for the change, which came from Detroit, may have been part of GM's attempt to make up for the losses incurred during the shutdowns in the U.S.

The workers gave management an ultimatum: the company must deal with their issues or face a strike by the end of the week. Meanwhile, they called the UAW in Detroit for assistance. On Friday of that week, during a meeting at which the two parties were going over the workers' demands, Hugh Thompson, an organizer from the UAW, arrived. In spite of opposition from the government's mediator, the workers insisted on hearing Thompson. That same afternoon, all 200 sheet-metal workers joined the union. They followed Thompson's advice to return to work while the union negotiated on their behalf, and Thompson set up an office to sign up union members.

Within a month, virtually every worker had joined the union. Even workers outside of the industry came to sign up, and the mayor himself became an honorary member. The worker demands included higher wages, shorter hours, overtime pay, seniority, an in-plant committee (stewards), and recognition of the UAW. In the course of the negotiations, the union got a boost when it was peacefully able to secure other agreements in Oshawa, including union recognition, at Coulter Manufacturing and Ontario Steel. On 6 April, the UAW in the United States extended the achievement of union recognition to Chrysler after a four-week sit-down in Detroit. However, the union did not reach an agreement with GM in Canada, and on 8 April 1937, the strike began.

Since the 1928 and 1929 strikes, there had been a number of skirmishes in Oshawa, but these had quickly faded. In 1937, there was a slight upturn in the economy, especially in auto. Although its own profits were at record levels, GM insisted on cuts in pay, just as it had in 1928. But 1937 was not 1928. This time, the workers' defiance established the UAW in Canada and the critical beachhead for the CIO. The workforce in Oshawa was no longer green; the earlier struggles to form the union were now an important part of their experience and history. A significant number of workers, although immigrants from England and Scotland, were now well established in Canada. Some, who had been active in the Independent Labour Party (ILP) before they came to Canada, were committed supporters of unionization.

In early 1937, GM announced wage cuts for the fifth time in five years. While output per worker was up and profits were now approaching predepression levels, actual wages were twenty per cent below where they were in the twenties. This discrepancy remained even after adjusting for the large

SUDBURY MINE AND SMELTER WORKERS' UNION, No. 239

I.U. of M.M. and S.W.

AFFILIATED WITH A.F. OF L.   AFFILIATED WITH THE TRADES AND LABOR CONGRESS OF CANADA

OFFICE: ROOM 205, HURON CHAMBERS
SUDBURY, ONT.

H. R. ANDERSON, SECRETARY-TREASURER

April 18th, 1937.

Mr. Hugh Thompson
Strike Committee,
Oshawa, Ont.

Dear Sir and Brother:

As representative of the local of the Sudbury Mine & Smelter Workers Union, who are at the present time conducting an organizational campaign, I have been requested to write you in the endeavour to prevail upon you to visit us upon the successful conclusion of the strike at Oshawa.

We have followed your campaign very closely and feel quite sure of victory in the near future. Realizing that this victory will be the start of many others in Canada, we naturally wish to capitalize on it. Our suggestion is that, following the successful conclusion of the strike in Oshawa, you visit us in Sudbury, where we plan to have a mass meeting. It would be necessary to have a few days notice as it is a difficult problem to procure the use of a large hall at a moment's notice.

Please advise us of the possibility of our suggestion becoming material, and may I assure you of our whole hearted support at all times.

Wishing you a speedy victory at Oshawa and again hoping you will be able to accomodate us, on behalf of the Executive and Membership of the Sudbury Local, I remain

Fraternally yours,

J. G. Munro

Secretary-Treasurer

JGM/HRA

Letter from the Mine Mill local in Sudbury sent to Hugh Thompson, the UAW organizer during the Oshawa strike, asking him to come up north and bring Mine Mill into the union. As it turned out, Mine Mill joined the autoworkers — fifty-five years later. (The road to that merger was hardly inevitable; it included bitter fights within labour and ultimately involved difficult and agonizing decisions.) Courtesy of Wayne State Archives.

decline in prices in that period. Although there were many accumulated frustrations — harassment by supervisors, unsafe conditions, long hours, insecurity, and the attempt to speed up the line that caused the work stoppage by the sheet metal workers — the wage cuts were the catalyst for the united response by workers throughout the plant.

From GM's perspective, keeping the union out was one way to offset the fact that the scale of Canadian operations was much smaller than that of American plants. This difference reflected the more general fact of Canadian labour relations: because of the structure of the Canadian economy — the smaller market, the shorter runs, the technological dependence — Canadian operations were less productive. But Canadian workers, who were as hard-working and capable as their American counterparts, weren't responsible for the structure of the economy, and they refused to accept second-class citizenship within any company's operations. Amongst skilled workers in particular and especially in border cities, the high mobility of workers already kept the wage differential relatively low. (Before World War II, auto wages in Windsor were comparable to those in Detroit.)

This gap between the expectations of the workers and the corporation's desire to keep profits high in Canada was partially offset by the high tariff on cars, which allowed the companies to charge more for their products. Whenever the tariff was lowered, the companies translated the drop into greater pressures for wage restraint and/or an increase in the line speed. Decreasing tariffs were a factor in GM's pressure on the Oshawa workers in 1927-28 and in the 1937 confrontations. When the Oshawa workers resisted the speed-up and the cuts in wages, and the incentive payments in February 1937, GM threatened (*Toronto Star*) that: " ... the parent company wants us to have all bodies manufactured in the U.S. and we can bring them in here, even with the duty, cheaper than it costs to produce them here."

Once the strike began on 8 April 1937, both the company and the Ontario premier, Mitch Hepburn, increased the pressure on the Oshawa workers. Quoted on the front page of the *New York Times* on 12 April 1937, the GM spokesman warned: " ... the competitive situation (facing Canadians) justified longer hours to lower production costs." Hepburn added: "In a competitive world situation ... the CIO drive would make [it] impossible [for the province to be] a great exporter of goods, would keep U.S. capital out of Ontario, and would prevent existing plants from expanding ...."

The facts, however, were that the Canadian operations were profitable in 1937, and GM, having conceded to unionization in the U.S., was unlikely to go through a long strike to block it in Canada. The catch was the intervention of the premier, whose aggressive anti-union position hardened GM's own position and encouraged GM to extend the strike. Hepburn was looking beyond GM and hoping to block the CIO's expansion into Canadian manufacturing and, especially, into the resource sector. Ontario's mines were a rich source of provincial revenue and the Canadian economy was generally more dependent on its resource sector than other developed countries. As Hepburn bluntly said to the *Globe and Mail* on 16 April 1937: "[I am] more concerned with the CIO's threat in the mine fields than in the automobile industry."

This statement led the *Toronto Star* on 23 April 1937 to refer to the Oshawa strike as a "miner's strike in a motors town."

Hepburn, a Liberal, had actually won on a mildly progressive, mildly pro-labour ticket in 1934. But, as with other politicians before and since, it was one thing to tell workers what was good for them and quite another to deal with an independent labour movement that could articulate and fight for its own demands. As early as 9 April 1937, Hepburn was warning in the *New York Times* that "... the entire resources of the province will be utilized ... to prevent anything in this country resembling that which is taking place ... across the line [border]." And a day later, he added: "If necessary we'll raise an army to do it!" (The workers referred to that private army of Premier Mitch Hepburn, which was recruited but never actually used, as "Sons of Mitches.")

When two cabinet ministers questioned Hepburn's aggressive anti-union stance, Hepburn insisted on cabinet solidarity and they eventually resigned, with one of them, Labour minister David Croll, bequeathing to posterity his immortal comment that "I'd rather walk with the workers than ride with General Motors."

Croll went on to become the mayor of Windsor later that year, defeating a prominent member of the city's business élite.

The Globe and Mail articulated the class perspective of business and the premier from day one. Its first report framed the confrontation as one between the head of an elected government and a foreign organization rather than one between Canadian workers and their employers. The banner headline of 9 April 1937 announced, "Premier Hepburn Declares War on CIO."

UAW female workers at Local 222 meeting April 1937. Courtesy of Wayne State Archives.

A front page editorial on 9 April 1937 ("A Menace to Be Stopped") set out themes that the *Globe and Mail* and the premier would hammer out on a daily basis: workers were really happy ("for years there seems to have been satisfaction with the treatment accorded"); the only problem was that the Canadian workers were being manipulated by "imported agitators"; the strike threatened violence ("Are we to be subjected to a reign of terror?"). This paper, which aggressively supported the largest American-based multinational in Canada, even argued, with no hint of shame, that the strike was about the CIO "dominating and dictating to Canadian industry." With the same straight face, the editorial went on to attack the CIO as being American and praised the no-less American, but conservative and decrepit, AFL: "Let it be remembered that their [i.e., the CIO's] primary purpose is to destroy the American Federation of Labour, which enjoys the world-wide distinction of high-minded craftsmen."

The workers answered GM, Hepburn, and the *Globe and Mail* by demonstrating the unanimity and solidarity behind the strike. Everyone walked out including, to the great interest of the media who featured this in their stories, the 260 women concentrated in the sewing department. Five hundred GM workers who were veterans of World War I marched through the streets of Oshawa wearing their war medals to challenge the insinuations that strikers were not "good Canadians." Clergy supported the strike, farmers brought milk and food, and shopkeepers supplied credit.

The *Toronto Star* reacted differently than the *Globe*. In an editorial published 14 April 1993, it acknowledged the real-world base of the changes taking place, arguing that "There is a natural feeling of antagonism between employers and employed. And to some extent there always will be. It is a natural product of our economic system ... No worker ever gets rich as a result of his toil. The capital and management often reap what the worker regards as fabulous wealth. That being the case, [the worker] ought not be handicapped in using what legal means he has."

On 12 April, the arrival of UAW president Homer Martin brought an amazing show of citywide support for what had become a community strike. That evening, 5,000 people rallied to hear speeches and to demonstrate their unity. Discipline — no drinking, no fighting — was rigidly maintained by patrols throughout the strike to avoid giving Hepburn reason to send in troops. The *Canadian Forum* reported in June, 1937, that: "Veteran labour leaders almost wept when they saw the amazing display of enthusiasm ... never in all the history of the Canadian labour movement had a town been so completely captured by the sentiment of unionism."

In order to boost morale, Martin had promised financial assistance and sympathy strikes, neither of which he had discussed with the CIO or UAW executive boards and which he could not honour. On Friday 16 April, eight days into the strike, he met with GM executives in Detroit and agreed that the Oshawa strike should be settled without recognition by GM of the CIO. Charles Millard, the president of the Oshawa local and now a full-time CIO organizer, was equally nervous and anxious for a settlement.

On Monday 19 April, Millard and Thompson confidently brought the proposed settlement to the workers, even though it wasn't in writing and it didn't include the recognition of the union that the UAW had won in Flint. The workers were clearly uncertain about what they had won and also suspicious, based on past unfulfilled company promises, of unwritten agreements. The press predicted support for a settlement as workers filed into the meeting, but the workers surprised their leadership and rejected the offer.

Yet by the end of the week, a written agreement was in place and the mood had changed. The reasons for the turnaround are not clear. It seems that with some gains made, with the leadership forcefully arguing that it could not do any better, and with it becoming evident that neither financial assistance nor sympathy strikes would come from the United States, workers concluded that they really had no choice but to end the fifteen-day strike. At the next meeting on Friday 23 April, the workers were buoyant and full of camaraderie. In spite of shortcomings in the agreement, they had gained a sense of achievement in taking on GM and enthusiastically voted — by a margin of 2205 to thirty-six — to return to work.

The settlement included wage gains, though wages remained some twelve to fifteen per cent below those paid at GM's American plants. There was seniority for lay-offs and rehiring, a nine-person bargaining committee, a grievance procedure, and a guarantee of no reprisals against union activists. The work week was shortened to forty-four hours with overtime pay of time-and-a-half; the regular week was nine-hour days Mondays to Thursdays and an eight-hour day on Friday. Canada's work week was still longer than the forty-hour week established at GM in the United States that March. And the union settled without achieving its original goal, the crucial goal won in the U.S. at both GM and Chrysler: recognition of the UAW. Hepburn immediately claimed victory.

Yet the fact that the workers had survived in the face of Hepburn's crusade against the CIO and after taking on the largest company in the world and the power of the state, meant victory was really theirs. The day after the Oshawa settlement, buoyant and optimistic CIO organizers and supporters were already distributing leaflets in the electrical and steel plants of Toronto and Hamilton. Others carried the CIO message across Ontario and beyond. In the *New York Times* on 24 April 1937, Charles Millard, the president of the Oshawa local, aptly summed up the situation: "I know and they know and the world knows the union has been recognized."

In spite of many initial successes, the drive to extend industrial unionism remained fragile. Workers carrying the CIO banner were harassed and often prevented from holding public meetings. They were fired and blacklisted, spied on, and confronted by strikebreakers. "Canadian governments," as Craig Heron stated in The Canadian Labour Movement, "were still most likely to respond with an iron heel to any efforts by workers to organize" and this attitude was "... probably the crucial difference between Canada and the United States in this period".

Unfriendly governments, the continuing absence of legal union rights, and unfavourable economic times left hostile companies with the upper hand. In late 1937, the economy experienced another severe downturn and organizing slowed down. Without a solid foundation in place, even some formerly unionized units were lost. Unionists expressed frustration about the difficulty of winning strikes when auto companies could undermine them by bringing in imports from underutilized American plants. (Canadian production was primarily for the local market at that time and so Canadian stoppages had only a marginal impact on U.S. production.)

Reflecting some of the divisions in the Canadian labour movement, the nationalist ACCL, which was opposed to the American-led CIO, went so far as to privately write to Hepburn after the Oshawa strike, commending him for his attempts to "curb domination by foreign agitators and Communists" and praise him in their publication for having done a "great service to Canadian labour."

Ironically, this Canadian nationalism echoed the AFL's opposition to the earlier Flint sit-down, when the AFL President commented: "... both personally and officially, I disavow the sit-down strike as part of the economic and organizational policy of the AFL."

After the growth between 1936 and 1938, the number of organized workers in Canada actually fell over the next two years. By the end of the thirties less than eighteen per cent of the Canadian workforce was organized, compared to twenty-five per cent in the United States. The UAW's membership dropped from about 10,000 in 1937 to under 5,000 in Canada, while it reached almost half a million in the U.S. Of Canada's dozen locals that existed a year earlier, only three were still active.

In Oshawa, the dues-paying membership fell to as low as 400 in a workforce of about 3,000. The local was desperate to recover its membership base, yet it was unable to deliver any material gains from the company. It therefore tried to maintain some links by way of social networks such as fishing/hunting clubs and bowling leagues, and through services such as credit unions. But it wasn't until 1943 that Local 222 signed its next agreement with GM.

Organizing had also slowed in the U.S., though not to the same extent as in Canada. In Flint, for example, only 500 of 32,000 workers were paying union dues in 1938. The crisis facing the American UAW, which also affected the Canadians, was aggravated by the economic downturn, but it stemmed essentially from an internal fight between its president, Homer Martin, and a group that included communists, socialists (such as the Reuthers), and other militants.

Martin, it seemed, had become president of the young union primarily on the basis of his skills as an orator and the absence of strong personal enemies in any section of the union. His lack of administrative and strategic skills soon became evident, but by 1938 his actions had become dangerously erratic. He made secret deals with the companies, and, apparently in return, Ford bought him a house when he eventually left the company. He arbitrarily fired board members who disagreed with him and he banned local union newspapers and direct contact between locals. He undermined wildcats (mid-contract walk-outs) and refused workers the right to ratify their agreements. Then, when the executive board rejected his direction, he even went so far as to set up an alternative union affiliated with the AFL.

Given the vulnerability of the new union, Martin's destructive actions seriously weakened the effectiveness of the UAW, even in plants where it had won recognition. The auto companies, and especially GM, argued that they no longer knew which union was legitimate (the CIO union or the Martin-backed AFL union) and refused to negotiate with either one. The turmoil seriously threatened the union's existence until Martin was finally deposed at the 1939 convention and replaced by R.J. Thomas. This change in leadership, combined with the upturn that followed the outbreak of World War II, brought a degree of stability to the union.

A parallel fight was taking place within the Canadian section of the union. Charles Millard, the president of the Oshawa local, had originally been appointed director of the Canadian region. Although this appointment was subsequently endorsed in an election, Millard's support was weak and the union was stumbling. His alliance with the unpopular Homer Martin, albeit temporary, didn't help his credibility. And Millard's focus on asserting the dominance of the CCF inside the union was generally viewed by both activists and members as being unnecessarily divisive, since there was at that time a strong working relationship within the union between CP members, CCF supporters, and independent militants. In 1939, George Burt, the secretary-treasurer of the Oshawa local, defeated Millard and became the Canadian director of the union.

The real growth and consolidation of unions in the mass production industries of Canada didn't come until after the war broke out. But the strike in Oshawa had broken the ground. The enthusiasm and activity that followed the Oshawa victory provided a base on which the new unions and organizing committees would build. Hepburn's belligerent escalation of the Oshawa strike and the union's survival of that attack gave the CIO and the UAW a stature, profile, and base that guaranteed its future prominence.

Charlie Millard came to GM after the depression destroyed his small business. After his defeat as Canadian director in 1939, he continued his conflict with Burt and the Canadian UAW in his role within steel. The staff of the Steelworkers Organizing Committee (SWOC) had earlier been fired because of frustration with both the apparent pace of organizing and their ties to the communist party. Millard was immediately made Executive Director of SWOC and became the head of the steelworkers union in Canada when it was established in 1942. He also played a key role in the development of other industrial unions like the United Packinghouse Workers.

Beyond Oshawa's City Limits

The Oshawa strike was organized and ultimately won in Canada. The American UAW was too new and distracted by the events exploding in its own country to offer support by way of strike pay, cadres of organizers, or sympathy strikes. Yet the Americans did the most important thing they could do: they acted decisively in their own country. This action created the space and led the way for Canadians to do the same.

The union had internationalized the struggle not because of any formal cross-border institutions, but by way of the solidarity of Canadians and Americans taking on, within their own spheres of activity, the common enemy. Victor Reuther, Walter Reuther's youngest brother and one of the leaders in the breakthrough at Flint, understood this principle when speaking, almost fifty years later, to the Canadian section of the UAW as it embarked on the formation of its own union: "... let us not stretch the ... importance of organic [i.e., institutional] unity as though without it, it is impossible to have an expression of solidarity."

THE CANADIAN COUNCIL

After the Oshawa strike, activists from each of the four locals in the Canadian section of the UAW began to meet regularly to deal with their common problems, give some direction to their activities, and impose some accountability on the director, whose internal support was weak. Frustrated because they had no formal status in the union, and learning that the UAW constitution allowed for just such a structure, they formed a regional committee at a meeting in Brantford in 1938 and then applied for and got a charter to establish the Canadian Council in 1939.

The radically democratic principle behind this clause was that delegates elected by the membership should have their own structure, parallel to the administrative structure of the union and with its own elected executive and independent financing, to act as a check on the regional director and the staff.

The director would be invited to each meeting — originally held six times a year but later quarterly — to give both an oral and written report on his or her activities in the preceding period. Over the years, it was almost unheard of for the director to be exempt, by reason of any extenuating circumstances, from providing the delegates a lengthy written report.

The council itself had no binding power on policy, but its authority — originally based on its democratic base but reinforced over time by the weight of tradition — meant that it became the real parliament of the union. The divisions within this emerging parliament were not so much the "administration" vs. the "rank-and-file," but ideological; it was at the council that so many of the ideological fights and ideological shifts got played out. As the ideological differences in the union collapsed, so did the notion of the council as an independent or parallel structure. But while this changed the tone of the council, it didn't undermine the crucial role it played within the union.

The council went beyond just monitoring the director and his or her activities. It was an exciting educational forum where the director could inform and raise the broadest issues; where new delegates could hear experienced debaters raising the issues and attacking corporations, governments, and each other; where those same new delegates would nervously make their first interventions in front of peers beyond their local; and where the director and the staff could get a better sense of the mood of the rank-and-file.

The council was also a cultural forum, especially when held in the workers' own educational camp. It gave local leadership precious time to socialize, catch up on personal matters, and informally discuss specific in-

plant issues. For the opposition, it was a chance to caucus regularly and reach potential recruits. The council was therefore an institution that linked the union together vertically (by creating

Canaadian Council delegates, 1948 (current CAW staff exceeds number of delegates there were then). Courtesy of National Archives, C107289.

relations between top leadership and activists), horizontally (by allowing activists to meet and work directly with each other rather than just depend on connections via the top leadership) and generationally (by establishing an ongoing continuity between past activists and traditions and emerging militants and issues).

The council structures never took hold in the U.S.; by the early fifties they were already dormant. The difference in Canada was twofold. First, Canada was a separate country and therefore needed a mechanism for having its own discussions and debates and, at times, for challenging or resisting the American leadership. Without its own national executive board and given the limits of injecting Canadian perspectives into an overwhelmingly American-based convention, the idea of a Canadian council had obvious attractions. Second, the Canadian section of the union included an opposition dependent on the council for access to other activists. Any attempt to undermine the council could be powerfully countered by mobilizing the members around democracy and nationalism. (In fact, no such move to get rid of the council was ever attempted.)

This Canada–U.S. solidarity did not preclude tensions. In fact, the relationship between the Canadians and the Americans involved, from the beginning, conflicting pressures and strains that would dominate the union's politics and evolution until the Canadian breakaway. The Canadians, as in other relationships between the two countries, were the dependent partner; the Americans, as senior partner, set the stage. The Canadians lagged behind in obtaining union recognition (not just at GM but at each of the Big Three companies), comparable wages, and other negotiated gains. Yet the Canadians, in large part because they were not simply another region of the UAW, also maintained a level of independence and cohesiveness. These elements would form the base for keeping alternative perspectives alive and, eventually, for developing the degree of self-confidence that would result in the union taking a different direction.

That independence was manifested in the creation of a particularly important and dynamic democratic institution: the Canadian Council. Although this structure was not unique to Canada — the UAW constitution set out the council's voluntary creation at the regional level — the Canadian section was alone in keeping its council over the years. The Americans had overcome a dangerous leader after a painful period by deposing him. The Canadians, who were not in a position to determine the North American leadership, took the issue of ongoing accountability one step further and deepened their own democracy with the establishment of this institution.

Beyond the effects on the UAW and other CIO unions, the Oshawa strike also had a crucial and lasting impact on the future direction of Canadian politics. The premier's rejection of the moderately progressive political space that the Liberals formerly held did not, at first, seem to hurt Hepburn electorally. Running on an anti-CIO ticket in the next provincial election, his Liberals swept the province. The virtual collapse of the Canadian UAW at GM in the late thirties was reflected electorally in the easy win by Hepburn's Liberals in the Oshawa riding. Yet this provincial victory was the Ontario Liberal's last hurrah.

The election reflected the facts that the Conservative Party had been discredited by its policies during the depression and the CCF had not yet gotten off the ground in Ontario (its vote was under six per cent). In the next election, with the CCF moving into the political vacuum that Hepburn and the Liberals had left in their attacks on the Oshawa workers, the Liberals lost and were not to return to office in the province for over four decades. The mercurial rise of the CCF — it was at or near the top of the polls in 1942–43 — shifted both the federal Liberals and Conservatives towards the centre-left, and had them advocating the rudiments of what would become Canada's social safety net after the war.

The victory in Oshawa can today be identified, in the words of an editorial in a church publication at the time, as "not just another industrial dispute [but] a phase in a movement of great significance" (*New Outlook*, 23 April 1937). Yet that movement remained very fragile. In the late thirties, it was stalled by the inevitable corporate counterattack, the difficult economic times, internal union problems, and a Canadian state that was at best indifferent and at worst openly hostile. Nor was any broader political alternative able to get off the ground.

In trying to assess the significant achievements of this difficult period, we won't find them so much in the specific gains made or the structures firmly established, but in the fact that the working class was stirring. It had begun to fight back in spite of the times and thereby build its self-confidence and organizing skills. Workers were challenging their companies, putting political élites on the spot, questioning past assumptions, and further testing and developing new structures, such as industrial unions, which covered all workers across companies and entire sectors, and the Canadian Council.

The significance of the Oshawa breakthrough therefore lay in its central role in a new beginning. The struggle in Oshawa established a base for the UAW in Canada. More generally, it created the crucial opening for the CIO, and, less directly, it set the stage for a shift in politics to the centre-left. From these beginnings — moderate in terms of immediate achievements but radical in terms of potential — emerged the more substantive gains of the coming decades.

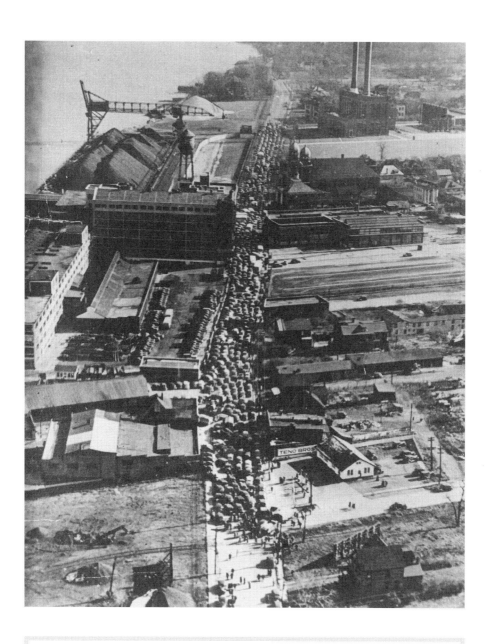

Ford blockade, 1945. Courtesy of National Archives, C107288.

CHAPTER 4

RECOGNITION

*Do we get dressed up when we go in to see the boss or
do we go in just the way we are in the factory?*
> — Shop committee member, Brantford

*All day long, whether rain or shine,
She's a part of the assembly line,
She's making history, working for victory,
Rosie — the Riveter.*
> — "Rosie the Riveter," Redd Evans and John
> Jacob Loeb

*… the "Rand remedy" [made] the Ford walkout of 1945
the most important post-war strike in Canada.*
> — David Moulton

The war economy between 1939 and 1945 provided the Canadian UAW with the opportunity to build on its earlier but very fragile success and establish the membership base which would define the UAW for the next four decades. This base included workers at the Big Three, at major independent parts companies, in aerospace, and in agricultural implements. In addition to the numbers, the specific responses of Canadian workers to this period had a significant impact on the emerging character of the union.

At first, the war, like most wars, tended to unite people around a common enemy and a collective goal. This tendency left workers hesitant to take contrary positions, and it legitimized pressures to keep production rolling. But as the war dragged on, the nature of the changes raised new questions about the organization of production in our society, about the everyday inequality that contradicted the call to a common purpose, about the subordinate role of workers relative to their employers in a country fighting for democracy, and — as women entered the workforce in such large numbers — about the role of women in the workplace and in society.

The War Ends the Depression

The war did something depression-era capitalism couldn't do: it provided jobs. Bankers stopped warning about the deficit, and corporate executives toned down their insistence that government stay out of the economy. Idle factories became busy, as the number of workers doubled in manufacturing and quadrupled in transportation equipment. Governments and companies even introduced child-care services to attract women into the workforce. The government's own Bank of Canada, along with Victory Bonds, financed a substantial portion of savings. (The bonds, which were sold by the government, carried lower interest but appealed to people's patriotism.) These options limited the dependence on foreign borrowing. Crown corporations were established to guarantee key supplies, such as oil, and vital materials, such as rubber. And a growing civil service introduced a measure of planning by way of the conversion to military production, partially regulated prices, and exchange controls limiting the export of capital as well as unnecessary imports.

None of these initiatives, it must be emphasized, undermined the basic power of those who owned industry and finance. In fact, by the end of the war, the productive capacity of Canadian business had been dramatically expanded, and profits were skyrocketing. This development wasn't solely the result of the strong and steady growth. The government had subsidized retooling, expansions, and new plants for military use. And as the war came to an end, the government subsidized the reconversion of these productive facilities to civilian use. Flourishing crown corporations were sold or virtually given to the private sector. Canada emerged from the war with sizable potential as a manufacturing nation, though the private sector was much more integrated with the United States in terms of ownership and trade.

Nor did the wartime planning regulate the economy to address the needs of working people. The strong economy and tight labour markets clearly strengthened labour's position. But the government counteracted with imposed delays on the right to strike, limits on picketing, and wage controls in 1940 which froze wages at their 1926–29 levels. In 1942, eighty per cent of manufacturing was involved in war production. Limits were placed on workers in war industries, preventing them from leaving their jobs for work elsewhere. And even when, after a period of both intense worker militancy and political gains, the government finally introduced legislation supporting unionization in early 1944, it made strikes against wage controls illegal and subject to stiff fines.

During the depression, when business was taking advantage of the large numbers of unemployed and desperate workers, one-sided labour legislation clearly presented a barrier for unions. However, the significance of such legislation declined with the strong wartime economy and tight labour market. The new conditions empowered any determined workers to establish their unions irrespective of, or at least in spite of, the absence of legislative support. Canadian labour, like business, came out of the war stronger. In 1939, union membership in Canada was at 356,000 (seventeen per cent of the workforce). By the end of the war it had more than doubled to over 724,000 (twenty-five per cent of the workforce). At the end of the thirties, the fate of the Canadian section of the UAW was uncertain: its prewar membership was down to 5,000. By the end of the war, membership had soared to almost 50,000.

Getting a Voice

The outbreak of war didn't immediately lead to rapid union growth. The drive to unionization was delayed by the shock of the war, the sense of relief at the availability of jobs, the lag in actual conversion to military production, and the intimidation of the state. In the fall of 1941, GM workers at McKinnon in St. Catharines went on strike for wage parity with Oshawa and learned first-hand about the rigidity of wartime controls. Uncertain about its own strength when the strike began and suddenly confronted with armed RCMP (Royal Canadian Mounted Police) officers, the union nevertheless survived the seventeen-day strike and made modest wage gains.

The turning point in the new drive to unionization again took place in the United States; this time at Ford. Unlike GM and Chrysler, Ford had survived the thirties without having to acknowledge the UAW. The company entered the forties confident that the situation would not change. In March, 1941, Henry Ford was quoted in the *Toronto Star* as declaring: "In my opinion the unions are losing ground and haven't a leg to stand on."

As long as Ford resisted, other major companies harboured hopes of rolling back the tide of unionism. For decades, Ford had led in the fight to keep workers in their place, depending in turn on paternalism, wage incentives, and threats. The company even monitored and spied on workers' personal lives, checking to see if they fulfilled Ford's "moral" standards. Ford tried to buy non-union subservience by paying higher wages (though only as long as the company's monopoly on assembly line development assured a flood of profits). Later, Ford hired an internal army of organized gangsters to monitor, spy on, and intimidate workers. Breaking the anti-union bastion at Ford was therefore crucial not only because of the new union members it would bring, but also because of the enormous symbolic weight a victory at Ford would carry.

Although the U.S. hadn't yet entered the war, its economy was already booming, and conversion plans were well underway. Ford found itself unable to hold out given the profitable opportunities it was missing. In April, 1941, workers went on strike for eight days, bringing in a massive cavalcade of cars to surround the sprawling River Rouge complex outside of Detroit — and the Ford workers won. Within a short month of Henry Ford's dismissal of the union as ineffectual, the company recognized the UAW. The American UAW had therefore "locked up" the Big Three and clearly established its

As part of mobilizing UAW members to fight Ford, executive board member Walter Reuther arranged for the distribution of 200,000 copies of Upton Sinclair's working-class novel *The Flivver King*.

permanence. Furthermore, the Ford agreement included union security, which had eluded the union at GM and Chrysler; Ford would deduct dues from workers' paycheques and send them directly to the union.

The Windsor workers had been trying to obtain a foothold at Ford since the twenties, and these attempts intensified, though without any immediate results, after the 1937 victory in Oshawa. The success across the river again inspired Canadians, as it did in 1937, to take hold of the new possibilities. This time, the workers had the advantage of war-time production demands and proximity. Skilled workers from Windsor, with experience in British trade unionism, had been meeting with the River Rouge workers even before the U.S. strike. Now they intensified their efforts in Windsor. Furthermore, the Americans were now sufficiently established to offer some material support.

In the fall of 1941, when Ford tried to exclude the Canadian UAW from the ballot by limiting unionization to a vote in favour of or against a company union, Canadian director George Burt and UAW president R.J. Thomas visited Ford headquarters. River Rouge was already in some turmoil, and Burt and Thomas threatened further workplace disruptions at River Rouge to stop Ford from shipping components for military vehicles to Windsor. Later, when Ford began flooding the air waves with the company message and no radio station in Ford-dominated Windsor would sell the union air time, the River Rouge local (Local 600) bought time on Detroit radio, allowing Burt to beam his message back across the river. With the help of their American brothers and sisters, the Canadian workers showed that the union could, quite literally, give the workers a voice.

The threat of parts shortages quickly got the attention of and a reaction from the federal government. Canada had entered the war before the Americans. Ford, one of the first to fully convert to military production, was already the leading producer of military vehicles. The government was concerned about its war orders and used its wartime legislation (it could place plants involved in war production under a government-appointed trustee) to pressure Ford into accepting a prompt representational vote.

Ford naturally exploited its access to every worker in the plant. But more significant, the company offered concessions to the workers if they rejected the UAW. Ford's promises went beyond the benefits of the UAW victory in Oshawa. The company offer matched GM in seniority rights, but offered a better deal in both wages and union structure. Ford promised, for example, to recognize not only a bargaining committee but also a steward system to

In 1941 at Kirkland Lake where Mine Mill had an organizing drive, a conciliation board ruled in favour of a vote so that workers could decide whether or not to join the union. The company refused to allow a vote and the government refused to intervene, claiming "neutrality." The workers went on strike, and the government demonstrated its neutrality in the form of the police marching into town to protect scabs. Although the strike lost, many future activists and leaders emerged from the protest and the government response reinforced the labour movement's commitment to win union recognition. Courtesy of National Archives, C107290.

handle grievances. But the Ford workers in Windsor had reached an irreversible stage in union consciousness and confidence. They had done the solid groundwork, organizing inside and outside the plant. A public meeting at Windsor's former Capital Theatre brought 2,000 workers together. Workers could now discuss the union without fear of company reprisal, and the union had won them the right to vote and a chance to be heard. The Ford workers were ready to launch the union. In November, 1941, they voted in favour of the UAW by a margin of three to two (6,833 to 4,455).

By January, 1942, the workers had an agreement. Because of the Americans' later entry into the war, the UAW in the U.S. didn't have to confront wage and price controls at that time. Wages at Ford U.S. had therefore moved ahead of those at Ford's Windsor plant. The Canadian agreement did not close that gap. It confirmed Ford's North American practice of a standard forty-hour week and also introduced company-wide seniority for layoffs and recall, a first amongst the Big Three in all of North America. And when long-term lay-offs did occur, the agreement — consistent with both the spirit of solidarity that existed at the time and the company's own preferences — required an initial stage of a four-day, thirty-two-hour week to limit the number of lay-offs. But most important, a major company had finally agreed to recognize the UAW.

> Excerpt from first UAW–Ford Agreement in Canada (Local 200), 15 January 1942:
>
> 8.(n)*If there be a general reduction in the number of employees in the Windsor plants the following procedures shall apply:*
>
> *First — Probationary employees shall be the first to be laid off.*
>
> *Second — As far as reasonably practicable the hours of work will be reduced to thirty-two hours per week and thereafter layoffs shall take place according to seniority.*

The negative side of the agreement was that Ford still denied Canadian workers the crucial breakthrough it had accepted in the United States: union security and the dues check-off. Moreover, the achievement of union recognition at Ford did not trigger a general pattern for the Canadian labour movement. Companies generally continued to fight the labour movement even where a union had the clear support of the majority of the membership, and the government endorsed this resistance directly and indirectly. Within the Canadian UAW, however, union recognition quickly

Workers at Motor Products, manufacturer of auto components, c. 1938. (In 1942, workers walked out to gain union recognition and got a government supervised vote, which they won.) Courtesy of CAW Archives, Port Elgin.

spread throughout southern Ontario.

Windsor workers had tried to organize Chrysler in 1938, after the momentum of the mid-thirties had begun to fade. The walk-out by a small group of activists wasn't supported, and the organizing drive petered out. In 1940, before the organizing momentum of the war period had begun, the Chrysler workers tried again. After a company lock-out, forty-seven workers — including UAW director George Burt — were arrested for interfering with the production of war materials while picketing across the street from the plant. This latest attempt to organize also failed, though an intensive labour lobby subsequently changed the law on picketing. Buoyed by the Ford victory, the 3,600 Chrysler workers in Windsor finally won. In April, 1942, they voted four to one (2,856 to 707) in favour of the union just as car production was being suspended for the duration of the war.

At one point, the Chrysler workers thought they had found a loophole in the law that allowed picketing if the picketers weren't on foot. They rented horses. The horses, one of the workers later joked, are still in jail.

By the end of 1943, the Canadian UAW had organized the main component plants in Windsor and won a narrow victory amongst the Ford office workers. Its agreements in total covered approximately 40,000 workers. The union had spread beyond Oshawa–St. Catharines–Windsor, to Amherstburg, Tilbury, Wallaceburg, Simcoe, Welland, Belleville, Sarnia, Brantford and Toronto.

The slow rate of unionization in the reactionary Toronto area had been reversed with the organization of 3,500 workers at de Havilland Aircraft and 6,000 workers in Toronto and Brantford at Massey-Ferguson (which manufactures farm equipment). Both previously had company unions. The fact that these units represented an expansion outside auto and therefore broadened the base of the union gave them an additional importance.

In Canada, one unionized worker in three participated in a work stoppage in 1942–43. This number was unprecedented in Canadian history and, for the first time, there were proportionately more strikes in Canada than in the United States. In the Canadian UAW, almost half of all workers participated in a stoppage in these two years.

A UAW organizing leaflet at de Havilland Aircraft argued that: "The only opportunity de Havilland workers have of bettering their wages is through comparison with the auto industry, since their wages are now as high as any paid in Canadian aircraft plants."

Unionization did raise wages significantly, but neither was auto standing still. In the early seventies, this demand for catch-up with auto turned out to be a crucial aspect of worker militancy in the Ontario aerospace industry.

"A Woman's Place Is..."

Within the trade union movement itself, the war brought to the fore a contradiction that, while not new, could no longer be ignored. The CIO and industrial unionism had crusaded for the equality of *all* workers, and working women, especially in the clothing industry, joined unions in large numbers. But wages in the sectors that employed women were low while in the new sectors such as auto, companies rarely hired women. Even when women got jobs in auto, their wages were about two-thirds of men's (or lower), and management restricted women to separate seniority lists.

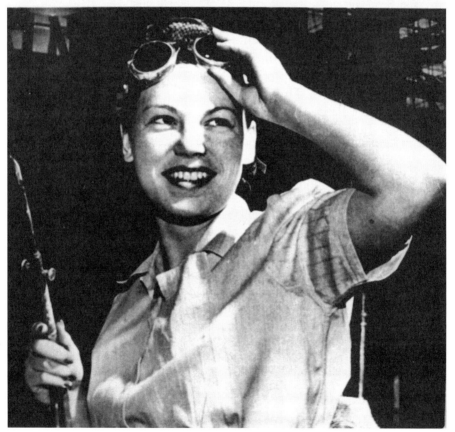

McKinnon recruiting poster for women during the war. Courtesy of CAW Local 199 Collection.

At GM, in the thirties, the Oshawa and St. Catharines plants each employed over 200 women. In addition, women reps sat on the bargaining committee, but they generally represented women who worked in segregated departments such as the sewing room. The original GM agreement of 1937 included a clause reading: "In any department in which both men and women are employed they should be divided into separate non-interchangeable occupational groups."

Soon after that agreement, when the economy slowed down and lay-offs returned, the union argued that positions should be found in other departments for those women with highest seniority. Although some inequities were later corrected, GM's Oshawa plant manager replied, at a meeting on 24 September 1937, that GM would unilaterally decide how many women to hire, adding that "the management did not favour mixing male and female 'help' in a department."

As young men left for the battlefield and the economy geared itself to the overseas war needs, Canada moved from unemployment to a situation where, by 1942, companies were competing for workers. For many companies and the government, women were the answer. Rather than attracting scarce workers with higher wages or better conditions, the companies could bring a new pool of labour into the factories and segregate these women workers in certain departments. Confident that the position offered to women — temporary, new to the labour market, separated from experienced union activists — would limit the development of their trade union consciousness and make them easier to control, the companies paid them lower wages.

In Oshawa, the number of women workers doubled (to 400); in St. Catharines, over one-quarter of the workforce was now women (1,200 of 4,500); at de Havilland, women (1,775) represented over half the workforce. In the auto industry before the war, only one worker in fourteen was female; this number more than doubled by 1943. In aerospace, the number of women was previously negligible; it rose to better than one in five workers (though they were still concentrated in certain lines of work). In agricultural implements, the proportion of women quadrupled from about five per cent to almost twenty per cent.

With popular culture supporting the inclusion of women in the workforce and with women participating in production, many thought that prevailing stereotypes of the role of women might change. After all, magazines now glorified the woman who left her home to produce for the war, popular

Woman involved in war production, GM Oshawa. Courtesy of CAW Collection.

songs such as "Rosie-the-Riveter" paid tribute to her, governments and companies not only endorsed but actually provided child-care services, and women showed that they were capable of heavy manufacturing and skilled work.

In spite of the apparent social support for women entering the workforce, their status remained inferior. The gendered division that the auto majors enforced was effective. If women had, for example, worked on the assembly line, doing the same work as men, the pressures from both the women and their fellow male unionists might have led to wage parity. But the company managed to avoid this outcome.

In motor vehicle assembly, employment increased by about 8,400 workers between 1939 and the wartime peak of 1942–43; but only 130 of these new workers, less than two per cent, were women. Even though the number of workers in the assembly sector increased by two-thirds between 1929 and 1949, the number of women — low as it was to start with — actually fell. Women were hired in certain sections of the parts sector, in traditional women's departments within the auto majors, or temporary divisions expected to disappear after the war. General Motors, for example, created a special Victory Shift for women which was to end when victory was achieved.

Some definite changes in attitude occurred. The Detroit office of the UAW established a Women's Bureau. With no automatic dues check-off, the union collected dues on an individual voluntary basis; this increased pressures to set out demands that would gain the support of women. Amalgamated locals such as Local 195 in Windsor and Local 397 in Brantford, which represented women in auto parts and miscellaneous manufacturing, successfully negotiated equal pay for equal work. Within the Big Three, Local 199 in St. Catharines was one of a number of locals who regularly raised the issue at the council, warning in June, 1942, that "unless the union is able to give leadership to the struggle for equal pay for equal work we will remain weak among the women."

The first strike of Ford Canada workers centred around the concern that Ford would replace men with lower-paid women. The union's demand was not to oppose the hiring of women, but to insist that they earn the same wages. Ford Canada's eventual response was that hiring women was worthwhile only if they were cheaper, and it refused to hire women at its assembly plants until 1977. Although the union leadership did raise the issue of equal pay with the broader public, the union did not launch a campaign to challenge Ford when it stopped hiring women in Canada. In the U.S., on the other hand, Ford was a major employer of women. This discrepancy may have stemmed from the differing structures of the company in the U.S. and in Canada. Whereas the Canadian operations were heavily weighted to assembly, the U.S. operations included an extensive parts manufacturing sector that could absorb lower-paid women workers.

After the war, many of these women, especially those who were married, were quite effectively returned to the kitchen. This trend was a matter of both company and government policy, reflected not only in lay-off policy but also in the closing of the extensive child-care centres that had been set up during the war. Yet women's return to the home also had a wide base of support amongst male and even female workers. There were isolated examples of resistance on the part of women, but as Pam Sugiman commented in *Labour's Dilemma*, her study of women in the Canadian UAW, the more common occurrence in the immediate postwar period was that "Married women disappeared as quietly and unassumingly as they had appeared in the auto plants."

Women's exposure to the world of work during the war did, however, have some lasting impact. In the decades after the war, the proportion of women in the workforce resumed a steady climb. Many of the married

The federal government had a nation-wide network of nurseries to "help working mothers in all industrial districts." Women not in the workforce provided voluntary assistance of a few hours per week to ease the staff pressures. Courtesy of CAW Local 199 Collection.

women who had entered the workforce in the war years and then returned to the home went back to work after their children grew up, influenced in part by their wartime experience. Furthermore, later studies indicated that women with wartime work experience passed on to their daughters attitudes that were more sympathetic to women's role in the workforce.

The story of women in the workforce during and after the war years contrasts in significant ways with the experience of black workers in the United States. The labour shortage and the relatively high wages in Detroit had attracted southern whites and blacks to Detroit. Racism against blacks was intense in spite of efforts by the UAW leadership to limit it: 100,000 person-days of wildcats occurred when whites (often but not always from the South) refused to work alongside blacks. The racism culminated in the horror of the Detroit race riots in the summer of 1943, when thirty-four people were killed. Yet, after the war, blacks, unlike women, remained a significant part of the auto workforce.

Black Workers

Little research has been done on black workers within the Canadian auto industry. There is little record of the kind of violently racist response that occurred in Detroit during the war, but that was fundamentally related to the small numbers of blacks then in Canada and the fact that social breakthrough into well-paying auto jobs hadn't yet started.

The main settlements of Canadian blacks were in Nova Scotia, where blacks came as part of the "loyalists" leaving the United States after the American revolution. While these settlements were far from the Ontario-based auto industry, GM recruited a few blacks from Nova Scotia along with a larger number from Toronto in the late thirties. They were hired in the St. Catharines foundry where the work was the hardest, dirtiest and most damaging to health. White workers generally avoided these jobs but those who had no choice regularly collapsed from the heat. Part of the rationale for recruiting blacks was the racist view that, being from Africa, they could better stand the heat. By the late forties, some blacks worked in St. Catharines. There were no blacks hired in Oshawa.

Another major settlement for blacks was Amherstburg, an end-point to the underground railway bringing escaped slaves to freedom. Yet even though Amherstburg was so close to Windsor, and even though tens of thousands of blacks were hired in Detroit, Chrysler didn't hire black production workers until after the war. That only changed after they lost a human rights case in 1946, initiated by the Canadian UAW and others in the labour movement and civil rights community. Ford, the largest private employer in Windsor, hired Chinese workers during the war as well as a few blacks. Again this was linked to the foundry and the worst jobs.

The difference, it seems, was that the role of blacks as paid workers wasn't generally challenged; the fight was over some white workers insisting that blacks be segregated. With women, on the other hand, it was their role as permanent paid workers that was not yet accepted. The truth was that the equality of women in the workplace could not be achieved unless the union addressed the broader role of women in the family and in society. As long as it was generally assumed that the role of women was primarily in the home, their role in the war would be viewed as temporary regardless of the rhetoric. Men might join in the fight for equal pay because they recognized this fight as being in their own self-interest; women accepting lower pay

A rare photo of black women in the early auto industry. These women are making parts in a St. Catharines components plant, 1944. Courtesy of *Toronto Telegram* collection at York University.

would be a competitive threat to their own jobs. But not so with seniority. Fewer workers with full seniority rights means more security for those with full rights (at least in the short run when solidarity is not an issue).

Indicative of these assumptions about the place of women in society was the role of the women's auxiliaries, organizations of wives of autoworkers established to assist the men in their struggles. The auxiliary in Oshawa, which became the largest such group in either Canada or the United States, was established before the 1937 strike began. These auxiliaries quickly spread throughout the union. They supplied coffee and sandwiches during strikes and sometimes joined the picket lines. They evolved into a social club for the participating women, who organized recreational and charity work.

But these women also saw themselves in broader political terms. In many locations — Oshawa is one example — they supplemented the work of the union by mobilizing within the community and sometimes nationally for better housing, rent controls, and national medicare. They supported key labour struggles outside the UAW, participated in the peace movement in the sixties, and addressed international issues.

Yet the auxiliaries and the working women in the UAW seemed to inhabit completely different worlds. Few links were established. As the participation of women in the workforce later grew, and as a feminist consciousness developed in the seventies and eighties, the membership of the auxiliaries correspondingly declined, especially amongst younger women.

When the war ended and lay-offs replaced labour shortages, the prevailing assumption that women's real role was in the home directly led to separate seniority lists. Even the fight for equal pay, as long as it was about equality in the abstract, rather than the pay of workers who were truly equal, would not attract the kind of commitment and mobilization needed to change the existing pay structures. Working women had not yet developed their own self-confidence and were not yet in a position to build on the experiences of the war to transform society's (and their own) view of women's role. They had little or no supportive resources inside or outside the union. The Women's Bureau, for example, was in Detroit and itself had limited resources. Changes occurred, but they came slowly and not before the notion of a broader women's movement was on the agenda.

The No-Strike Pledge

Before the war, equipment was sitting idle and skills and ideas were wasted. Suddenly the war demonstrated that productive capacities and formerly unskilled labour could be transformed to suit virtually any need. The car companies made military vehicles, armoured vehicles, tank hulls, Browning machine guns, naval gun mounts, automatic rifles, engines for the vehicles, and fuselages for airplanes. Ford's Windsor plant was the largest supplier of military vehicles in the British Empire. Massey-Harris manufactured shells and airplane wings. Early on in the war, de Havilland Aircraft, with an allocated workforce but no parts for planes, had the workers make toys and socks. Since war production could not be left to the market, a level of planning was necessary; the government had to closely supervise quality control and the allocation of production to ensure that the right demands were met according to plan. Plant closures couldn't be tolerated.

These accommodations eventually raised a series of questions: If we can plan for war, why can't we plan for peace? If the needs of war lead to full employment, why can't the peacetime needs of our citizens have the same result? By 1943, after the war clearly shifted in favour of the Allies, people began to think about the postwar world. How do we avoid another depression? How do we apply what we learned during the war to organizing our economy?

People questioned whose interests were being served by the structure of economic decision making and power. In the first days of the war, citizens patiently accepted the government's calls for sacrifices. But the calls for sacrifices also raised the issue of equality of sacrifice, and as the war went on, it became all too clear that wage controls worked much more effectively than price controls. The corporations could be conscripted into enforcing the limits on wages but controls on profits did not seem to work at all, especially after conversion to military production had been successfully implemented.

> It is undemocratic to attempt to call a halt to the free development of organizations of workers in the midst of a total war for freedom.
>
> — UAW (Canada) brief to the National War Labour Board

When workers asked for legislation forcing companies to negotiate with a worker-elected union, the government retreated behind its refusal to introduce mandatory requirements. Yet, it legislated mandatory wage controls. Unions challenged the inconsistency between fighting for democracy in Europe and denying basic trade union rights at home — such as the right to bargain. The patriotism that had been used to repress workers early in the war later became linked to democratic rights and justice at home.

Central to such debates was the government's request of a no-strike pledge. The war demanded steady production of war supplies and equipment. Although workers overwhelmingly supported the war and were generally very reluctant to interfere with production, they had their own grievances and demands, which had disruptive potential. The governments of both Canada and the United States responded with a call on labour to accept a no-strike pledge, which was eventually supported by wage controls and legislation that delayed or prevented strikes. Given that the industrial unions were still in their formative stages and given the significance of the strike as a weapon for workers, the response of the unions to the no-strike pledge could potentially have a profound effect on union philosophies, attitudes, structures, and internal politics.

In January, 1942, a month after the attack on Pearl Harbour, the leadership of the CIO met with Roosevelt. The American president offered the

Wartime government poster. Courtesy of National Archives, C87500.

CIO affiliates union security in exchange for no-strike pledges. Weekend work without premium pay was also demanded. The unions accepted. A special convention of the UAW in April confirmed the CIO patriotic pledge, formally including the Canadian UAW. But at a subsequent meeting of the Canadian Council, delegates refused to go along with their parent organization. The different responses in the two countries primarily reflected the distinct stages of the two labour movements and the contrasting legislative context each faced.

By the spring of 1941, after the decisive victory at Ford, the UAW had organized all the major auto companies in the U.S. and made major advances in aerospace and agricultural implements. Furthermore, and unlike its Canadian section, the American UAW had already obtained legislative protection. The additional union security offered by the government stipulated that workers who did not opt out within fifteen days of signing a contract would have to stay in the union and pay union dues (by a dues check-off). The government also established special labour boards to deal with any outstanding grievances.

The number of local educational committees in the UAW grew from seventy-five in 1940 to 240 in 1943. In 1941, the single one-week summer school had under 100 participants; by 1945 there were eight two-week schools for over 1,200 people.

The left-dominated UAW educational department also offered regional weekend schools, provided numerous pamphlets, distributed films, used radio extensively, and produced a regular weekly newspaper which included both union news and political analysis, reprints of key speeches, and reviews of relevant books, movies, and musical events. (The paper included a Canadian supplement.)

For the American UAW, with its major organizational goals largely achieved, this trade-off offered the chance to consolidate its new structures relatively free of company attempts to destroy them. The favourable political environment that had supported the union in the thirties was quickly fading, and the union felt vulnerable. Moreover, after Pearl Harbour and the appeals to defend American honour and prove that America was "Number One," American patriotism had reached a fever pitch. The union leadership and membership were not immune to the patriotic tide and were also sensitive to the risks of being isolated.

The UAW was walking the fine line between building the union's base and trying to limit the actions of that base. It had developed impressive educational materials and structures; it lobbied for creative national initiatives that would address both the war effort and domestic needs; and some leaders (the Reuthers, and especially Emil Mazey, the militant and popular president of the Briggs plant who was to become secretary-treasurer of the UAW in 1947) were less than enthusiastic in their support of the no-strike pledge. In terms of membership growth, experience seemed to justify the American UAW's acceptance of the no-strike pledge. By late 1943, UAW membership exceeded one million members (one-third more than the membership had fifty years later).

Significant sections of the membership were however, increasingly ready to take militant action despite the union's no-strike pledge. These groups included not only those workers opposed to the pledge because of the negative impact on the union, but also many workers who, hired as a result of the war, were new to the industry. While the activists of the thirties had focused on building the union, these new workers voiced other concerns. They were simply frustrated at the wage controls which kept wages far behind inflation, impatient with the company procedures for dealing with (or ignoring) their workplace grievances, and angry at the record profits the corporations were making from the war effort. In 1944, there were more strikes — most of them unauthorized — than in any year in American history, including the sit-down year of 1937; almost half of all union workers participated in a work stoppage that year.

The union's involvement in the no-strike pledge created a potentially dangerous gap between the membership and the leadership. The union was now in the position of disciplining, or at least pressuring, its members to "be more responsible" rather than leading them. The leadership's retreat from the strike weapon and the subsequent emphasis on technical presentations to government boards increasingly shifted the emphasis of the union away from worker mobilization towards centralization and professionalization.

The Canadian and American situations were fundamentally different. Until 1944, late in the war, Canadian workers were never offered legislated union security. During the war, the Canadian Manufacturers' Association (CMA) went so far as to argue that industrial unions be banned and that CIO organizers be jailed. Without effective legislation guaranteeing the right to bargain, the Canadian unions had little difficulty rejecting a formal no-strike pledge. Moreover, since the Canadian CIO unions were still organizing their sectors, their strikes were recognition strikes — the primary demand was for the basic democratic right of representation. Patriotism in this context didn't pressure workers to be more responsible; it challenged the undemocratic nature of the companies and the government.

In Canada, the union's top leaders were therefore actively working with the locals to mobilize and build the union. Since the government was directly involved in limiting wages and strikes, Canadian Council meetings directed attention to lobbying and challenging the government as well as the employers. And so, as the union grew, different relationships than in the U.S. developed between the members and their leadership, and between the union and the government. The Canadians' goal was not radical: they simply wanted the legislation the Americans had already won. Having to fight for it in the special context of a war economy, when the workers had some shop-floor strength, resulted in the development of confidence and independence. That drive extended to the Canadians also taking political action outside the mainstream parties — whether directly through demonstrations and lobbying or by way of a third party.

The different positions on the no-strike pledge taken by the Canadian and American sections of the UAW can't be understood apart from the different positions also taken by the communist trade unionists in each country. In both countries, the communists played a vital role in the development of industrial unionism in the mid-thirties. In addition to their own commitment and organizational skills, they also brought in activists from outside the labour movement, building a unique relationship between intellectuals and workers that developed mutual understanding. At the end of the thirties, communists were part of the alliance — along with social democrats such as the Reuthers and other militants — that fought to keep the union independent, democratic, and based on a strong shop-floor presence. This alliance was responsible for the ousting of Homer Martin in the U.S. and Charles Millard in Canada.

When the war started, the CP declared itself to be the organized opposition to the war and claimed that there was no difference between the sides involved in the European conflict. Then, in the summer of 1941, after Hitler invaded the Soviet Union, the CP abruptly changed its tune, becoming "red, white, and blue." In the United States, not only did the communists endorse the no-strike pledge but they showed their support with a passionate and ultimately self-destructive enthusiasm. The CP referred to striking workers as scabs against the war effort and attacked the UAW leadership

Wartime poster in Quebec. Courtesy of National Archives, C87504.

for not being aggressive enough in disciplining workers. It even went beyond the no-strike pledge, calling for incentive pay to increase productivity. The attempt to reinstate the piece-rate system, which workers had fought so hard to eliminate, turned out to be political suicide.

To top it off, the leadership of the American CP turned to American exceptionalism — arguing that class conflict no longer applied to the United States and that cooperation with business and government should continue even after the war. This latter change in direction led to a split in the American CP, the ouster of its leader, and a temporary discontinuance of the party.

The patriotic zeal of the CP and its move to the right did, it seems, appeal to some American workers. But these factors inevitably weakened and destroyed the credibility the CP had amongst activists. Their vision of building a new society might have kept the communists themselves going, but other activists were primarily interested not in their philosophy but in their militant daily actions. Now the communists were undercutting their own reputation for militancy. As it turned out, the CP's new-found and extreme Americanism didn't prevent it from being red-baited, but it did undermine the party as a force in the UAW before McCarthyism and the cold war finished it off.

The Canadian CP, tied to the Soviet CP rather than the American CP, did not show the same enthusiasm for a new era of cooperation with employers as its American counterpart. It did support the no-strike pledge, and some communist trade unionists, such as those at Massey-Harris, followed suit. But unlike those in the U.S., many communist trade unionists in Canada, especially in the UAW, refused to follow the party line. This resistance reflected, in part, the more general opposition within Canada to such a pledge when the trade union rights had not been recognized. It also reflected the unique position of communists within the Canadian UAW.

Alone amongst virtually all major labour unions in North America, the CP in the UAW was neither marginal nor dominant. It was neither so weak that it could be kicked out nor so in control that the Canadian UAW could be isolated as a "red" union. In the Canadian UAW there was a close working relationship between communists, leftist members of the CCF, and unaffiliated militants. And there was a relative balance between these groups and right-wing CCF members and anti-communists. That alliance and balance changed how the communists operated within the union; they refused to risk their effective relationships by following the party line. In addition, this dynamic preserved an organized and credible left in the union which affected the future UAW culture in Canada.

George Burt, the director of the UAW in Canada, reflected that balance. He was often criticized for drifting with the wind; he supported the left when it was the dominant faction in the union during the war and shifted towards the Reuther supporters when they became ascendant. But this weakness in choosing sides was also, from the perspective of the union's future, a strength. Burt avoided factional infighting, and, without preventing ongoing disagreements and debates about direction, he concentrated the union's efforts on fighting common enemies, building the membership, and strengthening the organization.

Alongside the different union responses in the two countries to the no-strike pledge was a more general difference in the changing political mood and directions. Politically, the U.S. shifted to the right, while Canada moved to the centre-left. In the U.S., the Roosevelt New Deal faded, while in Canada the CCF, a new political party with growing links to the labour movement, emerged.

In the U.S., Roosevelt's popularity had begun to fall after the recession that started in late 1937. Within labour, the AFL, fighting back against the CIO, was offering companies sweetheart deals to keep CIO unions out, while opposing progressive labour and social legislation, which the AFL believed would strengthen the CIO. Furthermore, with the outbreak of war and the return to full production, criticism of the corporations had abated in the United States. In Canada, however, both major parties had lost credibility during the depression. The extremely hard line against unions and the disruptions caused by strikes for simple recognition left unions with a measure of public support. In addition, since Canada entered the war before the Americans, Canadians experienced the contradictions of the wartime economy earlier, and resistance to the inequality of sacrifice came sooner.

In the February, 1942, federal by-election, the Conservative Party, with its very conservative leader, Arthur Meighen, lost to the CCF. The shock led the Conservatives to move their platform to the centre-left and absorb into their official name the word "Progressive" from Manitoba's Progressive Party of Farmers, which the new Conservative leader, John Bracken, had led since 1920. By 1943, the CCF's momentum had the establishment truly concerned. The CCF had come within a whisker of winning the 1943 Ontario election and the elected MPPs included the heads of the United Steelworkers of America (Charles Millard) and the International Union of

Mine Mill and Smelter Workers (Robert Carlin). In elections in British Columbia and Saskatchewan, the CCF came in second.

A month after the Ontario election, the CCF was in first place in a national poll (twenty-nine per cent compared to twenty-eight per cent for each of the Liberals and Conservatives). In a 1943 by-election in Montreal, the contest was actually between the communists and the CCF, with Fred Rose (CP) defeating David Lewis (CCF) for the seat. With the record strike wave in 1943 and the shift to the left in the popular mood, the Liberal government eventually adopted more progressive legislation such as family allowances and union rights to regain control over the pace of change, undermine the CCF support, and preserve their own future.

Once the government had conceded on the labour legislation, the UAW's Canadian Council resolved, in April, 1944, to limit its strike activity. The union was concerned about jeopardizing the permanence of the legislation as the war drew to a close. Over the next year, strikes were down, and the union turned its attention to a lobbying campaign to "Win the Peace". The emphasis was on implementing economic conversion, changing the labour code that unions would face after the war, achieving the forty-hour week plus extended paid vacations, and developing national social security plans.

This strike truce was, however, short-lived. When the war ended, Canadian workers acted quickly to build on the union recognition that they had won at the government level and to persuade employers to agree to union security. The momentum from that fight carried the union to a major national wage offensive.

The Day Ford Saw Too Many Cars

The fight for union security was the bridge between the end of the war and the beginning of the postwar period. At the height of the war (1943), 1.2 million Canadians were employed in the defence industries. By August, 1945, this workforce had been cut in half, while 50,000 soldiers were returning each month to the civilian workforce. For the UAW and others in the Canadian labour movement, the key threats after the war were the possible return of high unemployment and the concentration of corporate power, which threatened democracy. Labour's response included plans for postwar conversion that involved input from working people and wage increases to replace war demands with consumer demands. A strong labour movement was needed to support these objectives. The most immediate task was therefore to ensure that wartime union gains were irreversible and that unions became a permanent and accepted institution in society.

The first step towards the legitimization of unions was taken earlier, when the union won recognition from companies. The next came in early 1944, when the federal Liberals finally introduced labour legislation modelled on the American Wagner Act. This policy put in place mechanisms to certify unions and pressure the companies to recognize democratically chosen unions and bargain with them in good faith.

One crucial difference between Canadian labour law and the American Wagner Act is that in the U.S., unlike in Canada, workers can negotiate the right to strike over unresolved issues such as health and safety or production standards. This is a potentially powerful weapon in an era of just-in-time production, comparable to the "quickie" sit-downs during the earlier breakthrough of the union.

That Canadian law outlawing strikes during the life of the agreement did not seem to be a major issue at the time, given the prevalence of short-term agreements and the excitement at finally having some legislative rights and protections. But it limited Canadian trade union rights in a way that distinguished Canadian legislation from common practice in other developed countries. In the sixties, it resurfaced as a key issue for the union.

The final step in this process of securing trade union stability occurred when companies accepted union security clauses. These clauses had already been negotiated amongst major American companies and enforced by the American government in exchange for the no-strike pledge. But they were rare in Canada. The Canadian confrontation over this issue took place at Ford's Windsor operations — then Canada's largest manufacturing establishment.

By 1944, Ford employed 14,000 production workers who were anxious to address their grievances, including union security, by going on strike. But they wanted to avoid an all-out strike during the war at this crucial plant. Ford had never fully accepted the union, and there were mini-strikes between 1942 and 1944 over speed-up and the firing of union militants, as well as over equal pay for women. The union had, from the day of its first contract, continued to build its membership and steward body. David Fraser, in his thesis, "Years of Struggle," quotes a local 200 steward: "On Sunday we have a full day frequently holding as many as ten meetings. Wherever possible we have an election of sub-stewards to carry our gospel into the plant and so far we have elected 367 sub-stewards. [Note: sixty-four of these were company-recognized stewards]."

There was little or no concern that establishing union security might undermine the union by freeing stewards from direct contact with each member in collecting dues, and that the steady dues might give the leaders too much autonomy from the members. There was overwhelming consensus in three areas: the financial base provided by of a dues check-off was crucial to the union's survival, the union needed to devote its time to activities other than collecting dues, and the lack of union security constantly provided the company with opportunities to divide the membership and even destroy the union when tough times recurred. The issue was therefore never whether to fight for the dues check-off but how to replace the loss in membership contact.

On 12 September 1945, a few months after the end of the war, the Ford workers in Windsor officially opened postwar labour relations by going on strike. The strike was clearly a test for the Canadian labour movement as a whole, but it also divided the movement along ideological lines. Communists and their allies, now freed from their wartime cautiousness, argued for broadening the struggle to include other locals and other unions; the Canadian Congress of Labour (CCL), representing the majority of the industrial affiliates, disagreed with that strategy. Both the CCL and the CCF were also concerned that this strategy might strengthen communist credibility in the movement.

As they did during the Oshawa strike, the *Globe and Mail* and the *Toronto Star* articulated two poles within the establishment (the *Globe* reflecting the more dominant tendency):

[It is time] to clear the communists out of the trade unions and [the strike offered] ample excuse for making the cleaning nation-wide.

— *The Globe*, 21 December 1945

Those who do not relish socialism should be the first to advocate ... changes in the capitalist system which fall short of complete socialization but make concessions to the growth of socialist sentiment. ... in doing so, capitalists will be preserving the system which they support.

— *The Toronto Star*, 7 November 1945

The union had previously been successful in persuading conciliation boards to recommend union security, but the companies generally ignored these nonbinding recommendations. Before and after the strike began, the union — confident that the ruling would be favourable — suggested resolving the issue of union security by way of binding arbitration. The company refused, and the strike dragged on.

After five weeks on the picket line, the union moved to escalate the strike by preventing the non-union security guards from entering the plant. When the police tried to escort them in, thousands of pickets blocked the path. The province looked to the federal government to send in the RCMP, and in anticipation of that assault, one of the most dramatic events in Canadian labour history occurred.

First, the Local 195 leadership, generally led by the left, decided to hold a sympathy strike with the Ford workers. The international executive board of the union did not support this tactic, but the Canadian director, George Burt, supported the Windsor local (though he opposed its call to shut down all Canadian UAW plants). The response of the Local 195 membership was remarkable: the local included workers at GM, two dozen components plants, a few miscellaneous manufacturing firms, and 3,600 members at the Chrysler plant. These workers shut down their own operations and joined the Ford picket lines, and then, at a time when the union provided no strike pay, they demonstrated their solidarity with the Ford workers by refusing to return to work for almost one month.

The sympathy strike began on 5 November 1945, and later that day, the union acted to block any police or RCMP action. The workers chose the same strategy the Ford River Rouge workers had used in the U.S. in 1941: a car blockade. The event was planned by strike leaders with participation from the national office, though carrying it out involved creative and spontaneous intervention by many rank-and-file workers. Roughly 8,000 Ford workers participated in the protest with the help of 6,000 members from Local 195. Workers brought not only their own cars to the Ford plant, but also trapped over 1,000 cars and twenty-five street buses (some estimates ranged up to 1,500 vehicles) that were — willingly or unwillingly — caught in the traffic. The blockade, in which workers defended their strike with products they themselves produced, covered twenty blocks. The union had prevented a violent confrontation, and negotiations resumed.

The strike had strong support within the community. The mayor promised to pay welfare to any family in need (though a conservative majority within the city council soon reversed this pledge). Small business in the community took out a newspaper ad supporting the strikers. Church groups backed the strike, and some even joined picket lines. Especially militant in their support were the young soldiers recently back from the front lines. Rallies took place across the country with the city of Windsor alone bringing 15,000 supporters together. UAW locals in Sarnia and Brantford stopped work in a day of solidarity, and other UAW locals in St. Catharines and Oshawa took votes of support for any action they were called on to do. American locals sent financial support. Workers in Fort William and Ottawa expressed their clear support, as did mineworkers from Nova Scotia, rubberworkers from Kitchener, and steelworkers from Hamilton.

The leaders of the Canadian labour movement were, however, divided in their attitudes to the strike and in their choices over strategy. Without their united support, a more general national work stoppage wasn't possible. From then on, with the workers' actions having peaked, the strategy of Ford and the provincial and federal governments became simply waiting the strikers out. Towards the end of November, the parties reached a compromise. Ford wasn't ready to give in to union security, but if the workers returned to work, Ford would accept the union's original offer of binding arbitration. The committee was divided, but George Burt and most of the committee members favoured ending the strike.

Fifty-two per cent of the members, however, rejected that recommendation. Tom McLean, even though he was Burt's assistant, voiced his strong opposition to the compromise at the membership meeting, and sufficient numbers agreed. He reasoned that the workers couldn't trust an arbitrator and had to win this fight on the picket line. (Others argued that McLean should be fired for his insubordination but Burt never pressed the issue.)

However, with no way to escalate the fight and with the members and the leadership split over ending the strike, the membership had few options. Two weeks later, the union held another vote on essentially the same offer, with the added understanding that the arbitrator would be sympathetic to the union. The committee, including Tom McLean, was satisfied, and of the 6,000 workers who voted, seventy-two per cent were in favour of ending the strike. Justice Ivan Rand was appointed arbitrator, and his decision endorsed full union dues check-off, even for those workers who chose to stay out of the union. Justice Rand essentially argued that since all employees benefited from union struggles and union representation, all workers should pay their share.

STRIKE

OF

WINDSOR

10,000 Workers on Strike
THEIR VICTORY IS YOUR VICTORY

CANADIAN BROTHERHOOD OF RAILWAY EMPLOYEES
AND
OTHER TRANSPORT WORKERS

The Ford strike at Windsor, Ont. is still in progress and at the moment there is no prospect of a settlement. The Management of the Ford Motor Company still refuses to grant the demands of the Union.

With the strike now in its ninth week, the United Automobile Workers of America (CIO) is faced with a heavy burden in the feeding and maintenance of many of its members. It is estimated that the union is now feeding over nine thousand persons, and the expectation is that this number will increase. It will, therefore, be seen that in order to maintain a fighting position on behalf of its membership, the union must have greater support as soon as possible.

Funds are urgently needed, and it is absolutely essential that every member of our Brotherhood appreciate the nature of the fight being waged by the workers of the Ford Company. This fight is the fight of every member of the labour movement. It is the front line fight of all working men to maintain present wage levels, with reduced hours so as to maintain full employment. To lose this fight would be a serious blow to every member of our Brotherhood.

You are urged to give, and give generously so that this most important fight may be won on behalf of Labour.

CBRE poster in support of 1945 Windsor strike. Courtesy of Wayne State Archives.

This ruling was very rapidly applied to UAW agreements that followed. By the end of 1946, twenty-three other agreements in Windsor, including those at Chrysler, contained the Rand formula, and GM conceded in 1947. It was soon common across all regions and sectors. In the late-seventies, Quebec legislated the Rand formula; in the early eighties, Ontario followed suit.

This strike against the largest employer in Canada, in the critical early period after the war, was a national event, and its outcome was clearly a victory for Canadian workers. But that victory also had an explicit price tag. In exchange for union security, Justice Rand established a new responsibility for the union: *policing* wildcats. This bargaining followed the pattern of the Roosevelt wartime offer of union security, which included a no-strike pledge, and it expanded on the new Canadian labour legislation which gave workers the right to have a union but prohibited work stoppages during the agreement's term. Rand went one step further; the union's responsibility was not only to oppose wildcat strikes, but also to end them. Workers who went on wildcat strikes could face fines and lose years of seniority in proportion to the length of time they illegally stopped work, while the union could lose its dues check-off for up to six months.

In the United States, although the UAW seemed divided between a communist-supported group and the emerging Reuther group, the traditional left-right identifications lost most of their meaning during the war. One result of the consensus on the no-strike pledge within the United States was that neither group mobilized the growing frustrations of the membership. This lack of cohesiveness became evident at the 1944 special UAW convention on the war, when a significant minority of delegates refused to go along with the proposals of either caucus. It was also expressed more generally in the unauthorized strike wave of 1944. As the war came to an end, the American UAW seemed to be in chaos, and strategy at headquarters was geared to reestablishing a measure of control. Victor Reuther, in an interview cited in Eric Mann's *Taking on General Motors*, later commented on the thinking behind the first significant postwar strike in the union: "The GM strike was designed to take the ball out of the hands of stewards and committeemen ... and put it in the hands of the national leadership."

The Canadians experienced their own disappointments and divisions during this period, but the leadership's relationship with its members was maintained and strengthened. The concentration of the industry in southern Ontario provided the union with the potential for cohesiveness, but the development of this potential rested on a more profound, worker-built base.

The Canadian Council provided the regular forum for collective discussion, debate, and leadership. The actual decisions that were made reflected rank-and-file pressures and led in creating a clearly independent working class orientation. The strong independent locals provided the mechanism for workers to express in-plant demands, challenge "the top" when necessary, develop new leadership, and effectively carry out agreed-on policy. Supported by such structures, and with the resourcefulness, solidarity, and determination of shop-floor (and sometimes office) workers, the union won crucial victories.

At the end of the war, the two largest locals among all of Canada's unions were CAW locals: Ford Local 200 and the amalgamated local in Windsor, Local 195. (Third was Mine Mill Local 598 in Sudbury. CAW Local 222 in Oshawa — now the largest — was then seventh.)

While trying to establish itself during one social crisis, the depression, the UAW was confronted by another, World War II. The depression made organizing difficult because, for most of the period, the threat of disrupting production carried very little weight since most of the economy was already down. In contrast, the war made organizing difficult because the threat of disrupting production, and therefore the war effort, carried so much weight that governments placed severe limits on strikes and walk-outs.

The Canadian section of the UAW entered the war uncertain and lagging behind its American counterpart in numbers, strength, supportive legislation, and social programs. It emerged as the largest union in Canada, with a base in key industrial sectors spread across the communities of southern Ontario. Along with the rest of Canadian labour, the union essentially caught up to the New Deal reforms won earlier in the United States. While these reforms came later to the Canadians, they also provided a momentum heading into the postwar period that the Americans had lost.

The war and its aftermath established union recognition for the Canadian UAW from both the state, through the legislation of collective bargaining rights, and employers, through union security clauses won by direct action. In spite of internal conflicts, the struggles and mobilizations that led to this achievement left the Canadian UAW relatively healthy and confident as it prepared to address the next stage of its development. Having established its existence, and with the war over, what kind of union would the Canadian UAW become?

Walter Reuther on the cover of Time *Magazine, 1955.* Courtesy of Time Inc.

CHAPTER 5

Delivering the Goods

What made the prospect [of unionization] seem especially grim in those early years was the persistent union attempt to invade management prerogatives … We have moved to codify certain practices, to discuss workers' grievances with union representatives, and to submit for arbitration the few grievances that remain unsettled. But on the whole we have retained all the basic powers to manage.

— Alfred P. Sloan, (former President of GM)

We are the vanguard in America, in that great crusade to build a better world. We are the architects of the future and we are going to fashion the weapons with which we will work and fight and build.

— Walter Reuther

Ever stop to think how we crawl here bumper to bumper, and crawl home bumper to bumper, and we've got to turn out more every minute to keep our jobs, when there isn't any room for them on the highway?

— Harvey Swados

107

The UAW was born on the shop floor, out of struggles to limit management's power to decide arbitrarily who worked and who didn't, out of conflicts over the pace and organization of work, and out of resentment over arbitrary rules and daily harassments. The war, especially in the United States, provided the transition to a focus on workers as consumers; that is, on how workers live outside the workplace. For the American UAW, this change came alongside two other transitions; one political, the other internal. The war turned out to be a passage from the heady days of the New Deal to the conservatism of the cold war. It was also a passage from a union divided along ideological-factional lines and fragmented amongst strong and independent locals, to a union that was highly centralized, both ideologically and administratively.

In this period, the UAW established its basic structures and direction, as well as its reputation as an innovative leader in social unionism. The Canadians played a secondary role in shaping these basic overall structures (ninety-five per cent of the members and a higher proportion of the industry were centred in the United States). But the Canadians did not simply inherit the American system. The process by which the American UAW structure and philosophy was translated to Canada involved both resistance and attraction. The outcome, as the fifties came to an end, was a Canadian section that was the same but different.

The Treaty of Detroit

From the beginning of the union in the thirties, the corporations' main concern was to retain complete control over production. Forced to recognize unions, the corporations insisted that the unions must also recognize management. The companies would remove some of their arbitrary practices, but management rights — the right to hire, lay-off, invest, choose products, schedule hours, and determine the methods, organization, and pace of production — would be written into the agreements and enforced by both the company and the union.

During the war, full production had allowed workers to resist this unilateral management power on the shop floor, and this resistance often created tensions with the top leadership of the union. But in the United States, the more lasting development of the war was the establishment, through government initiatives, of grievance procedures and arbitration boards to channel workers' frustrations away from direct action. Once the war was over, companies were more determined than ever to restore any management rights and control they had lost to workers and stewards during the war. Walter Reuther, who became head of the UAW's GM department in 1939, challenged the company's pricing policy in 1946 and insisted that workers and the public had a right to influence it. The management endured a 113-day strike to assert that it would not relinquish management rights either in the workplace (dealing with workers) or outside (issues of pricing, products, and investment). And GM won.

Immediately after the GM agreement was signed, large numbers of workers walked off the job to join demonstrations against the attack on labour launched by the Taft-Hartley Act. The act was introduced in 1947 to weaken labour, particularly its ability to engage in solidaristic actions. While making it easier for management to interfere in organizing drives, it reinstituted injunctions, outlawed mass and secondary picketing, and encouraged states to ban "union shops." It also denied services and legislative rights to any union whose leaders didn't sign affidavits rejecting support for or belief in communism. This denial proved to be the most divisive aspect of the act and was instrumental in undermining labour's overall attack on the legislation.

In response to the worker demonstrations during working hours, GM fired local leaders and activists and then entered into negotiations with the union over reducing some of the penalties. This tactic, of firing militants and putting the union on the defensive to bring the workers back, quickly developed into a basic corporate strategy for dealing with militancy; Ford and later Chrysler adopted its use. The companies were reinforced by the conservative times, the new labour legislation, and the backing from the labour boards and the courts. Workers were intimidated and the negotiated compromises, reinforced by the trade-off inherent in judgements like the Rand decision, committed the union to limiting further occurrences.

But as in the thirties, discipline was not enough. Stability would require both channelling union energy elsewhere and showing that there were specific benefits for workers if they moderated shop-floor militancy. In 1948, GM offered, and the union accepted, a quarterly cost-of-living allowance (COLA) over and above the wage increase, in exchange for a two-year agreement. The company hoped this term would lead to greater workplace stability. (Previous agreements were for only one year.) This turn of events set the stage for the 1950 agreement, which *Fortune* dubbed the "Treaty of Detroit."

The 1950 bargaining round with GM represented the most systematic attempt by both sides to shape a coherent and stable relationship. The company wanted a five-year agreement so it could plan production without concern over a national walk-out every year or two. In addition, it especially wanted to consolidate management rights and remove them from the union's bargaining agenda.

The trade-off GM offered, after listening to the union demands, included continuing the 1948 wage principle of both an annual improvement factor (AIF) and a quarterly COLA; negotiating a comprehensive health and insurance plan cofinanced by the company (any previous benefits were outside the agreement and unilaterally determined by GM); accepting the principle of a company-paid pension plan (recently won after a long strike at Chrysler); extending paid vacations (to three weeks after fifteen years of service); and expanding recall rights from two years to time-for-time (i.e., for each year of work, there is an additional year in which to exercise the right to recall if the company is hiring).

> You work in the factory all of your life,
> Try to provide for your kids and your wife.
> When you get too old to produce any more,
> They hand you your hat and show you the door.
>
> Chorus:
> Too old to work, too old to work
> When you're too old to work and you're too young to die,
> Who will take care of you, how'll you get by
> When you're too old to work, and
> too young to die.
>
> — "Too Old to Work Too Young to Die," Joe Glazer, inspired by a Reuther speech and the Chrysler pension strike in 1950

The subheading on *Fortune*'s analysis of the agreement read, "GM Paid a Billion for Peace. It Got a Bargain." Although workers rebelled in 1953 and forced a wage reopener, the principles behind the 1950 agreement, especially that of longer-term agreements as three years became the norm, remained intact. GM president Alfred P. Sloan, looking back from the vantage point of the early sixties, observed in *My Years With General Motors*:

> At the time I write this, it is more than seventeen years
> since there has been an extended strike over national issues
> at General Motors. To those of us who recall ... the thirties
> ... [this] record is almost incredible. And we have achieved
> this record without surrendering any of the basic responsi-
> bilities of management ... The issue of unionism at General
> Motors is long since settled.

In the mid-fifties a new wave of technology that integrated procedures developed during the war swept the industry. The trend was called "automa-tion," and its introduction raised fears about replacing and changing exist-ing jobs. The restructuring inside the plants was used to further reinforce management control and tighten production standards.

There was ongoing worker resistance to some of the changes. In response, the UAW tried to initiate a national debate on the social implica-tions of new technology. Walter Reuther, in a pamphlet in the early fifties on the wide-ranging implications of automation, wrote that

> An important step towards minimizing the potential social
> dislocations during the coming decades ... would be the
> reduction in the length of the workweek ... The reduction
> in the workweek to 35 or 30 hours in the coming decade
> can be an important shock absorber during the transition to
> the widespread use of automation.

The union, however, subsequently shifted its response to income security and sharing the fruits of the technology rather than influencing the imple-mentation or role of automation in the workplace. A total rejection of new methods of production clearly made no sense. But the union made no concerted effort to influence how the emerging technologies and organization of work stations could be more sensitive to workplace conditions.

Moreover, and in spite of pro-gressive rhetoric suggesting further

Had autoworkers since the mid-fifties been able, as a response to accelerating technology, to take one per cent of their annual two to three per cent increase in the form of reduced work-time, the four-day week — and tens of thousands of new job opportunities — would be here by now.

111

PATTERN BARGAINING

In a relatively short period of time, the UAW and the companies had developed a tightly-conceived bargaining system and strategy referred to as "pattern bargaining." It was this strategy, as much as anything else, that reinforced and legitimated the centralized structure of the union and was generally credited for the UAW's collective bargaining successes. This strategy was put in place in the U.S. in 1950, with the Treaty of Detroit. Canada didn't completely follow suit until the late fifties.

Sectoral Bargaining

Postwar talk of a pattern for all the CIO unions died quickly. The UAW based its strategy on establishing a pattern at the Big Three. One company was targeted, while the others were left waiting. Striking only one company at a time, and threatening it with a loss in market share to the others, put competitive pressures on the target while also minimizing damage to the overall economy (especially if imports were low). Once an agreement was established, it was taken to the other major companies and copied in detail. Then it was extended with some inevitable flexibility in smaller units — to the parts industry, aerospace, and agricultural implements.

Focus on Economics

The content of national bargaining focused on economic issues; these united the membership around common demands. Issues related to working conditions and work environment were negotiated locally. In the U.S., workers had the right to strike during the agreement's life over certain issues not specified in the collective agreement (production standards and health and safety) but these were also centralized in the sense that they required the prior approval of the international office in Detroit.

Long-Term Agreements

The original plan was for a five-year agreement, but after the members rebelled, the union moved to the three-year agreement of today. That longer agreement gave the union a chance to focus on other issues and agreements outside the Big Three, but it necessitated some provision for security against economic changes during the terms of that agreement.

Real Wages

At the core of the wage agreement were two principles: the right to share in technology/productivity, and protection against the erosion of wages to inflation. This formula seems to have first come from GM, though it was clearly a response to the militancy and expectations of its workers. The "right to share" led to the provision of an AIF tied not to the company, but to general trends in the economy. If the companies did better than that, which they normally did, they could use the excess for their own purposes or, as the union argued, increase benefits to workers and distribute it to consumers in the form of lower prices.

Cost-of-living bonuses were first introduced during the War to limit the growing resistance to wage controls. Similarly, COLA, like the AIF, supported the union argument that workers were not to blame for inflation: COLA provided quarterly protection against inflation (only) *after* prices went up. The COLA originally represented 100 per cent protection against inflation (under ninety per cent today) and it is linked to other forms of pay — when workers work shifts or overtime, and get vacation or holiday pay, the COLA is added on and treated as part of regular pay.

Wage Differentials

The union-negotiated pay structure within each of the Big Three is relatively egalitarian (i.e., relative to other countries and other industries). Janitors get about 5 per cent less than assemblers and skilled workers get about twenty per cent above assemblers. The AIF was briefly a fixed amount but quickly (it took longer in Canada) became a percentage increase. COLA (which has generated about two-thirds of wages since the end of the forties) remains the same for all workers and therefore represents a higher percentage for lower-paid workers. If the wage structure should get out of line with community standards for skilled workers, special additional increases are negotiated for the trades (i.e., the structure is biased to pinch differentials but there is flexibility in the system).

When auto was first organized, women were either excluded from auto jobs or segregated into certain departments. But even when doing the same job, their wages were significantly lower. Such differentials for doing the same work did not disappear until the end of the fifties.

Paid Time Off

In both countries, the government introduced the principle of one-week vacations during the war. The union introduced paid holidays in the late forties and extended the paid vacation time in the fifties. While a standard demand of the union from its very beginnings, the union never made a pattern breakthrough beyond the forty-hour workweek.

Company-Paid Benefits

The costs of benefits (health care, income protection, pensions) were at first divided equally between the companies and the workers, but fully paid company plans became the general pattern on both sides of the border by the early sixties. Benefits like pensions (negotiated in 1950) and income security (negotiated in 1955) were integrated to government plans to make them both less expensive and more rational.

Pensions

The pension plans were based on a defined benefit per year of service and supported by a fund supervised, but not controlled, by the union. Improvements were negotiated during each round of bargaining and these included improvements for those already retired and not part of the workforce. Over time, the pension plans became more flexible and complex with the addition of benefits like early retirement and survivor's options.

Income Security

In the debates over how to respond to automation in the mid-fifties, the opposition pushed for a longer-term solution of reduced work-time, but Walter Reuther channelled this demand into a program to achieve a guaranteed annual income to overcome the short-term cyclical nature of the industry. That program, which evolved into SUB (supplementary employment benefits), provided a top-up for those laid off for a period of time linked to seniority.

possibilities, discussion of sharing the ultimate benefits of the
higher productivity was narrowed to wages and benefits.
The option of dramatic reduc-

Striking workers at Massey-Ferguson.
Courtesy of the CAW collection.

tions in work-time to correspond to the liberating potential of the new
technology was largely ignored, even though the subject came up in popular discussions. Writing in *Fortune*, one of the best-read and most influential business magazines, Daniel Seligman noted in July, 1954, that "Most
businessmen shudder at the thought, but the four-day week may be coming
anyway — and sooner than you might expect. If and when it does come, of
course, it will create some 'insurmountable' problems. But remember,
please, so did the five day week."

Through the fifties and into the sixties, the union expanded its negotiated programs and introduced new ones. The strategy of "pattern" bargaining
served the union well as it took the price of labour out of competition
amongst the Big Three. The authority that came with that pattern after it
was won also spread, though unevenly, to the independent parts sector,
aerospace, and agricultural implements. There were repeated protests

115

Family Auxiliary in support of Massey-Ferguson strikers. Courtesy of the CAW collection.

against increases in the speed of the line and working conditions, especially after a renewed management offensive during the recession at the end of the fifties. But these protests remained largely invisible to the popular perceptions of the happy and complacent worker — until the workers themselves temporarily returned the issue to the agenda in the later sixties.

Reutherism

During the fifties and sixties, no name was more identifiable with social unionism than that of Walter Reuther. Future labour leaders and activists, in both Canada and the United States, remembered when they first met Walter and when his oratory and vision first moved them. Walter Reuther marched with Martin Luther King and Cesar Chavez, befriended and dined with John F. Kennedy, discussed world affairs with the social democratic leaders of Germany and England, argued with the head of the Soviet Union on the merits and future of capitalism and communism, and relished public debates

with the presidents of the largest companies in the world. The Sunday *Times* of London, after a Reuther speech to Britain's labour central, rapturously reported that "Throughout the Congress ... one man spoke like a ... prophet." In 1955, *Time* put him on its cover.

UAW Local 399 (Toronto, amalgamated) at educational in FDR-CIO camp in Port Huron, Michigan (Black Lake wasn't built until 1970). Courtesy of Wayne State Archives.

Walter Reuther was a first-generation American, the son of German immigrants. He was born in 1907 in the industrial centre of Wheeling, West Virginia, and, like his younger brothers Roy and Victor, he was clearly influenced by the commitment of his father to trade unionism and democratic socialism. At nineteen, he moved to Detroit, where he was active in socialist circles at work and at university, which he attended while he was a diemaker at Ford. In the early thirties, he and Victor travelled through Europe, visited China, and worked for eighteen months at an auto plant near Gorki in the Soviet Union. They returned in 1935 to witness, and participate in, the birth of the UAW.

Detroit was then seething with strikes and pressure from workers for recognition of elected stewards and the union. In 1936, Walter went to the crucial founding convention in South Bend, Indiana, and, confident and articulate, he emerged as a member of the UAW's executive board. He quickly built a base as the president of the powerful amalgamated Local 174 on the west side of Detroit, and in 1939, he became head of the GM department. In 1946, Walter Reuther was elected president of the UAW.

Reuther first attained national prominence during the war with his detailed plan for industrywide conversion of automobile plants to airplane production as a means for overcoming the early difficulties in moving to a war economy. As the war came to an end, he grabbed public attention with equally well-developed and well-publicized retooling and reconversion plans. One idea Reuther presented was the setting up of commando units of engineers, designers and skilled trades, to assist smaller firms in getting access to the available pool of technology, knowledge, and expertise. After the war, he gained notoriety by broadening the scope of union demands to include corporate decisions affecting the public. In 1946, he called on the automotive companies to open their books so their pricing policies could be challenged, and in 1949, he argued for the production of a fuel-efficient, nonpolluting, safe and affordable small car.

The base for all of these gains was, of course, the UAW's achievements in bargaining. Led by Reuther, workers at the Big Three more than doubled their wages in the fifteen years after the war — an increase of over one-third after inflation. (To put this in perspective, hourly wages for American Big Three workers have increased by less than three per cent after inflation in the fifteen years ending in 1995.) The UAW's agreements with the companies modestly increased paid time off, introduced company-paid health protection for workers and their families, pioneered an income protection policy to deal with lay-offs, and developed pension plans to allow workers to retire comfortably. The UAW set the direction and standards for American, and also Canadian, labour.

When Reuther was elected UAW president in 1946, it was by the slimmest of majorities: less than one and one-half per cent. The executive board elected at the same time was overwhelmingly loyal to his opposition. That opposition was communist-led, and with the war over, the communists' militant line of the thirties had returned. The communists themselves made up a very small proportion of this postwar left, which included various socialists and many workers who were simply militant with no clear political orientation.

Reuther's victory was closely linked to both his role as the head of the GM department and the union's first test after the war, the 113-day strike at GM. From the perspective of the union's stated goals, the strike was a defeat. But workers' struggles, as Reuther then well understood, have a logic that is both more straightforward and more complex than checking off gains and losses. Workers were frustrated; they wanted someone to articulate that frustration publicly, and they were ready for a fight. Reuther showed that he was ready to lead, and he was rewarded for that insight and action.

Reuther had positioned himself to steer a particular course through an increasingly conservative America. Having preempted the media, business, and the state from red-baiting the UAW by leading the attack on communists himself, he tried to carve out a space that would achieve concrete gains for the union's members while simultaneously resurrecting the broader progressive New Deal agenda that had faded in wartime. His underlying vision was to build a progressive alliance, with the organized working class in the lead, to win the material and liberating benefits of mass production and its accelerating technology. For very powerful reasons, this strategy led him to focus on democratizing consumption.

With the end of the war, the inevitable focus on material well-being dominated working class demands. For almost two continuous decades that included the deprivation of the depression and the disruption of the war, Americans and Canadians had made sacrifices. Now that they were on the winning side of the war, they wanted to share in the benefits and promises they were owed by that victory. The public longed for a normalcy most had long forgotten or never known, and the people looked to their unions and politicians to deliver it. In contrast to an emphasis on the workplace itself, the focus on compensating workers as consumers for selling their labour presented, from Reuther's perspective, three further advantages.

First, any focus on management rights would inherently shift power to the locals, while Reuther was instead trying to centralize the union. Given the unevenness and sectionalism in the union, a decentralized strategy could fragment and weaken the union's potential influence. For example, some locals might be strong enough to oppose management in the plants or win special wage gains, while others were not; some local battles might have their own logic but undermine broader strategic goals of the union as a whole; and workers were divided by race, ethnicity, and occupation. Reuther wanted to concentrate on those national issues that would mean common gains for all workers and would therefore unite the membership.

Second, a focus on increasing workers' purchasing power and benefits was a less radical demand since, unlike an emphasis on management rights, it didn't challenge private property rights. Rather, it channelled militancy towards making gains within the system and was therefore less likely to isolate the union. Moreover, this strategy could even be articulated as a progressive weapon in the cold war: the most effective way to undercut communist arguments was to show that America delivered on its promises of greater benefits for all.

Third, and perhaps most important, it was becoming increasingly clear that fighting over management rights would mean an all-out battle with very uncertain chances of success. American management emerged from the war conscious of the profitable opportunities that lay ahead. Not only was productive capacity back on its feet, but the war had also left companies with a backlog of technology and had expanded their assets, making them hungry for new opportunities. Their primary concern was that they be free to manage production — free, that is, from union interference.

Companies such as the Big Three didn't expect to eliminate unions altogether. They had learned to live with the unions during the war and certainly didn't want to risk reviving the battles of the thirties. Instead, companies wanted a particular trade-off: "We'll recognize you, but you have to recognize us, which means our right to manage and plan production with some stability". Reuther was fully aware of both America's potential wealth and the corporations' fundamental desire for a measure of labour stability. He set out to take maximum advantage of that situation.

The eighteen months following Reuther's initial election saw an intensification of the internal battle for control over the union that had, in one form or another, dominated the union since its inception. Reuther came out of this infighting as the undisputed leader of the union, winning reelection in 1947 and sweeping his allies along as together they took eighteen of twenty-two executive positions.

That triumph was the result of both successful organization and the exploitation of the increasingly anti-communist environment in America. Even without a majority on the board, Reuther had been able to retain control over the departments of education and communications — crucial areas in an emerging organization. He combined this control with exciting ideas and plans for the future direction of the union. But he also reinforced the red-baiting that was seething in American society and used it to isolate both the left and many of those who refused to "choose sides" and denounce communists.

Once he had the levers of power, Reuther acted quickly and ruthlessly to solidify his hold. Seventy-five staff members, as well as the head of the legal department and dozens of support staff whose loyalty to Reuther was in question were fired. Many of these people had made vital contributions to the struggles of working people in the past and still had much to offer. (There was some attempt to justify the firings on grounds of "economy," but in the following decade, membership rose only fifteen per cent while the number of staff members reached levels fifty-five per cent higher than those before the mass firings.) With the staff under control, the next step was to crush locals that remained under the leadership of either communists or those labelled "communist sympathizers." After 1949, the caucus was tightened and essentially became another instrument of Reuther's executive board.

Reuther then turned to the CIO, playing an active role in expelling unions which had democratically chosen to retain its left leadership. Of the thirty-five CIO unions, a dozen had been labelled communist-dominated and another half-dozen were labelled communist-sympathetic. Irrespective of the struggles these unions had earlier led and their membership now faced, Reuther and the CIO leadership picked out eleven of these unions, representing twenty per cent of the CIO membership, and began to implement plans to raid them.

> The United Electrical Workers (UE) had been the third largest CIO union, behind the autoworkers and steel, and one of the most militant. The American UAW participated in the subsequent raids of UE. In Canada, when UE was similarly expelled and other unions were called on to support a raiding drive, the Canadian Council of the UAW — by the narrowest of margins — voted to stay out of that campaign against UE.

It was one thing to defeat those on the left; it was another to target the total destruction of the opposition. The climate created as these witch-hunts were unleashed throughout the union led to the expulsion of many experienced and talented activists. It brought out the worst in the membership and undermined the ability of the union to later carry out progressive work at its base. Furthermore, this preoccupation diverted attention and resources from the crucial need to bring unionization to the South, where the communists had established some links to the black community. And the leaders generally emphasized loyalty over ability and commitment,

121

... those who sought to combine principled anti-communism with an on-going commitment to democratic radicalism in the union were overwhelmed in a tide of repression that sharply narrowed the spectrum of legitimate debate in labor circles.

— American labour
historian Robert Zeigler

encouraging the growth of bureaucratic tendencies. (This charge does not apply to the loyal and exceptionally talented "brain trust" around Reuther himself.)

The prevailing atmosphere stifled debate, closed off any fundamental questioning of American foreign policy, and guaranteed that the eventual merger of the CIO with the less-than-progressive AFL would, as Reuther later experienced, be on the AFL's terms. Even though the rank-and-file retained the ability to challenge the leadership on some issues, those challenges could only be marginally effective and certainly couldn't be sustained without a coordinated opposition or alternative mechanisms to give them weight. In spite of its later achievements, the union paid dearly in the long term.

Victor Reuther, who headed the union's education department at that time, later captured one aspect of the implications in a 1986 interview cited by Eric Mann in *Taking on General Motors*:

> You know I am proud of ... the accomplishments of what is known as the Reuther years. But I am seeing one mistake we made ... The administration caucus ... was maintained many years after that battle was over. Essentially a great deal of authority got concentrated at the top. The vehicle of the administration caucus is [now] used to prevent open debate in the union.

The impressive success in gaining a share of the wealth for UAW members was not matched by the growth of the broad social alliance Reuther had worked and hoped for. The main reason for this lack of growth was that the American labour movement would not move in any serious way to lay the foundation for any permanent new politics. Reuther himself had, in the early thirties, assumed that significant social change simply couldn't happen without a socialist party based on the working class. In August, 1940, he could still bring workers to their feet at a UAW convention by raising the issue: "Some day in this country people are going to lose confidence in the existing political parties to a degree that they will form their own party." Even in 1946, Reuther joined other prominent liberals and social democrats in the call for a National Education Committee for a New Party.

But the idea no longer seemed inevitable. Victor Reuther had raised the idea of a radical popular alliance well before the war was over, outlining the need to start preparing for such a

In 1943, a Michigan group inspired by the near victory of the CCF in Ontario formed the MCCF (Michigan Cooperative Commonwealth Federation). It received no substantial support and soon disappeared.

In 1945, the Flint local, with support in other GM locals, endorsed the idea of a third party.

In the 1948 election, both the United Electrical Workers and Mine Mill broke ranks with the CIO (and paid dearly) to support the candidacy of Henry Wallace, former vice-president under Roosevelt. Disenchanted with the direction of the Democrats, Wallace was running for the Progressive Party.

new political alliance, and a postwar conference did occur. The labour movement was, however, too divided to generate the necessary momentum for such an initiative; these divisions stemmed from competition between the AFL and CIO and from right-left conflicts. Even more important, it seems, was the fear of losing links with the Democratic Party and wandering alone in the woods for an indefinite period.

A poll in 1947 amongst CIO officials showed that a significant base favoured setting up a labour party. One out of four officials wanted to create a new party in the next two or three years, and half looked to the founding of a new labour party within the next ten years. But confronted with the immediate choice between working towards such a party and risking the defeat of the Democrats in the upcoming election, the labour leadership stayed with the Democrats. By the early fifties, the idea of a third party was, for Reuther, dead and buried. At the Detroit Economic Club in 1953, he stated: "I felt in 1932 ... that it [socialism] might be a better way to do things. I have long stopped believing that Socialism is the answer."

Reuther continued to place consumer-oriented demands on the bargaining table, arguing for union input into the price of cars, the responsiveness of cars to the environment, and car safety. But this focus naturally brought the debate back to overall management rights. Companies were not going to concede at this level, having generally blocked the union's challenge to management's rights in the workplace. And the union could not force their hand given that it had neither the support of a political movement to take on the companies, nor any prospect of making these issues a priority amongst the membership. Workers could not be expected to fight over these challenges with management since they had not been mobilized to fight management over more specific workplace issues.

Reuther never stopped lobbying for more general benefits for all citizens; the UAW was a leading force within the United States for a national health care plan and for the expansion of public pensions. But, unable to achieve European-style social benefits, the union drifted towards establishing a "parallel (or private) welfare state" for its members through collective bargaining. As a result, autoworkers, having met their own needs, became less and less interested in joining others to fight for universal programs. A disappointed Reuther remarked, in 1968, that "I have been much saddened by the fact that the American labour movement has not played the decisive role which it must of necessity play."

For the American UAW, the postwar period was the golden era. Led by the charismatic Reuther, the UAW established its reputation as a progressive force in a conservative period and made enviable gains to bring to their members a middle class level of consumption and benefits. But that effectiveness outside the workplace stood in contrast to, and sometimes came at the direct expense of, the union's ability to deal with life in the workplace. Furthermore, the collective bargaining gains were not matched by the development of an independent politics; negotiated gains and the union itself remained vulnerable to future changes in the economy and in society.

That vulnerability raised uncomfortable questions about the union's future. Would this union, so dependent on its leader's powerful presence, be the same after Walter Reuther moved on? Would this union, which emerged in the toughest of economic times and was structured to make gains in good economic times, be able to mobilize workers when the bad economic times returned (as they would in the seventies and eighties)? With the opposition crushed, with locals increasingly dependent on UAW headquarters, with the bureaucracy growing, and with the spirit that gave birth to the union fading, the "best of times" seemed to bear the seeds of the "worst of times."

Male Choir at Ford Local 200 performing along with the Harmonettes Female Choir at Ford Local 240 (office) at the installation of officers of Locals 200, 240, and 195 at the Vanity Theatre in Windsor, 1947. Courtesy of Wayne State Archives.

Canada: The Same but Different

Developments in the United States inevitably had an impact on Canada; the Canadians worked for the same employers, confronted an increasingly integrated continental economy, faced similar pressures, had many of the same needs and, of course, remained tied to the American UAW.

The American headquarters influenced both the bargaining direction and politics of the Canadians. Sometimes, as in the case of the Flint sit-down, this influence was indirect and came by way of positive examples of what workers could achieve. Other times, it was more direct and based on the resources and supportive pressures the UAW could bring to fighting the companies. But on a significant number of occasions, this influence took the form of Detroit, with support from sections of the union in Canada, imposing its perspective on the recalcitrant Canadians.

In 1959, the UAW conducted a trial of members of the 1955–56 GM bargaining committee who were accused of consulting, during those negotiations, with communists. Other than George Burt, the trial committee consisted entirely of Americans: UAW top officers from Detroit and an American lawyer. Amongst those charged was Cliff Pilkey of Local 222 in Oshawa, who had run against Burt for president. Pilkey and the other local leaders were all exonerated for lack of sufficient evidence. Pilkey was subsequently elected to the provincial parliament as an NDP member and later became president of the Ontario Federation of Labour.

But Paul Siren, a long-time member of the UAW staff, was found guilty and fired from his position. He had previously refused to go into Toronto-area locals and join others to eliminate the opposition. He did not consider that to be the proper role of the staff. The recently established Public Review Board (an independent board set up by the union in 1957 to give members a court of final appeal against arbitrary internal decisions) ruled in his favour. Siren refused to return given the circumstances and went on to play a central role in the building of the actor's union (ACTRA).

In 1947, when Reuther fired many staff members, seven candidates for termination were Canadian. In that earlier period, Canadians voiced resistance to these political firings, and, pushed by the Canadian Council, Director George Burt confronted Reuther. A compromise, while embarrassing to Burt and the Canadians, was negotiated. By the end of the fifties, however, Burt himself had joined the investigation of local leaders and a staff member for "consorting with communists."

Similarly, when the Americans signed the Treaty of Detroit in 1950, Oshawa and the Canadian Ford and Chrysler committees refused to discuss a five-year agreement. Yet by 1958, the Canadian agreements were virtually indistinguishable from those of the Americans in terms of dates, wage changes, and benefits. By the end of the fifties, it therefore seemed that any lingering differences between the directions of the unions in the two countries had disappeared.

Concentrating on the similarities of the unions on both sides of the border at that time would, however, overlook crucial differences. Emphasizing these differences isn't simply a matter of clarifying the record. They are, rather, the key to comprehending central developments in the history of the union, including the Canadian union's eventual split from the American union. Unions are more than the sum of their daily achievements. At least as important, if not more so, is the transition from one point to another. It's that *process* that shapes the culture and soul of a union — its decision-making procedures and principles, its leadership's views of the membership and of the union itself, and its potential to survive future struggles and achieve success.

After the war the Canadian section of the union was confident and aggressive. The 1945 Ford strike for union security had sparked similar successes in other sectors, and in 1946, Canadian workers, like workers in the U.S., engaged in a militant push for postwar wage increases. Within the Canadian UAW, Chrysler workers led the way in a 126-day strike while the rest of the union, especially outside the auto majors, made sure that no other agreements were signed that might undercut the Chrysler workers' efforts. The main victory in that strike, apart from wages, was the winning of three paid holidays.

Largest Unions in Canada, 1950

1. UAW (United Automobile Workers)*	60,000
2. USWA (United Steel Workers of America)	55,000
3. Carpenters/Joiners (United Brotherhood of Carpenters and Joiners of America)	38,000
4. Pulp, Sulphite, Paperworkers (International Brotherhood of Pulp, Sulphite, and Paper Mill Workers)	33,000
5. CBRT (Canadian Brotherhood of Railway & Transportation Workers)*	33,000
6. IAM (International Association of Machinists)	27,000
7. UMW (United Mine Workers of America)	26,000
8. Mine Mill (International Union of Mine, Mill, and Smelting Workers)*	25,000
9. UE (United Electrical Workers)*	25,000
10. Carmen (The Brotherhood of Railway Carmen of America)*	22,000

*Now in CAW

After the home of a fellow Local 222 member (Clarence O'Connor) was destroyed by a fire, the other workers in his department, Body Shop 9 at GM, Oshawa, came to build a new one for/with him. Early 1950s. Courtesy of Wayne State Archives.

The recently elected American leadership attempted the same kind of "housecleaning" in Canada that Reuther had introduced in the U.S. But it would take much longer in Canada and be less thorough because the left within the UAW had a much wider base of support amongst activists. Within this left grouping, communists in fact formed a small minority; the remainder consisted of many committed members of the CCF, and as in the U.S., solid militants outside any left politics.

This left subgroup had a number of advantages that didn't exist in the United States. It had the credibility of its record of defending the membership during the war. The Canadian left could also, in any fight with the American leadership, appeal to not only rank-and-file democracy, but also democracy linked to nationalism and Canadian autonomy. In addition, the Canadian Council acted as a mechanism for responding to or resisting Detroit. The relative compactness of the Canadian union at the time, being essentially restricted to southern Ontario, simplified the logistics of communication. And the Canadian state was not, like that of the United States, leading the international fight against communism; consequently, it was less aggressive-repressive than the American state in its attack. (Canada was of course still linked to and part of that American crusade; the preference of the Canadian state was, however, that labour be left to do the dirty work itself.) Together, these factors provided the Canadian locals with a shield their American counterparts, picked off one by one, did not have.

Although we now look back with nostalgia to the fifties, these years were not blissful, even for the organized sections of the working class; two-thirds of workers then, as now, had no union. The mid-fifties saw a significant downturn in the economy which, combined with the growth of automation, hit auto particularly hard.

Between 1953 and 1960, the Canadian market for vehicles increased by fifteen per cent but output fell by fifteen per cent and employment fell even faster. The apparent contradiction lay in the changing relationship with European industry. The revival of Europe's productive capacity reduced Canadian overseas auto exports one-quarter while imports into Canada quadrupled. In the U.S., the overseas import share rose to about ten per cent; in Canada it rose to well over twenty-five per cent. When Local 707 in Oakville joined the Ford strike in 1955, more than two-thirds of the workers were already on lay-off.

The 1958 recession was very severe, aggravated by the reversal in auto trade: Canadian auto exports were falling while imports were rising dramatically. Plant closures, and especially plant relocations, were increasingly common. (Bob White, then a local president in his mid-twenties, was put on the organizing staff on a temporary basis to deal with these plants.) Then, at the end of the fifties, came Black Monday. The Canadian government cancelled production of the AVRO Arrow in response to American insistence that Canadian defences use the U.S.'s Bomarc missiles. Virtually overnight, 14,000 aerospace employees were left with no place in Canada to apply their skills.

The Canadian economy and society were continuing to move towards greater integration with the United States and greater reliance on resource exports. Massive public projects, such as the Trans-Canada highway, the St. Lawrence Seaway, and pipelines, were introduced to facilitate that integration and reliance. Similar public intervention to build the social infrastruc-

McKINNON MACETTES — CITY AND DISTRICT JUNIOR CHAMPIONS

Front row, left to right: Irene Davey, Jacqueline Carr, Carol Cadot, Doreen Pepperall, Judy Pepperall, Frances Smell, Ann Gaines. Foreground, Alvin McPhail (bat boy), Back row: Coach Bill Gaines, Jacqueline Stockwell, Florence Argent, Marilyn Woodcock, Beverley Bell, Pauline Montague, Ass't. Coach Ossie Hill, Manager Bert Gaines. Absent from photo, Doris Barnas.

The McKinnon People

Page Fifteen

(Top) Local 200 baseball team, c. 1950. Courtesy of Wayne State Archives. (Bottom) Women's softball team, McKinnon (GM), St. Catharines. Courtesy of CAW Local 199 collection.

ture of the Canadian welfare state wasn't yet on the agenda, and trade unionism was endorsed as long as it was moderate.

During the fifties and into the early sixties, Canadian workers fought the companies, their international union office, the government, and occasionally each other. The Canadian UAW lobbied and demonstrated against the relocation of plants and organized a cavalcade of unemployed workers to take their demands for jobs to Ottawa. Workers fought internally over the future direction of the auto industry and its integration with the United States, and presented no less than four briefs to the royal commission on the future of the Canadian industry. They went on strike against some company attempts to implement American UAW directions in Canada, but they also went on strike to copy and catch up to other American achievements that the companies refused to implement in Canada.

Playing Catch-Up: GM workers in the U.S. got the formal forty-hour week in 1937; Canadian GM workers, who came out of the Oshawa strike with a forty-four-hour week didn't get to the forty-hour week until 1954. Ford accepted a national master agreement and union security in the U.S. in 1941, but it forced its Canadian workers to strike for ninety-nine days in 1945 (union security) and over 100 in 1954 (master agreement). Similarly, while GM plants in the U.S. had parity with each other, in 1948 the workers in St. Catharines had to strike for three and a half months simply to reduce their gap with Oshawa.

Key Canadian locals resisted longer agreements, opposed profit-sharing, fought management on production standards (e.g., the speed of the line), and argued for reduced work-time instead of SUB (supplementary unemployment benefits). As the *Toronto Telegram* reported on 14 January 1958: "Clifford Pilkey (Local 222) said the local's delegates ... will press for higher pay and the shorter day. The Oshawa stand opposes that of President Reuther who said yesterday the union will NOT seek a shorter day but will demand part of the auto companies' profits above 10% [also opposed was Detroit's Local 600, the UAW's largest local]."

In 1950–51 Ford workers were involved in a battle that included thirty-four wildcats in a matter of weeks and the firing of one-quarter of the elected steward body. Workers held wildcats over attempts to speed up the line at Chrysler, Ford, GM, and Massey-Harris in the early fifties, and over discharges at the trailer manufacturer Fruehauf after plant-gate protests against

Excerpts from editorials during the 1954 Ford strike, which became the focus of a more general attack on the Canadian UAW for not bending enough during the mid-fifties recession:

Remember too what happened in South Bend, Indiana just a few weeks ago when Studebaker workers themselves voted for a wage cut rather than see their plant shut down.

— *Financial Post*, 4 September 1954

Evidence has been presented that we are quickly pricing ourselves out of the markets of the world.

— *St. Catharines Standard*, 9 September 1954

The strike is a slap in the face … for Canadian autoworkers who obediently shout the slogans read to them; who obediently go on strike against their best interests; and who obediently raise or lower their arms whenever the string puller at a so-called strike vote tells them to do so.

— *Financial Times*, 5 November 1954

It could safely be said that 70% of the men on strike at Massey and Ford's would gladly go back to work at their present good rate of pay but are prevented by a disgruntled few with communist leanings.

— *The Toronto Telegram*, 22 November 1954

employees working overtime in spite of lay-offs. While Ford and GM in the U.S. were in the middle of a relatively peaceful decade as far as nationwide strikes were concerned, Canadian workers were on strike in 1954–55 at Ford for 109 days, Massey-Harris for eighty days, GM for 148 days, and de Havilland Aircraft for 155 days. There was turmoil within GM as the Oshawa local elected a group of young militants who refused to enter into the GM master agreement. And even after stability was achieved at the end of the sixties, Chrysler workers held a week-long strike to protest production standards and to reduce the term of the agreement to two years.

In some cases, the Canadians were able to establish better practices than the Americans. Workplace conditions were generally superior in Canada; there was less overtime; GM workers managed to get one more holiday than their American counterparts; Ford workers won paid medical benefits seven years ahead of the U.S. union; and Canadians retained across-the-board increases, which were more egalitarian than percentage increases for a longer period of time.

The secret to the Canadian difference didn't, however, lie in such specific achievements. The Canadian UAW was shaped by several factors: distinct domestic economic conditions, a different role in the world and therefore a

Members of Local 200 involved in various kinds of recreation at their hall in the fifties. Courtesy of Wayne State Archives.

different kind of nationalism as compared to that of the U.S., a state that postponed effective bargaining rights until the end of the war, the creation of lasting democratic structures such as the Canadian Council, and the survival of a left opposition. This combination of factors affected the union's spirit in Canada; Canadians were putting up resistance, fighting back, refusing to wait patiently for change, rejecting partnerships with the corporations, and debating issues and directions even at the risk of internal division. The Canadian UAW was challenging the stereotypes of Canadians as polite and passive. The union culture reflected Canadian culture, but in a quite distinct way, linked as it was to the experiences of the working class and this particular union.

The UAW and the CCF

The political battles between the left in Canada and the Reuther forces were tied to the conflicts over the CCF. The CCF believed that it could not have a base in the Canadian UAW until the communists were ousted; therefore, it was very sympathetic to, and worked closely with, the Reutherites, who were on the same track. In 1947, when Reuther won his second term, George Burt was part of the left, and the Reuther supporters in Canada ran against him. David Lewis, national secretary of the CCF, indicated the extent of the Reuther-CCF ties in a letter to Walter Reuther on 10 December 1947 saying: "I am only sorry that our people were unable to deliver a victory in the Canadian region. My impression is that it is only a matter of time now."

Although the CCF was founded in the early thirties and exploded onto the electoral map in Ontario in 1943, the Canadian UAW did not officially endorse the CCF until December, 1948. The barrier did in fact relate to the CCF-CP conflict over influence within the union. The communists called for an alliance between all "progressive forces," which included the CP-based Labour Progressive Party (LPP); the CCF refused. The CP, with its credible base within the Canadian UAW that went back to the thirties, was able to rally other activists — including many who weren't particularly supportive of the CCF and some who argued for a labour party — against support for any one party.

In the CCF's surprise showing in 1943, all three provincial seats in Windsor went to the CCF. The *Windsor Star* reported that "No matter what the sentiment in the rest of the province, the victory here belonged to the CIO (UAW)."

These circumstances led to a spectacle in the 1945 Ontario election: the UAW endorsed three candidates in Windsor, who were in turn endorsed by the LPP and the Liberals, while the CCF ran competing candidates. The UAW slate included George Burt, the president of the union; Alex Parent, the communist president of the second largest local in the UAW (Local 195); and Art Reaume, the former conservative and mayor of Windsor who had supported the Ford workers in their fight for the Rand formula. In the previous provincial election, the CCF had won all three seats on the basis of UAW support. Now the party lost by a small margin in each seat; of the three UAW candidates, only Alex Parent won. The other two narrowly

missed election because of a split vote. The resulting bitterness remained on all sides for years.

The left's strength in the union waned, and Burt himself shifted away from the CP after Reuther's

Local 397 float in Labour Day parade, Brantford, 1946. Courtesy of the CAW collection.

ascendancy was clear and the cold war intensified. The union thus moved steadily towards the CCF. By the early fifties, the UAW, along with other key unions such as the United Steelworkers of America and the Packinghouse Workers (now part of the United Food and Commercial Workers), became the organizational backbone of the party. But that support remained at the level of leadership and staff and was not reflected by the general membership. With the Liberals making some concessions on progressive programs and, more important, the union making crucial social gains in collective bargaining, the need for a third party became less urgent. The locals did not affiliate with the CCF until after it was revived in 1961 as the NDP (New Democratic Party). In fact, as late as 1957, de Havilland Aircraft workers comprised the only UAW local affiliated to the CCF.

There were two implications of this relationship between the Canadian UAW and its eventual political arm. First, the union never limited its defin

Autoworkers prepare a cavalcade to protest unemployment during the 1958 recession. Standing in the middle is Charlie Brooks, president of the Chrysler local and later the Canadian Council. Brooks was assassinated in 1977 by a frustrated worker when the union failed to get the worker's job back after a third discharge. Courtesy of the CAW collection.

ition of politics to electoral activity. The UAW developed and maintained an emphasis on independent lobbying in a number of ways. It sent cavalcades to Queen's Park and Ottawa, organized the unemployed, and buttonholed MPs (i.e., it sent staff and council delegates as teams to meet and lobby members of Parliament). It also worked with the rest of the labour movement on campaigns for labour legislation, met with mayors of auto communities to garner support for tariff and taxation policy, and established solid community links through union-led services such as co-op housing and community health clinics.

Second, even as ties with the CCF/NDP grew, a healthy level of skepticism prevented the relationship from being reduced to one of unconditional loyalty. The union would, when necessary, challenge the party's direction. This independence became more evident in later periods when, at critical times (usually at a new stage of economic restructuring), the NDP went in one direction while the union went in another (wage controls, free trade, the "social contract"). But even in the fifties, as the NDP moved towards a "social democracy that reflected giving up on socialism," there were hints of such differences. In March, 1952, George Burt, addressing and apparently reflecting the mood of the Canadian Council, wondered whether the move shouldn't instead be to reaffirm earlier social

The creation of the NDP in 1961 was a response to both the failure of the CCF to make a breakthrough in popular support and the merger in 1956 of the TLC and the CCL to form the Canadian Labour Congress. The merger forced a discussion of the relationship to the CCF which the CCL had supported and the TLC had not. Out of that discussion came the agreement to work towards the creation of a rejuvenated social democratic party (the NDP) with close ties to labour.

democratic touchstones: "Unemployment ... can only be solved by ... planning our economy to develop ... the utmost use of our resources. This means the exercise of government control over our natural resources and the resources of industry."

By the early sixties, the American section of the union had remained relatively stable for fifteen years, and observers began to note an emerging bureaucratization. In spite of Reuther's eloquence, the UAW's education programs (including the use of radio and TV in a way that American and Canadian unions today would envy), and the development of many superb pamphlets on automation, production standards, health and safety, democracy, and the failures of capitalism, an ill wind was blowing. Harvey Swados, a writer who had worked in an auto plant and who was sympathetic to the union, reflected on the UAW in *Dissent* in October, 1963. He observed the link between ongoing struggles and the potential of the working class:

> ... struggles themselves function as educational forces for the participants — and the leaders. It is when struggles are postponed or aborted that the fabric of democracy must deteriorate. It is when people are in motion, and are led towards an ethical goal, that they are most receptive to challenges to receive wisdom; more than that they themselves become innovators and discover that they are capable of an inven-

tiveness and an intellectual audacity of which they themselves could scarcely conceive in less adventurous times.

Walter Reuther, looking back at the UAW two years before his death, was also sensitive to the dangers of the American labour movement's drift into complacency. At a 1968 UAW convention, he noted: "A labour movement can get soft and flabby spiritually. It can make progress materially and the soul of the union can die in the process."

The Canadians shared in the gains made by the Americans and fought struggles of their own. They couldn't escape the pressures the Americans faced — when necessary, the Americans made sure of that. Yet, different circumstances and past experiences influenced the Canadians as they shaped their own union culture. The Canadian section of the union had emerged from that same fifteen-year period differently, if only because it endured greater turmoil and the stable UAW pattern did not settle in until the late fifties. There was therefore less time, before the greater disruptions of the sixties, for the establishment of any bureaucratization.

Even by the end of the sixties, after Burt had moved ideologically towards Reuther, and the remaining opposition to Reutherism in Canada had suffered both electoral defeats (for example, it lost control of the Oshawa local) and collective bargaining defeats (it was forced to accept the American pattern), an oppositional base remained within the union and key locals. That opposition got a new lease on life with an upsurge of Canadian nationalism that was based on the reaction to the growing American dominance over the economy and on the in-plant rebellions of the sixties.

The fifties were a mixed blessing. Unions and workers were invited "in" but at a price: they had to develop the proper table etiquette and leave their "bad" manners outside. The issue to come in the sixties, in both Canada and the United States, was whether unions were still a leading force in the movement to challenge the status quo.

PART THREE: NORMAL ISN'T NORMAL ANYMORE

In the sixties, a new generation rebelled and raised basic questions about the values and direction of society (Chapter 6). That social offensive was met, in the seventies, by a corporate counteroffensive to regain the initiative (Chapter 7).

SKD striker arrested on picket line, August 23, 1969. Courtesy of *Windsor Star.*

CHAPTER 6

THE OTHER SIXTIES

*I think the movement is in better condition than it ever
was ... We no longer march in the streets. We no longer
have sit-down strikes ... Labour to some extent has
become middle-class ... when you have no property,
you don't have anything, you have nothing to lose by
these radical actions. But when you become a person
who has a home and has property, to some extent you
become conservative.*

— George Meany

*Some people say I'm a dreamer
But I know I'm not the only one.*

— John Lennon

*If I were a sociologist, I would take the wave of strikes
in 1968, the black revolution to the south of us, student
demonstrations here as elsewhere, the apparent
consumer interest, the quiet revolution in Quebec, and
the hippy movement, and I would place them all in the
same sociological bag because all of them in one way or
another are a clear manifestation of obvious
dissatisfaction with the status quo.*

— Dennis McDermott

The sixties have come to mean a time of generational revolt. Throughout the developed capitalist countries, young people who had never experienced the depression, who were born after the war and, uninspired by the fifties, refused to play the game by the old rules and challenged established authority. The public's memory of those times centred on student unrest, but those who entered the workforce were part of this same rebellion, and even when they were hostile to some aspects of it, they were still influenced by it. As workers, they expressed their dissatisfaction with the status quo not by dropping out or participating in political protest; rebellion found expression in their attitudes to the workplace.

Yet even in the workplace, the issues were penetrated by the politics of an emerging English Canadian and a rising Quebec nationalism. In the United States, the antiwar movement fought against an aggressive American nationalism; in Canada, progressives saw nationalism as a positive force based on our role in the world, our specific relationship to the United States, and our history as a federation of two nations.

Gold-Plated Sweatshops

Gary Bryner, the young president of the Lordstown, Ohio, local which became a symbol for the "Blue Collar Blues," captured some of the changes in the attitudes of young workers in a 1972 interview:

> ... someone said Lordstown is the Woodstock of the working man ... long hair, big Afros, beads ... Fathers used to show their manliness by being able to work hard and have big strong muscles ... the young guy now doesn't get a kick out of saying how hard he can work ... Father felt patriotic about it ... obligated to that guy that gave him a job to do his dirty work ... the young guy believes he has something to say about what he does ... Hell, he may be ten times more intelligent than his foreman ...
>
> What I have to say about what I do, how I do it [is] more important than the almighty dollar. The reason might be that the dollar's here now ... I can concentrate on the social aspects, my rights ... That's how I got involved in this whole stinkin' mess ... Fighting every day of my life ...

142

The targets of the workplace revolt and anger often included the union itself, which had focused so exclusively in the fifties on wages and benefits and neglected working conditions. The report of the 1968 Royal Commission on Labour Relations (the Wood's Task force) commented: "The fact that worker dissatisfaction sometimes runs as deeply against the union and collective bargaining as against management is reflected in the rebellion of union members against their leaders."

With the economy on a roll and this growth providing workers with some power, this "other sixties" exploded in a wave of rebellion of young workers. In 1963, one-third of UAW local officials in the United States were unelected. An internal UAW poll of the American membership showed general satisfaction with the national leadership who successfully negotiated the economic package, but two-thirds of workers were disenchanted with the local leadership whom they held responsible for working conditions. In Canada, contract rejections became common, and the number of strikes grew rapidly. Companies lost more time to strikes in 1966 than in any year since 1946. A record number of these strikes were wildcats: during the sixties, roughly one-third of strikes in Canada were illegal work stoppages.

The UAW responded by negotiating increases in relief time, more holidays, reductions in the amount of time it took to process grievances, and later, a substantial health and safety program. Some leaders were aware that the problem went deeper. Leonard Woodcock, then head of the GM department, talked about "gold-plated sweatshops," and Reuther, in the period just before his death, often suggested that there was a need to rethink basic values.

But the union remained unwilling and/or unable to develop a national challenge to the companies over the work-

> *There is a new breed of workers in the plant who is less willing to accept corporate decisions that pre-empt his own decisions ... there is a different kind of worker than we had twenty-five or thirty years ago.*
>
> — Walter Reuther, *Wall Street Journal*, 20 April 1970

> *We are in trouble because our values are all mixed up in America. We have been more concerned by the quantity of our gadgets and the brightness of the chrome on those gadgets than we have concerning the quality of life ... we have forgotten what is important and what is unimportant ...*
>
> — Walter Reuther, address to 1970 convention

place conditions. The basic position remained: "Let them produce the gold-en goose and we'll share in carving it up." In the U.S., the potential of a revival of the union initiated by these young workers was soon lost. The deep recession and the energy crisis in the mid-seventies consolidated that loss and brought discipline back to the workplace. The revolt was essentially over.

Not so in Canada. Although the Canadian social protest movements were relatively weaker, the labour movement was stronger. The defiance of workers lasted longer, and the political influence of Canadian labour was actually more powerful in the seventies than in the sixties. In fact, the unions themselves became an important vehicle for placing social issues on the national agenda.

The economic climate in Canada and the deepening of unionization helped to sustain the movement. The Canadian economy benefited from both the growth in the United States and the devalued Canadian dollar, which lowered the costs of exports relative to imports. In the sixties, Canada's workforce grew faster than the workforce in any other major devel-oped country, and unionization kept pace. Workers in manufacturing may have been rebelling against their union leaders, but it was equally clear that the workers wanted to sustain their unions. The Canadian UAW regularly led all other UAW regions in organizing during this period, and it also entered the new telecommunications sector by organizing Northern Telecom in 1967.

Led by the highly politicized public sector workers in Quebec, unioniza-tion in the Canadian public sector erupted in 1965 when most of these work-ers gained the right to strike. Postal workers and railworkers took on the fight over the right to negotiate the introduction, and not just the fruits, of tech-nological change in the workplace. Such battles in the private and public sectors reinforced the confidence of the entire Canadian labour movement.

Unlike the United States, Canada wasn't polarized — or paralyzed — around a dominating international issue. As a result, the door was open for significant social reforms. Those gains increased workers' security and there-fore the strength of the Canadian labour movement. In the mid-sixties, the minority Liberal government, supported by the NDP, responded to the mood and pressures of the times by introducing the Canada Pension Plan and national medicare.

The situation in auto was particularly important. Not only was auto pro-duction running at a high rate, but the auto industry was moving towards an integrated market with the United States via the Autopact (the Canada-U.S. Automotive Products Agreement). Canadian plants had been designed for the domestic market and thus included a wide range of models. While management had always pressured Canadian workers to maximize production at minimum cost, the nature of the production process in Canada — regular model changes and diversity in jobs and work cycles — gave Canadian workers a relatively greater degree of in-plant bargaining power than workers in standardized single-product plants.

When the Pact went into effect, the corporate demands for tougher production standards and greater management flexibility, especially in terms of overtime, increased in Canada. This change was not surprising given the greater cross-border interdependence of production, the expensive investments, and increases in Canadian wages (wage parity) that accompanied the Autopact. New managers and consultants, who were more familiar with the organization of global-scale plants and were often American, were brought in to implement the changes. Their single-minded drive to recast production facilities along American lines added to the disaffection already brewing in the workforce.

Ratification

The assembly over,

The workers stood

Huddled together

In small accusing groups

And with critical eyes

Examined my face

As I humbly left

A frigid union hall

Where moments before

I had asked a sullen audience

To confront reality.

But reality is not an easy sell,

Better for me

Had I fooled them,

Offered them much

While delivering little,

Conveyed my ignoble message

In cunning political prose

Delivered with an austere

Yet confident voice

As if in deceit

They would find promise.

Ron Dickson

145

The Canada-U.S. Automotive Products Agreement (Autopact) was a trade agreement between Canada and the United States introduced in 1965. It more fully integrated the auto industries of Canada and the United States, providing the Canadian operations a chance to benefit from larger and more specialized production runs. But it also recognized the need for safeguards to protect the Canadian industry because of its dependence on the U.S. in terms of both ownership and size. This was done by enforcing commitments on multinational corporations. Those commitments said that if the auto companies wanted to sell in the Canadian market, they also had to reach certain levels of production in Canada.

Under this managed trade, companies that produced 50 per cent or more of their vehicles in North America (Canada and the United States) could freely ship vehicles and components north or south across the Canada-U.S. border. On the Canadian side there were additional conditions that had to be met to get duty-free status: companies had to assemble roughly one vehicle for every vehicle sold in Canada, and for each dollar of sales in Canada, companies had to offset this with 60 cents of value-added production in Canada. (This last condition was accomplished through direct agreements between the Canadian government and the auto companies rather than legislatively.)

In the American auto plants, many of the wildcats were led by workers who, while young, had been in the plants for a decade or more and simply refused to accept the never-ending speed-ups (almost two-thirds of the American workforce was over 30). In Canada, where the Autopact had led to a rapid expansion of the workforce, the popular stereotype of new workers leading the walk-outs — with the tolerance and often the support of the old guard — was more accurate.

The restructuring brought on by the Autopact caused job losses in certain plants. But because the pact was introduced during a period of rapid growth, it resulted in the construction of ninety new plants and twice as many major expansions. Prominent examples include Chrysler car assembly in Windsor; GM truck assembly in Oshawa; Ford car assembly in St. Thomas; GM car assembly in Ste-Thérèse, International Harvester heavy-duty trucks in Chatham; car and truck frames at Budd in Kitchener and Hayes-Dana in St. Catharines; and car trim at GM in Windsor. In these locations, thousands of young workers were hired. The UAW's American membership in 1969 was an impressive thirty-five per cent higher than in

1960; in Canada, the increase for the same time period exceeded seventy per cent. Autoworkers' recollections may exaggerate the mood, but they capture the confident shrug with which many young workers then viewed employment in auto communities: "In those days, if they canned you in the morning you could just go down the street and get another job before lunch. And if you didn't like it there, you could be working somewhere else that afternoon."

U.S. assembly plants operated on the basis of fixed shifts. The first thing young workers consequently learned about seniority and union principles was that it stuck them with night shifts. In Canadian plants (with the later exception of Ste-Thérèse) workers rotated shifts every two weeks, removing that particular barrier to gaining union support from young workers.

Although the pay in the auto plants was relatively good, the nature of the work was a shock to the young people flooding in. At the same time, the reality of the power small groups can exercise in assembly plants was well known, and jobs in the auto communities were plentiful. With the discipline of the market temporarily in abeyance and revolt in the air, the workers' readiness to take action against inhumane conditions, arbitrary management, and compulsory overtime was hardly surprising.

When, for example, Chrysler tried to establish compulsory overtime as the norm, members of Local 144 wildcatted for overtime to be voluntary after eight hours each day and forty-eight hours weekly. At de Havilland Aircraft, Local 112 had a wildcat to limit overtime when other workers were laid off. In St. Thomas, wives and girlfriends picketed the Ford operations on Saturdays to challenge the weekend loss of their partners. One particular Saturday, the St. Thomas workers threatened job action if management didn't let them off early so they could cheer for fellow workers in a local hockey tournament. The workers got to the tournament.

The resistance to overtime was, however, increasingly ambivalent. In fact, while workers disliked being forced to put in overtime, their growing dependence on it was becoming a matter of concern. In February, 1965, George Burt observed: "Workers have established brand new standards of living based on overtime and I'm afraid persistent overtime is going to endanger their health."

This period was crucial to the history of the Canadian UAW in that many of today's top leaders and activists were introduced to the union at

147

this time. They surfaced at a time of shop-floor militancy and social protest, and this atmosphere shaped, even if it did not determine, their future atti-tudes. In contrast, the first generation of American UAW leaders enjoyed a longer reign and passed the torch to the generation from the fifties, skipping potential leaders who emerged in the sixties.

Within the union, women had fought alongside men for common work-place improvements like limiting speed-up and improved washroom facili-ties. Yet female members still faced the bias of separate seniority lists. The economic restructuring that followed the Autopact both aggravated and highlighted this inequity. Women with high seniority lost their jobs as departments were closed or cut back, while lower-seniority male workers remained. When expansions later occurred in departments that traditionally excluded women, companies often hired new workers, ignoring the women who had been laid off.

At that time, the Human Rights Code of Ontario prohibited discrimina-tion on a number of grounds, but these did not include the sex and marital status of the worker. In 1970, the legislation was finally amended after a long and intensive lobbying campaign and the introduction of a private member's bill by member of Provincial Parliament (MPP) Cliff Pilkey, the former president of GM Oshawa Local 222.

UAW women in Oshawa played a decisive role. No doubt, the emer-gence of a broader women's movement helped give them the support and confidence they needed to win seniority rights. That this amendment took so long to achieve was not simply a matter of corporate resistance, though corporations were the source of this discriminatory practice. It is also a reminder of the difficulty of changing broader social assumptions, especially those steeped in tradition. The powerful lesson was that sometimes change in the workplace occurs only as part of broader social change.

The expansion of unionization in the public sector, with its high propor-tion of women, and the emerging feminism of the sixties provided that broader context of change. With a base in the rapidly grow-ing public sector and with links to the minority of women in the industrial sector, working women pushed the male trade union leadership to act, and, eventually, many did respond.

Between the early sixties and mid-seventies, the number of women in unions tripled, increasing by over half a million.

But Don't Forget Wages ...

Labour militancy in the sixties was generally based on both workplace and pay issues. Inflation was accelerating, the newly organized public sector was making up for lost time, railworkers and workers on the St. Lawrence Seaway were setting high standards, and Canadian autoworkers' discussions at the Big Three were finally turning to wage parity with the Americans.

The principle of wage parity with American autoworkers — the same pay for the same work — had been a demand by Canadian workers from day one. But the smaller Canadian market, with its less efficient production runs, remained a barrier to winning that equality. The Autopact integrated Canada into the same market and productive system as the U.S. (with some Canadian safeguards) and gave Canadians a clear rationale for demanding equal wages: they were now as productive as Americans. The pact also gave the UAW in the U.S. a good reason to insist on parity: it did not want to compete with an equally productive neighbour that paid lower wages.

After three decades of unionization, the implementation of wage parity with American Big Three workers was relatively straightforward. The policy was phased in during the 1968 agreement. Parity committees studied jobs on each side of the border, and workers performing the same tasks received the same basic wage in their own currency. Wages differed according to the inflation rates in each country, but this discrepancy was erased in 1973 by the introduction of a Canada-U.S. COLA formula which provided workers in both countries with identical cost-of-living increases.

Canada-U.S. wage parity in the Big Three, and especially the large wage increases that went along with it for the Canadians, immediately led to a series of wage-related comparisons and confrontations across the independent parts, aerospace, and agricultural implements sectors. Workers still confronted the occasional employer when the issue was a wage freeze or concessions (e.g., the 134-day strike at Dominion Forge, an auto components plant in Windsor), but the dominant issue in the union, especially in the auto parts sector, was matching the increases at the Big Three. The overwhelming majority of legal strikes in the late sixties occurred amongst these independent suppliers to the auto majors.

In aerospace, the issue was less direct. Of particular significance was the two-month strike at McDonnell-Douglas in 1971. The U.S. had introduced wage controls, and the American negotiators seemed to have reached a settlement within those guidelines. The Canadian bargaining team rejected the offer. When the continuing strike threatened to disrupt American plants, the union's international office — with the support of the Canadian director — eventually ordered the local to vote on the offer. The argument was that the Canadians had essentially achieved their objective of matching the Big Three pattern increase, and therefore no longer had a reason to continue the strike.

While there were grounds for debating whether the pattern was completely met, events and the locals' own wage demands had moved the confrontation beyond the technicality of how the pattern should be applied to McDonnell-Douglas in Canada. At the subsequent membership meeting, a group within the union stormed the stage and prevented a vote, arguing that the meeting should have only been informational. After bitter recriminations between the local and the national office, the members voted to return to work in defiance of the local leadership. But the local leadership in turn received a strong endorsement in the subsequent elections in defiance of the national and international offices. Hostility between the local and national union, not to mention the international union, didn't abate for almost two decades.

The significance of these events is not restricted to the internal conflict in the union; it extends to the many issues this conflict straddled and in some ways foreshadowed. This instance was the most visible of a number of postparity conflicts. Since the formation of the union, Canadians had tried to catch up to Americans in each sector. Now they were rejecting parity with their American aerospace counterparts and looking to Canadian comparisons such as the gains made in Canadian auto plants. This change in attitude was part of a more general trend in which Canadian workers were no longer viewing the U.S. as their role model. That trend was later a key factor in the mobilization of massive opposition to the Canada-U.S. Free Trade Agreement (FTA).

Furthermore, the readiness with which the Americans accepted voluntary wage guidelines was one indicator of the UAW's future readiness to accept concessions. Similar discussions between the Canadian government and the unions had been unproductive, and the Canadian labour movement fought controls even when they were mandated by law in 1975. In a sense, the McDonnell-Douglas fight was therefore also an early skirmish against such limits on bargaining. In terms of strategy, that strike was one of the few instances where a Canadian shut-down had a major impact on American facilities. It was therefore a precursor of later developments that revealed the

McDonnell-Douglas workers on strike, October 1970. Courtesy of the *Toronto Telegram* collection, York University.

workers' potential bargaining power in a system where the flip side of international restructuring is specialization and just-in-time production, which leave companies vulnerable to disruptions anywhere in the production chain.

Most important, however, the McDonnell-Douglas conflict was an indicator of a new surge of nationalism in the country which linked economic demands to political perspectives. The immediate tension may have been over the American leadership's response to wage demands, and the changing demands of the local's bargaining team may have been questionable. But the emotional side of this strike could not be understood without consideration of the intensifying debates over American domination of the Canadian economy. The arrogance of this American multinational company, the weakness of the American UAW's response to wage controls, and the apparent order from Detroit to end the strike fed into and reinforced a growing left nationalism in Canada.

Dave Monie of the United Electrical Workers (UE) being dragged away by police at Artistic Woodworkers' strike in Toronto. Courtesy of the Laurel Ritchie collection.

The union involved was the Canadian Textile and Chemical Union (CTCU). The main speakers at the rally included Andreas Papandreaou, then active in the Greek community and later Prime Minister of Greece, Jim Hunter of the Canadian Brotherhood of Rail and Transport Workers (CBRT), and Abe Taylor of Local 222 Oshawa. The CTCU, UE, and CBRT are now part of the CAW. One of the workers from McDonnell-Douglas who came to the protest was arrested. He and six other sympathetic Douglas activists showed up for work late and they were suspended. This led to a sick-in by the union membership; five of the key leaders of the local at Douglas were subsequently fired.

Which Side Are You On?

The Canadian UAW, like the American UAW, did not easily cope with the social movements outside the union. In Canada, despite the conflicts accompanying those movements, the union itself eventually integrated much of the spirit of rebellion and moral challenge to the status quo which the movements represented. In the United States, the divisions grew deeper.

The two most intense and divisive movements of the decade were based in the United States: the civil rights movement, which began the slow march to citizenship for the black population, and the mobilization against the war in Vietnam, which led hundreds of thousands of young people to question what America stood for. It was in the civil rights marches and non-violent sit-in campaigns of the American South that young white students from the northern states got their first taste of activism. They returned to apply their new-found organizing skills at the community level and then in the antiwar demonstrations on campuses.

The songs of protest sung in the early sixties were often based on the labour songs of the thirties. This influence reflected labour's history as the most important and lasting movement of that earlier period, but also high-lighted the extent to which labour's link to other movements was now only by way of its past. American labour couldn't comprehend the urban rebel-lions and black rage. It was generally absent from the civil rights protests and the antiwar demonstrations.

There were some exceptions, the most notable being the UAW and Walter Reuther. Reuther had joined the civil rights marches in the South, and in turn, Martin Luther King spoke at UAW functions. But this alliance never became permanent nor did it lead to sustained organizing break-throughs in the South. As the black movement mobilized and became radi-calized, the UAW faced several choices. The choices the union leadership ultimately made, within both the Democratic Party and the UAW itself, blocked closer ties to the civil rights movement.

In 1964, the delegation from Mississippi to the Democratic Convention included blacks. When the nonracial Mississippi Freedom Party held its own statewide democratic convention to choose delegates for that same conven-tion and insisted that it be seated in spite of the presence of the official all-white delegation from Mississippi, Reuther — concerned about internal party turmoil — supported the party establishment.

Later, when angry young blacks, influenced by the growing militancy in their community, fought management over workplace conditions in the Detroit factories and simultaneously challenged the union on the lack of black representation on staff and the executive board, they were branded "extremists." Frustrated young black workers watched Reuther marching on television with Southern blacks and asked, "Why isn't he doing that in

Detroit?" They noted the eventual moves to bring blacks in as union officials and acknowledged that the UAW had gone further than other unions.
However, they complained bitterly that those black leaders chosen were not
based amongst the militants but were politically safe.

The ties to the student antiwar movement followed a similar path. In the
first days of that movement, when the students were developing a broad
challenge to the overall direction of American society, the UAW was directly supportive. The American student left even drafted its manifesto, the
Port Huron Statement, at the UAW summer camp. The UAW financed the
first organizer of the Students for a Democratic Society (SDS), and contributed to their community campaigns and other projects. The bridge
between the movements was often labour families crossing the generational
divide. Labour activists from the thirties were now in influential union positions and their sons and daughters who were now in "the movement" sought
and received financial support.

> Used to positions at the forefront of social
> change, labour leaders found themselves
> attacked by radical activists and student
> demonstrators as part of the
> establishment.
>
> — Robert Zeigler, Professor of
> History, Wayne State University

But these links couldn't survive the antiwar protests. Emil
Mazey (UAW secretary-treasurer) and Paul Schrade (UAW
director for California) voiced
their opposition to the war
early, and Victor Reuther tried
to encourage his brother Walter,
to take that position as well. But
Walter Reuther refused, caught
again within the politics of the
Democratic Party: any such action by as prominent a democrat as the leader
of the UAW would embarrass the presidency of Lyndon Johnson — which
was, of course, precisely what the antiwar movement wanted. Reuther's
eventual announcement in 1970 of his opposition to the war was a welcome
moral statement, but it came much too late to overcome the damage done
to the potential ties between the UAW and the young antiwar activists.

Reuther, concerned that the labour movement was being marginalized,
eventually broke from the AFL-CIO to create a new, more progressive
alliance of labour. But this attempt was also destined to fail. Quick to criticize
the AFL's extreme integration with the American state department, but hesitant to break with the most important aspects of that policy (the Vietnam
War), there was no basis for a relationship with the student movement. To

the surprise of very few, the new alliance with the Teamsters, the main union outside the AFL-CIO, did not lead to new directions on social policy.

The Canadian left had the advantage of being energized by the American movements without having to confront, to anywhere near the same degree, the bitterly divisive issues of race and war. Canadian politics wasn't about the forceful capture of black slaves, the denial of the most fundamental citizenship rights to a large internal minority, the bombing of civilians in a country thousands of miles away, or the maimed war veterans who came home to tell the stories of those who didn't. While the American left fought against its country's aggressive nationalism, the defining issue for the left in both English and French Canada was the assertion of a defensive and emerging nationalism.

This nationalism differed from American flag-waving because Canada wasn't a superpower intent on making the world safe for American capitalism. In fact, Canada's sovereignty was based on finding a way to escape the domination of that superpower and to prevent it from stifling Canadian potential. In the case of Quebec nationalism, the focus was on liberation: Quebecers were simultaneously recovering something lost while shedding a conservative past that held back the province's creativity and promise.

Because the main vehicle for the increasing penetration of the U.S. into Canada was economic — foreign investment and trade — Canadian nationalism was debated in economic terms. This emphasis put the Canadian UAW at the centre of political debates within the left. Could Canada challenge economic integration with the U.S. and follow nationalist industrial strategies such as developing a Canadian car? Could international unions play a role in a nationalist movement? Would the international unions limit nationalism in the NDP?

In each case, the Canadian UAW leadership found itself at odds with the nationalist left, which included sections of its own membership. The union supported the Autopact, arguing that the industry was already so integrated with, and dependent on, the American companies that a Canadian car was simply not on the agenda. Canadian safeguards for a fair share of the industry, along with income protection for those affected by the restructuring, were therefore the main goal. The union defended its ties to the American-based UAW, arguing that the measure of a union was its internal democracy and direct achievements, not its nationality. In addition, the top leadership emphasized that internationalism as applied to worker solidarity was quite different from, and even essential to taking on,

A Canadian Car?

The CAW council supported the principle of the Autopact, though it rejected the actual agreement because of its inadequate support for those affected by the possible restructuring. In addition to the official Canadian UAW brief, three other briefs — each taking a left nationalist perspective — were presented: Local 444 (Chrysler); the GM inter-corporate council (though they had divisions); and the Windsor Council of the Unemployed (linked primarily to Local 444 and Local 200). These alternatives to further integration with the American industry pointed towards building a Canadian car.

While Canadian nationalism had significant support in even some conservative circles, this support would go up in smoke once the radical implications of a Canadian car were spelled out. The legacy of dependency had left the Canadian industry without the industrial structure and skills to compete head on with the Americans. To keep prices reasonable we would have to limit imports in order to get economies of scale. But this meant limiting consumer choices in the face of options which readily existed across the border; risking retaliation which might impact on other sectors such as steel; and shutting some Canadian plants as we moved away from a wide range of models. While jobs would be expanded with the higher Canadian content in a Canadian car, many of these jobs would be in other communities, for other workers. Moving to a Canadian car would therefore have meant addressing all kinds of complex issues for which, in spite of the enthusiasm, there was no economic and political base.

The argument that the pact would further integrate this crucial industry with the United States, further limiting Canadian sovereignty, was correct (though the industry was already virtually completely American-dominated). Nor did the pact provide the Canadian industry with the crucial aspects of any independent industry — research, design, development, process engineering, and high-technology parts production. The opposition to the pact was, however, wrong in warning that there would be a net shift of jobs away from Canada. The restructuring that followed the Autopact did mean closures and "rationalizations" that spelled job loss for many, but the overall impact *did* increase jobs.

Employment in the Canadian auto industry went from 32,000 in 1964 to 60,000 in 1973. With access to the American market, a lower dollar, and the safeguards to maintain assembly plants, Canada got new investments to make the existing plants world scale. This gave us the advantage of having the more modern plants in Canada and it created the opportunity for parts plants to produce larger runs for these larger plants producing standardized product. Having this higher efficiency, it increased the opportunities for parts plants and assembly plants to export to the United States. (American tariff reductions were a less significant factor.)

Although the debate over the Autopact continued for years, that debate gradually merged into a consensus that essentially accepted the logic of the Autopact. When the Americans tried to erode the pact, there was unanimity within the Canadian UAW in defending the importance of the safeguards; even those originally opposed recognized that Canada was now more vulnerable to their withdrawal. And when the Americans shifted their focus elsewhere, the continued imbalance in favour of assembly lead to unanimity within the union to strengthen the safeguards to get more parts production and some research and development.

internationalism as applied to capital. As for the NDP, the union played an active role in expelling the Waffle group from the party, arguing that the group's focus on long-term radical utopias would undermine the NDP's electoral chances.

The Waffle group was one central expression of Canada's new left, full of intellectual and organizing potential. Its nationalism was unashamedly part of a socialist project, and its strategy was based on the working class as the main motor of social change. This fact in itself would have, sooner or later, led to a direct confrontation with the NDP establishment and much of its base. The

Within the nationalist left in the union, there was overlap between the old left of communists and ex-communists (many of whom had left the CP after the invasion of Czechoslovakia in 1956), and a new left of independent socialists and left-CCF members who became active in the Waffle group in the NDP. The Waffle-sponsored conference on the Autopact in Windsor on 9 January 1971 was endorsed by the presidents of five of the six largest auto plants in Ontario. The speakers included well-known Waffle leader Jim Laxer as well as Ed Baillargeon, the president of the Windsor Labour Council, Charlie Brooks of Local 444 and president of the CAW Council, and Ed Broadbent, then the federal MP for Oshawa.

NDP had already defined itself as primarily an electoral party, whose main goal was to come to political office. The Waffle's idea of a socialist party placed immediate electoral success second.

The Waffle group included different tendencies, but to its key activists, the main point of a party was to educate, organize, mobilize, build understanding, and expand the number of activists. The Waffle's goal was to lead and coordinate campaigns and struggles, and eventually unify workers, unions, and other progressive groups into an unstoppable political force. To lifetime NDP stalwarts such as Dennis McDermott, who had taken over the helm of the Canadian UAW in 1968, the Waffle's increasingly radical ideas and actions threatened the NDP's electoral chances. In 1971, McDermott told the Canadian Council:

> Labour desires a change in the social order now and not 50–100 years from now ... It is my belief that the end purpose of political and ideological belief is to bring that belief to fulfilment and in one's own lifetime. Fulfilment means power, power means government, and government means changing the social order now ...

This assessment had some short-term validity, and after the Waffle was expelled, the NDP was in fact successful in a number of provincial elections. But as the future history of the NDP showed, the loss of committed young people with ideas and vision cost the party dearly. Ironically, many of these people later returned to work with the labour movement — in some ways more productively. Having been excluded from the NDP, they and other young people disenchanted with the NDP drifted into other forms of politics. Some ended up in coalitions which became part of the impressive alliance with labour that almost defeated the FTA. A good number became union activists through their jobs and have since risen to important positions within the labour movement. Others found work directly in the union movement as staff, and many joined the feminist movement. Within the trade union movement, groups such as Organized Working Women (OWW) lobbied for changes in structures and policies. These socialist feminists, refusing to write off the trade union movement even in difficult times, established — to a degree unique to any country — strong links with the labour movement.

In Canada, unlike in the United States, the conflicts with the new movements did not become the dead weight of a renewed and false stability. Although the nationalist left was defeated in Canada, the labour movement and others eventually adopted much of its perspective. As a result, militancy and politicization continued and even expanded within the labour movement. The evolution of the Canadian UAW's positions from the sixties to the mid-eighties and beyond is one of the best examples of change within the movement. By the mid-eighties, the union that, a dozen years earlier, had been the leading defender of its international connections had bolted from its own international union; it ended up playing — by way of the anti-FTA fight — a leading role in the battle against further integration into the U.S. and it increasingly attacked the NDP from the left.

That evolution reflected more general trends in the Canadian labour movement, the Canadian UAW's own political make-up and culture, and the particular response of the union's new leader to the criticisms and challenges facing the union. Dennis McDermott was one of a generation of activists inspired by and devoted to the social unionism of Walter Reuther. McDermott was keenly aware of the instability of the times and determined not to lose the young militants either to the left or to cynicism. He also had his own strong nationalist impulses.

Dennis McDermott relates the following story: Growing up Irish in England, he was listening as his teacher showed the class the vastness and riches of the empire. The young Dennis naively asked, "Why, if it is so great, were there so many poor people in it?" On his next report card, the teacher warned: "... this child has bolshevik tendencies."

Though he didn't hesitate to marginalize those who challenged his authority as leader, he set out to accommodate certain pressures from the left and to establish a militant, progressive, and Canadian face for the union.

Within months of taking office in 1968, McDermott announced his opposition to the U.S. role in Vietnam, even though Walter Reuther and the UAW executive board remained mute on the subject. Soon after, confronting an employer (North American Plastics) that was determined to break the union, McDermott took an unusual but dramatic last-resort step: he called for a sympathy walk-out at Ford and informed GM and Chrysler that shut-downs at their plants would soon follow. North American Plastics eventually accepted the union.

Dennis McDermott, Director, Canadian Region, with Cesar Chavez at United Farmworkers rally in California, 1969 (Bobby Kennedy poster in background). Courtesy of Wayne State Archives.

The next year, and continuing into the early seventies, McDermott adopted the struggle for an issue that had historically been led by the left: the shop-floor demands for reduced work-time and especially the frustrations over forced overtime. He also led the fight within the international union for voluntary overtime. Though the Canadian union extended the strike at GM in 1970 to try and win voluntary overtime, the lack of interest in the United States undermined that goal. This divergence in attitudes towards control over work-time became another factor that

Ontario legislation provided for voluntary overtime after forty-eight hours, but there was no mechanism to enforce this. Consequently, the Chrysler workers fought for and won language to get this right put into their agreements, where it could be arbitrated.

weakened the American UAW's role as a model for the Canadian union.

Local 112 float in Labour Day parade. Courtesy of the CAW collection.

The struggle of the Canadian UAW to control overtime and reduce work-time was part of a larger demand across the labour movement. At that time, the movement seemed to have enough drive to lead the respected H.D. Woods, in Queen's IR Scene in Canada, to conclude in 1973 that: "The 1970's may witness a dramatic decline in hours of work due to the growing demand for shorter hours and the four day week."

Anxious that the union reach the young workers in the industry, McDermott pushed to expand the union's emphasis on education and to link the opportunities for more education created by the large number of strikes. In many of the large units, the companies did not challenge the union with scabs during strikes, making mass pickets unnecessary. However, pickets were an important educational tool of the union. To compensate for this change, the union insisted that workers who didn't picket had to attend strike classes as a condition for receiving their strike pay. The classes dealt with union structure and union history, and provided information for new members.

McDermott moved the Canadian office from Windsor to Toronto, officially to be closer to the national media but unofficially to create some physical distance from Detroit. Remarkably, the UAW, one of the most powerful unions in Canada, did not have its own research department or its own newspaper. Instead, the American UAW paper had a Canadian supplement. McDermott successfully set up a research department and a national paper and raised the status of Canadians at the meetings of the International Metalworkers Federation from merely being part of an American UAW delegation to representing workers in a sovereign country. McDermott's nationalism also included a sympathetic appreciation of the nationalism of others, in particular Quebecers.

Quebec: The Not So Quiet Revolution

No part of Canada experienced more change during the sixties than Quebec. With the death of the reactionary and iron-fisted Premier of Quebec, Maurice Duplessis, Quebec emerged from the *Grande Norcier* (Dark Ages) and entered a decade of capitalist reform and modernization that witnessed the explosion of both militant trade unionism and nationalist sentiments.

During the sixties, the number of organized workers in the province almost doubled, and Quebec's rate of unionization became one of the highest in North America. The Quebec Federation of Labour (QFL) moved from being a modest provincial body to a labour body at the centre of decisions on bargaining and the political direction of its affiliates. The Catholic-based central union dropped its religious ties, establishing the primarily public sector-based CNTU (Confederation of National Trade Unions). The existence of the CNTU pushed the QFL in a more nationalist direction. Though its competition with the QFL would later become bitter, the two centrals brought a new dynamism to the Canadian labour movement. The two centrals joined in fighting the War Measures Act and, in 1972, organized — along with the teachers' central — a virtual general strike in Quebec. In the process of this mobilization, the educational material prepared by these centrals added radical socialist ideas to the nationalist analysis.

The UAW's presence in Quebec came late. The UAW had been slow to bring Quebec workers into the union. White Consolidated, organized in 1946, was Quebec's first UAW unit. During the war, the opportunities within Quebec were great, but the UAW made no significant inroads: it was preoccupied with the competition from other well-established unions in Quebec, the demands of organizing in Ontario, and the lack of additional resources coming from Detroit. In 1947,

Unless we are prepared to set up a separate organization in Quebec, it seems that our efforts would be better regarded by cleaning up and consolidating our membership in Ontario than attempting a Quebec campaign without the necessary tools, i.e., men and money.

— Report by Harry Rowe to Canadian Council, 19 December, 1943

the union again considered the potential for growth within Quebec, focusing unsuccessfully on approximately 17,000 garage workers. (These workers eventually joined the CAW by means of the Canadian Brotherhood of Railway Transport and General Workers.) While the UAW did experience growth in Quebec through the fifties, the real breakthroughs came in the mid-sixties, with the establishment of GM's assembly plant in Ste-Thérèse and the successful vote at United Aircraft (now Pratt and Whitney).

The War Measures Act, which took away civil liberties in Quebec, was introduced in 1970 under the pretext of fighting terrorism. It is now generally known that the actual goal was to weaken Quebec's nationalist movement; the federal government already had the police powers to deal with terrorist activists and the murder of Pierre Laporte, Quebec's minister of labour. Few individuals or institutions outside Quebec escaped the resulting hysteria, but the UAW's Canadian Council, with McDermott leading the argument, eventually passed a resolution exposing and condemning the actions of the federal and Quebec governments. Subsequently, in 1977, the UAW also passed a resolution recognizing Quebec's historic claim as one of the founding nations of Canada.

Two UAW strikes during the sixties and early seventies, both strongly supported by the national office in Canada, played a prominent political role in Quebec. In 1970, GM workers at Ste-Thérèse included as a major demand their right to work in their own language. As the *Financial Times* subsequently reported on May 16, 1977:

> The assemblers [in Ste-Thérèse] ... are proud of their achievements following a three-month strike that turned a routine company-wide strike ... into a cause celebre throughout Quebec and turned the local into the spearhead

for language reform ... Premier Bourassa intervened near the
end with the promise of language legislation, laying the
groundwork for the 1974 Official Language Act.

At the beginning of 1974, the workers at United Aircraft in Longueuil
(Local 510) launched a strike that was originally over issues such as upgrad-
ing their lagging wages and benefits but eventually focused on the more fundamental issue of union recognition. As the strike dragged on, the union
successfully mobilized funds and special monthly contributions from its
locals across Canada. But in August, 1974, eight months into the strike and
while the Canadian director was out of the country, the international secretary-
treasurer did something inexplicable. Without consulting McDermott, Emil
Mazey sent letters to the strikers and all Canadian locals, accusing the local
union of fraud in obtaining extra benefits. The accusation was technically
true, but the additional funds were not going into anyone's pocket. They
were being channelled into emergency relief for the strikers. Mazey's letter
threatened to undermine support.

On his return to Canada, a furious McDermott, foreseeing the implications not only for the strike but also for the Quebec labour movement and
the UAW's role in Quebec, arranged a loan from the QFL to continue strike
payments until the issue was resolved. At the next council meeting, he put
forth and received support for an unprecedented resolution condemning
Mazey's actions. There had been many conflicts with the international
office over the years, but for the first time, a Canadian director had led the
criticism on a major policy issue and demanded a reversal by the international union with the support of the Canadian secondary leadership. Since
Mazey was embroiled in other conflicts in the union at the time,
McDermott wasn't as isolated within the international executive board as
he might have been. Mazey's policy was reversed and when McDermott
introduced Local 510 leadership to the Canadian Council in June 1975,
they were welcomed as heroes.

This first significant crisis in the relationship between the Canadian
UAW and its parent organization had, interestingly enough, occurred within Quebec. In a strange twist of events, sensitivity to Quebec nationalism
had led to a crucial expression of *Canadian* sovereignty and nationalism.

The long and bitter United Aircraft strike ended in August, 1975, after
almost twenty months. It had included professional strikebreakers, dogs, violent confrontations, mass demonstrations and cultural events, and then a

desperate factory occupation that ended with a brutal police assault. The strike occurred at a particular point in Quebec's development when nationalism was directly linked to questions of class and corporate power and when workers were playing the leadership role in that

Union meeting of United Aircraft workers in Longueuil, Quebec (Local 510) during bitter 1974–75 strike. (Picket reads "United Against United.") Courtesy of the CAW Local 510 collection.

nationalism. The strike consequently came to symbolize the refusal of Quebecers to be treated like colonials by a foreign-based multinational which refused to accept standards that had become common in neighbouring Ontario.

The negotiated settlement did not include union security, but the workers returned to work with a political commitment, from an embarrassed provincial Liberal government, to introduce the Rand formula through legislation. The legislation was implemented in 1977 after the Parti Québécois (PQ) came to power with a social democratic and nationalist mandate.

By the mid-fifties, it seemed that capitalism had attained a new normalcy in North America. Conflicts between labour and management were contained within fairly narrow limits, steady material progress was assured, and the only threat was externally based — the Soviet Union.

Suddenly, in the United States, a generation stood up and challenged the morality behind the normalcy. It questioned society's commitment to the democratic values that were repeatedly expressed but were absent in the schools, in the workplace, and in America's foreign policy. It questioned society's commitment to equality for blacks and for women. The American labour movement, however, proved incapable of tapping into this energy and potential, as did the UAW. The UAW had failed to make strong connections with and channel the angry energy of its own members; it could hardly be expected to form lasting bonds with external movements. The UAW — for all its achievements — had been drained of its own spirit.

That failure condemned American trade unions to a long and steady slide to marginalization. Walter Reuther's death in 1970 may have symbolized the death of an era for American labour, but labour's fall was by then well established. For American unions, the sixties offered the last chance for revival or even transformation. That chance was lost.

In Canada, the countermovement was neither as intense nor as explosive as in the United States but, especially in the labour and women's movements, it lasted longer. The Canadian UAW's relationship with the new movements was hardly smooth. No formal or informal ties of any significance emerged. Yet the Canadian union was influenced by surrounding events and emerged from this turbulent period with greater militancy and a stronger sense of its role. There was no breakthrough in political power or dramatic achievements in relating to the Canadian movements, but unlike their American counterparts, Canadian unions remained a relevant social force. This modest achievement was crucial given the impending attack on labour.

The social unionism of Walter Reuther couldn't take root in the United States because of both the conservative climate and the way the seeds were planted. The great irony of the UAW was that any hope of Reuther's ideals taking hold seemed narrowed to the one region of the union that had historically retained some significant opposition to Reutherism.

WE JUST WON'T TAKE IT!

UNION MEMBERS AND LEADERSHIP REACT TO WAGE CONTROLS

A 16 mm. colour—55 minute film

directed by Jim Littleton

On October 14, 1975, the Liberal Government introduced wage controls. The labour movement saw that this program attacked one of the few instruments working people have for defending themselves in an unequal society—collective bargaining through their unions. This film covers the period between March 22—the historic demonstration in Ottawa—and April 10 and 11—the UAW collective bargaining conference. It shows workers and their leaders discussing the controls at their place of work, at their union halls, at their conventions and on the way to Ottawa. The film expresses their opposition to the controls, their determination to fight the government program and their growing confidence as they struggle collectively to defeat the controls.

EXCELLENT FOR USE AT UNION MEETINGS, RALLIES, PUBLIC MEETINGS, EDUCATION SEMINARS, ETC.
EVERY WORKER SHOULD SEE IT

Distributed by Sam Gindin, UAW Canadian Headquarters, 205 Placer Court, Willowdale, Ontario. (416) 497-4110

Purchase Price — $500
Rental — $75

10

Flyer for Canadian UAW film on wage controls and the union response. Courtesy of the CAW collection.

CHAPTER 7

THE CANDY MAN'S GONE

I hate to tell you but the candy man's gone …
— Bruce Cockburn

… it will be a hard pill … to swallow — the idea of doing with less so that big business can have more … nothing that this nation, or any other nation, has done in modern economic history compares in difficulty with the selling jobs that must now be done to make people accept the new reality.
— Business Week

We'll put a few union leaders in jail for a few months and others will get the message.

— Prime Minister Pierre Trudeau

The excitement of the sixties stemmed from a feature common to other rebellious periods: the people seemed to have grabbed the initiative. But by the mid-seventies, the corporations held the initiative once again. Although the seventies were a period of great labour militancy in Canada, that militancy was becoming defensive.

Ironically, this reversal was rooted not in capitalism's success, but in its immediate failures. By the early seventies, the evidence was growing that falling profits, rising unemployment, and accelerating inflation weren't simply cyclical problems; instead, they were signals that the postwar economic boom was over. With no alternative force to initiate a progressive redirection of the economy, this potential crisis on the right — the failure of business to provide stable economic security — became a crisis on the left. The agenda and momentum moved quickly towards an even greater dependence on strengthening corporations and the business climate.

Since the seventies, the corporations have retained that initiative and used it to restructure both the economy and expectations. At best, the Canadian labour movement slowed down the corporate agenda and kept some alternative values and ideas alive — limited yet crucially important achievements.

Lowering Expectations, Redefining Progress

The sixties had raised expectations by asking fundamental questions about the alleged democratic values of capitalism. By the end of that decade, another issue was emerging in North America: capitalism's capacity to provide a constantly rising material standard of living.

The unique conditions central to the postwar success of the United States, and therefore Canada, had disappeared. Manufacturers faced a profit squeeze, and the U.S. economy faced growing trade deficits and an outflow of capital. The era of access to cheap raw materials and America's overwhelming economic dominance was coming to an end. Demands for raw materials grew, while the most ready sources of supply dried up, and some Third World countries had room to insist on better prices. The U.S. was diverting resources to fight the war in Vietnam, while Europe and Japan, fully recovered from the war, were advancing economically on the United States. The results were intensified competition and the steady transformation of the relationship between these blocs.

The energy crisis of 1973–75, when oil prices quadrupled, aggravated this economic crisis. Companies tried to protect their profits in the face of added material costs and increased competition by limiting wage increases. When workers resisted, the companies raised prices to maintain their profits and protect their stockholders. And when workers then responded to the high rate of inflation with militant wage demands to protect their standard of living, this conflict over the distribution of income led to accelerating inflation. The higher prices, in turn, fed concerns about the loss of international competitiveness.

Every country felt compelled to increase its exports of manufactured goods, thereby providing jobs and additional national income, while limiting its imports. This strategy would alleviate the rising unemployment and pay for the escalating costs of raw materials. The catch was that one country's exports were another's imports; the unanimous adoption of this strategy resulted in everyone producing more but buying less.

The result was "stagflation" — high unemployment and high prices. Since the fifties, people had taken on faith that modern capitalism would no longer have to face wild fluctuations in economic activity and prices. By the mid-seventies, that confidence in capitalism's ability to provide steady and stable growth was profoundly shaken. Along with this realization came a profound change in the lives of working people. From this point on, reducing inflation would be a central goal of Canadian economic policy; the underlying assumption was that, with zero inflation, all other economic problems would iron themselves out. In the interim, high unemployment would have to be tolerated. An indicator of the changing times was the fact that the lowest unemployment rate after 1975 was still higher than the rate in any year between 1941 and 1975.

The economic and political élite attempted to persuade and/or force workers to reduce their demands so that inflation would fall and the economy's relative competitiveness would be strengthened. This situation had the makings of a political crisis. Workers previously considered greater job security, higher wages, and a more equitable distribution of wealth to be the fruits and even the essence of progress. Now these benefits were being redefined as problems standing in the way of competitiveness. In the past, trade unions could justify such goals as being good for the economy because they maintained purchasing power; now the unions were attacked for inhibiting the ability to sell internationally.

Capitalism's inability to justify itself either morally or materially created the perfect scenario for a challenge to the system. There was, however, no social force in Canada or the United States that was interested in, or capable of mounting, such a challenge. As a result, capitalism not only rode out this storm and its occasional bumps, but also used it to become stronger.

This situation was clearest in the United States, where the hopes of the sixties had been dashed. It wasn't that worker struggles had faded. Mineworkers suffered through a long confrontation to win compensation for lung disease, and the UAW fought tough battles at International Harvestor and Caterpillar, manufacturers of farm machinery and other heavy equipment. Also, the UAW made a major breakthrough in 1976 with an innovative program on reduced work-time that revived the possibility of a transition towards the four-day week. And, in the late seventies, UAW president Doug Fraser led an attempt to form a new alliance with promises of returning to the organizing style and militancy of the thirties.

But the American labour movement was constrained by its history and the self-fulfilling prophecies of its leadership. Its mobilizing and organizing skills had been laid off for too long, and rust had set in. The leaders' claim that the members were too demoralized or too complacent to fight was, because of American labour's recent past, partly true. But it was also true that the leaders used this argument as an excuse for not attempting remobilization.

Lacking confidence in itself and fearing that militant national campaigns might further isolate it and undermine the electoral chances of the Democratic Party (on whom it depended for better legislation), the American labour movement slid into irrelevancy. Its response to Nixon's call for voluntary controls in the early seventies was weak and confused. The labour movement was unable to persuade sympathetic (Democratic) administrations to improve America's unsympathetic labour legislation; instead, the movement faced increasingly antagonistic labour board interpretations of existing legislation. American labour possessed neither an alternative strategy for fighting legislation nor a means of using its still impressive resources to spread unionization to new regions and sectors.

In June 1981, when President Reagan legislated air traffic controllers back to work as the American labour movement watched meekly, he exposed organized labour in the U.S. as a paper tiger. On behalf of employers, he declared open season on all workers. By the early eighties, the acceptance of concessions within the UAW — still considered to be the leader within the movement — confirmed that American labour had virtually given up.

The distinguishing factor of the Canadian response to "the new reality" was that, in spite of Canada's tight economic integration with the United States, the movement showed sustained signs of resistance, and therefore life. One dimension of that distinction was captured by the electoral moods and trends as the sixties ended.

In 1968, Nixon, with a strong anti-union and antiprogressive history, became president of the United States. That same year brought Trudeau to power in Canada, riding a sixties image and carrying a banner calling for a Just Society. In 1972, Nixon was reelected in the U.S. In Canada, the NDP, led by David Lewis, won the balance of power. Although the Waffle group had been expelled, its influence on NDP politics left a residue, and the country itself was open to the left-populist slogan of the Lewis campaign: taking on the "corporate welfare bums." Later, when the Tories called for wage and price controls, Trudeau — desperate for worker votes and with the NDP breathing down his neck — ridiculed the idea. Trudeau won a majority government in 1974. The provincial election of left-leaning and left-dependent governments led to significant labour law reform in Canada. NDP governments were elected in three provinces: in Manitoba in 1969–77; in Saskatchewan in 1971–82; and in British Columbia in 1972–5. The PQ, in power from 1976 to 1985, also clearly leaned towards social democracy.

These events seemed to have the makings of the NDP's moment in the sun. During the heady sixties, even the Liberals were proposing social democratic policies and therefore competing with the NDP. But as the Liberals began to retreat from recent definitions of progress, the field was left to the NDP. The establishment had always called on workers to restrain their demands but now, for the first time since the war, it clearly stood for the bitter medicine of lowering people's expectations and insisting they stifle their demands. Canadians had not signed on yet and the NDP took advantage of the opportunity.

The NDP attacked corporations for demanding that others take less while the corporate élite took more. It revived the issue of American control of Canada's resources and economy, resurrecting some themes of the exiled Waffle group. It argued for price controls on certain necessities, and it challenged the logic of creating more jobs by reducing purchasing power. In office, or where it was influential, the NDP led in the introduction of health and safety legislation and progressive labour reform.

The NDP's programs were, however, based on an assumption of steady

Northern Telecom workers, organized in the late sixties, were out on strike in 1973 for greater security. Courtesy of the National Archives, PA-182814.

growth and stable prices. Now the country was facing a serious economic crisis and high inflation. Old solutions — such as stimulating the economy — would no longer work in the new environment unless they were supplemented by greater control over prices, investment, and capital flows. Any such attempt to democratize the economy and move towards planning meant taking on the corporations, especially the Canadian banks. The NDP no longer seriously considered this option. With neither an alternative strategy nor an inclination to lead a movement that would fundamentally challenge the status quo, the NDP could not sustain its momentum when the recession deepened in the mid-seventies and the economy plunged still deeper at the end of the decade.

Although the Canadian labour movement was strengthened by both the existence of the NDP and the party's role in supporting working class positions and arguments, the most significant resistance to Canada's new direction came from the labour movement itself. The labour movement became more directly politicized as workers, through their unions, took concrete action to challenge both existing legislation and the lack of legislation. They fought legislated wage controls, battled employers and police to formalize the right to union security, and assumed control of plants in a desperate protest of the corporations' unilateral right to rob communities of the tools that allowed workers to use their skills.

During the sixties, the strike records of Canada and the U. S. were similar. In the seventies, time lost due to strike activity in Canada was almost double that in the United States. In fact, Canada lost proportionately more days to strikes during the seventies than any other developed country. Public sector workers and their new unions continued their fight to bring their wages up after the lag in the pre-union period, and workers in the resource sector took advantage of the boom in their industries. Workers in the manufacturing sector increasingly shifted their focus away from wage comparisons with the United States and looked to comparability within Canada.

One-third of the strikes in the seventies were wildcats, which were illegal in all Canadian provinces except Saskatchewan. This number was proportionately higher than even that in the U.S., where wildcats were, under certain conditions, legal. In Canada, wildcats were led at the local level and, while McDermott did not sanction them, he made no concerted attempt to discredit the frustrations these protests reflected. At GM Canada, there were fifty-nine wildcats in the ten years after the long 1970 strike, and at Budd, a major stampings plant, there were 150 wildcats during the period from 1976 to 1979. De Havilland workers were on strike for an incredible 468 days to negotiate three new agreements during the seventies. And on 14 October 1976, Canadian labour held a one-day national strike — the first national work stoppage in North American history.

By the mid-seventies, the deterioration of the economic situation in Canada forced the hand of the Liberal government. Canada's resource base should have left it with a unique advantage amongst the major capitalist economies, especially with the

Campaigning in Timmins, Ontario in 1974, Trudeau had mocked the Tory controls, arguing that they merely masked an attack on working people while protecting the powerful: "So what's he going to freeze?" Mr. Trudeau shouted. "Your wages! He's going to freeze your wages."
— *The Toronto Star*, 28 October 1975

rising prices of resources. But Canadian business, operating under its own profit-maximizing rules, had not translated this natural wealth into a stronger manufacturing base. Furthermore, Canada was linked to a declining power that was increasingly "looking after it own." As a consequence, pressured by Canada's powerful banks with their priority of reducing inflation, and concerned that the strength of Canadian labour relative to that of the United States would undermine competitiveness, the nervous Liberals reversed their election promise and introduced compulsory wage controls effective October, 1975.

Controlling Wages, Controlling Unions

Wage controls — legal limits on what workers could negotiate — were directed at breaking the momentum of the Canadian labour movement, which kept resisting corporate pressures and refusing to accede to government lectures on economics. The labour movement was united in opposition, recognizing that acceptance of controls in any form, especially since they included no offsetting benefits, risked the union's alienation from the membership. The government offered no trade-offs, such as equitable tax reform or enriched social programs to buy labour's compliance. But as collective agreements expired, labour generally had no concrete response other than the rhetoric of opposition.

The Canadian UAW's response began with the recognition that wage controls differed from other attacks on working people such as tax increases, which affected workers as individuals or family units. Wage controls constituted an attack on the organization itself. Controls undermined unions by imposing the most severe limits on their ability to fulfil workers' expectations in negotiating the price and conditions of labour. In contrast, the government made no attempt to control corporate power over price determination and the direction of investment. (The focus of the Liberals was not surprising since they were trying to improve the "investment climate" as defined by private corporations.) If unions were to retain the confidence of their membership, it was essential that they not only avoid any role in endorsing controls, but also actively mobilize all aspects of their organizations to fight them.

Because controls were not universally popular, the government conceded some flexibility in the program (e.g., historical relationships to other groups and appeal procedures). The UAW's bargaining strategy was to build on, and take advantage of, this flexibility. In each set of negotiations, bargaining was to occur as if the controls didn't exist. Any agreement should exclude recognition of the controls apparatus and would have to be fully implemented by the company or a strike would begin or continue. With the contract in place, the bureaucracy of the program worked in the union's favour. If the Anti-Inflation Board (AIB) ruled against any settlement, the union called on the appeal procedure and used any delaying tactics it could. The companies — nervous about introducing a reduction in pay — were put in a position that strongly encouraged them to support the union arguments. In contrast to a process in which workers depended solely on technical arguments and then waited anxiously to see if Ottawa approved the negotiations, this situation allowed workers to continue to receive full pay.

This strategy was taken to the Canadian Council and the staff. The union set up meetings with activists (local leaders, bargaining committees, stewards, education committees) on a regional basis. It distributed pamphlets and addressed the issues in local union papers and at union educationals. The campaign for Canadian content in auto was linked to the fight against wage controls and provided workers with an alternative focus and policy to the controls. If the central issue was jobs, then the answer was mobilizing to put restrictions, such as the Canadian content requirements, on companies rather than on workers. All bargaining was centrally monitored to ensure as close adherence as possible to the policy. With this base, the union worked within the Canadian Labour Congress (CLC) towards a broader political protest against the controls, which eventually led to the National Day of Protest on 14 October 1976.

The significance of the UAW's response on the issue of controls to the future role and direction of the Canadian UAW cannot be underestimated. The struggle over wage controls was ultimately about worker concessions. This early fight against concessions developed workers' confidence in their union and provided the ideological argu ments and understanding that were

In the spirit of the On-to-Ottawa trek of the thirties, the Canadian UAW chartered a train to leave Windsor and pick up passengers at selected stops on the way to Ottawa. The problem was the train was full before it left Windsor. Bus/car caravans were hastily arranged to get others there and back.

the base for later opposition to concessions and to the positions taken by the American union.

If the union's opposition was only at the level of rhetoric and the membership felt that the controls would still be accepted, workers would have shown little or no interest in educational material. But because the union was actually engaged in a struggle, workers sought out this material and discussed each wave of bargaining. Leaders wanted to be able to answer members' questions on whether controls were a good idea, whether they should be fought, whether they could be fought if they were "the law," what the implications of fighting were, and so on.

Moreover, the experience of challenging the controls reminded workers of the vital importance of their union. Ultimately, the union was really the only institution they could count on. Companies were, of course, never on their side; governments, as Trudeau showed, couldn't be trusted; and even the NDP's record was spotty (the Manitoba and Saskatchewan NDP governments supported the controls). But the union was there, fighting the companies, the law, and the bureaucracy. It was protecting the wages workers had negotiated or limiting their losses, and unambiguously leading and fighting alongside the members.

At de Havilland, workers were on the verge of a settlement in their long strike when wage controls came into effect. Since the company would not, however, agree to implement the agreement in full, their service rep, Frank Fairchild, made the case to McDermott that the union should call for a rejection of the agreement. McDermott agreed, though he was concerned that, given the length of the strike, this was demanding an awful lot from workers. The workers did reject the agreement and eventually forced the company to agree to full implementation.

When wage controls came into effect in October, 1975, Canadian Salt (Local 195) and de Havilland (Local 112) were both in the midst of long strikes and in both cases the strikes were extended to force implementation of what they had negotiated. The de Havilland strike, lasting three and a half months, concluded with full implementation of the negotiated agreement; the Canadian Salt strike went on for over seven months and it too ended with the workers getting virtually everything they negotiated. At Mussens, Quebec workers who serviced

The CAW and Wage Controls

The controls attack our unions, demand sacrifices by working people, do not control prices, and do nothing about unemployment or income distribution ... They represent no 'alternative' to real solutions — which would mean challenging (not reinforcing) corporate power ...

That is why labour opposes controls. That is why, on October 14, UAW workers will close down their plants and offices as part of the National Day of Protest called by the Canadian Labour Congress.

— excerpt from UAW Canadian Council Statement on Wage Controls

Wage controls covered about four million of the ten million workers in the economy at that time. This included two out of three organized workers (smaller units were exempt). In the UAW, sixty-five per cent of agreements (ninety per cent of membership) were covered.

About thirty-five per cent of all workers under controls settled above the guidelines; for the UAW that percentage was almost seventy-five per cent (fifty-five per cent if we exclude the Big Three, who followed the American pattern which was slightly above the guidelines but accepted by the AIB).

The goal wasn't to break the guidelines but to ignore them. There were about 100 strikes within the union during the program, which ran for less than three years. About half of those strikes didn't lead to any involvement by the AIB, either because the settlement occurred early on when the guidelines were relatively high or because the settlement was acceptable to the workers even if within the guidelines.

A UAW study of 110 non–Big Three agreements (of 121 that exceeded the guidelines) found that:

• In seventy per cent of the agreements, covering ninety per cent of workers, the UAW eventually had the agreement approved or the workers kept everything they had coming because the union forced the companies into some "creative" accounting.

• In fifteen per cent (six per cent of workers), the union achieved more than the guidelines but did suffer a rollback.

• The remaining fifteen per cent, covering 1500 workers, who were generally in smaller units, ended up rolled back to the guidelines (three cases involved strikes that took them to the highest appeal level under the program).

heavy-duty equipment suffered a roll-back in spite of their long and bitter strike — fourteen months — against the controls.

In spite of limited successes, the labour movement did not defeat the controls. The strategy of choosing one particular set of negotiations where the workers had an argument that could attract national support, and rallying the labour movement around that case as a challenge to the entire program, was never attempted. The trade union leadership was not, it seems, confident enough to aim at defeating rather than just protesting the controls. The impressive Day of Protest turned out to be an isolated event, and, rather than indicating the beginning of a massive public campaign, it signalled the end.

Though the number of strikes within the Canadian UAW during the controls was about the same as in the previous three-year cycle, the overall number of strikes by the Canadian labour movement fell significantly. The rationale for controls had included the repeated arguments that they would lower inflation and increase jobs. In fact, inflation was higher in the three years after controls than it was in the period that preceded them. (For one thing, Canadian inflation depended on U.S. inflation.) Unemployment, which had risen in 1974 to a relatively high 6.4 per cent, continued in the seventies to rise and never again returned to within even one per cent of that "extremely high level." Wages were reduced, though the more significant impact on wages came with the deep recession of 1979–81. And as the weaker firms were pushed aside in the restructuring of the economy, profits took off. Future governments returned to controls, but limited them to the public sector, leaving the market and record unemployment rates to provide the less overt controls in the private sector.

Concessions: You Don't Need a Union to Go Backwards

In 1979, Chrysler was in serious financial trouble and the UAW agreed to postpone part of the pattern settlement until later in the agreement. By early 1980, with Chrysler staring bankruptcy in the face, the American Congress made long-term worker concessions a condition of loan guarantees to the company. The savings from worker concessions would help to pay off the bank vultures, who faced no corresponding conditions. The American UAW accepted those conditions but the Canadians rejected them, arguing that Canadian workers weren't going to be bound by a foreign legislature.

A year later in January, 1981, Chrysler returned, this time without Congress but with its own demands and Lee Iacocca's threat of immediate bankruptcy. The Canadian Chrysler workers, who had been the most committed to ties with the Americans, were now part of an overall union vote. (They were, unlike workers at Ford and GM, part of a formal international agreement.) The result was that Chrysler workers lost their current COLA ($1.15/hour), along with future wage increases and some of their paid time off.

Soon small employers were lining up demanding the same "sensitivity" to their plight. It had never been unusual for specific companies to argue for concessions based on unique and temporary circumstances. Trying to isolate such demands to Chrysler was, because of its size and prominence, difficult enough. But when the American Ford and GM agreements were opened to negotiate concessions in the spring of 1982, which was before the three-year term was up, broader concessions independent of circumstances were legitimized, and a devastating new chapter began for the American UAW.

In the 1981 vote on Iacocca's ultimatum, the Canadian leadership took the rare step of making no recommendation to the membership. While the total U.S.-Canada vote was clearly in favour, the largest Canadian local, Local 444 in Windsor, voted — by the slightest of margins — against the agreement. (Counting all the Canadian units, Canadian workers voted fifty-one per cent in favour.) The Canadians subsequently left the international agreement.

Some union leaders naively argued that these circumstances actually provided an opportunity: if the companies were so desperate for wage restraint, why not trade it off for shop-floor control? This strategy was nonsense. Workplace improvements could emerge only out of organizational strength, not out of weakness. The companies' goals were to restructure their costs *and* their operations; they wanted both. Once the union and workers accepted the logic of wage concessions, the same logic — and threats — would be applied to workplace concessions. With American wages (after concessions), still generally the same across one company's plants, workers were given the so-called freedom to compete for jobs by lowering their own workplace standards. Workers were much more vulnerable to such decentralized local changes. The wage concessions were therefore

ALL THAT SHINES IN THE DARK IS NOT NECESSARILY CHARITABLE

Today I began negotiations
for a contract at Fleetwood Tool & Mold,
the owner of which informed me,
in an attempt to impress, that he read
the King James version of the bible every day
to improve his writing, invigorate his mind.
Yet, when I asked him to consider
a cost-of-living clause for the poorly paid,
he told me he would consult his King Jamie
and get back to me. While I was hoping
for something glorious about the kindness
of strangers, he advanced a curious parable
about the poor someday inheriting the earth,
with only his swelling pinky ring to illuminate the gloom.

Ron Dickson

the prelude to the much more important corporate objective of restructuring the workplace to maximize profits.

In the early days of the auto industry, companies had taken advantage of the desperate desire for work by forcing workers to undercut each other. One of the first goals of unionization was to overcome this competition between individual workers. After the war, GM was concerned about the bargaining power of autoworkers. It had initiated the Treaty of Detroit and accepted "continuous improvement" in workers' wages and benefits. Soon "continuous improvement" would take on quite a different meaning. The companies now wanted to recreate the past competition between workers at a higher level. Companies pressured employees to compete with workers both at other companies and at different plants within the same company.

The companies were essentially saying that centralization and consideration of worker's concerns may have been tolerated in the past, when workers had bargaining strength and used it to leap frog each other in settlements. But with the decrease in the relative bargaining power of workers, the companies had decided to change the rules. They were no longer interested in centralization but in competitive decentralization. Bargaining would no longer centre on workers' demands, but company demands.

The UAW's new direction was dangerous in that it robbed the union of its independent role and virtually transformed it into an industrial-relations arm of the companies. The *union* was now selling the company line and ideology. If the union was supporting concessions, did this mean that the union had negotiated too well before and would never negotiate that forcefully again? If GM and Ford needed help, who didn't? If the union believed workers needed to work harder for less, then why was a union necessary? As one exasperated worker said, "We don't need a union to walk backwards; we can give things up just as easily on our own ..."

The dynamic of the union endorsement of concessions undermined every facet of the union's life: its outward stance, its internal democracy, its educational structures. By accepting concessions, the union allowed the companies to shift the focus of America's problems on to workers' shoulders. The public debate centred on whether autoworkers would make concessions, and this emphasis diverted attention from more fundamental causes of the industry's problems: high interest rates and the banks; the corporate failure to build small, quality vehicles; the overvalued dollar (and undervalued yen); and the diversion of resources and skills to the military, which reflected the competitive costs of America's imperial role.

One casualty of concessions was the emerging drive towards reduced work-time. The new program of paid personal holidays (PPH) had been introduced in 1976 as a long-term measure in negotiations headed towards the four-day week. Now the union gave up PPH as part of the concessions package, essentially removing shorter work-time from the union's agenda. That the surrender of paid time off was justified in the name of job security further exposed the futility of this new direction.

In spite of pressures from the companies, the media, and their own union, American workers did not immediately buy into the new direction. At GM, workers originally voted

The objectives of the PPH program were to provide workers with an increasing amount of paid time off, allow the companies to utilize their facilities fully, and create new job openings. This program gave each worker a given number of paid days off per year: six at first but it was originally hoped this would soon rise to twelve (providing a four-day week each month), then twenty-four (a four-day week every second week), and so on.

With a given number of workers off each day, replacements would be needed. Example: an operation requires 100 people. The company hires 125. On a rotating basis, twenty-five are off each day of a five-day week. Each worker would therefore work only four days (paid for five), but the company has the 100 workers it needs daily. (This could also be adjusted for six-day schedules.)

against reopening their agreement before it expired and, even when they were softened up by union-company pressures, forty-eight per cent still voted against the concessions. Because of such resistance, the insecure union leadership interfered with the workers' ability to collectively deal with these questions across workplaces and companies.

In 1982 for example, the scheduled Collective Bargaining Conference, the purpose of which was to set the general directions for all sections of the union, was cancelled. Locals that defied the leadership were isolated and weakened with threats and rumours of their plants being next on the closure list. Union democracy could hardly flourish in such an environment; the roles of union education and the development of activism also faded in this context.

These events should not obscure the pressures faced by the Americans. The industry was confronting its greatest crisis in over half a century. It was becoming increasingly common to hear rumours that the auto industry was essentially dead in North America and that autoworkers should all move on. American autoworkers, earning almost fifty per cent more than the average worker in manufacturing (plus far superior benefits), attracted little public sympathy for their wage losses. The UAW members themselves were acutely aware that even a lower-paying auto job was much better than other alternatives. Politically, the right was on the rise; the union was therefore even further isolated in terms of hopes for more meaningful alternatives.

This situation was part of a more general economic and social transition taking place in the United States in the seventies and eighties. The U.S. had, since the late sixties, experienced a relative loss in stature as international competitors eroded its once dominant status. In the late seventies, two events symbolized America's frustration: the Japanese were making inroads into the most American of all products — the car — and a Third World country, Iran, held Americans hostage while the U.S. sat helpless, watching CNN with the rest of the world. Furthermore, the Soviet Union had just invaded Afghanistan, and this was used to rekindle the cold war.

Reagan emerged with the promise to restore the "good old days," when America, as the undisputed leader in all things important, was shown proper respect, and when Americans knew they would achieve a standard of living that exceeded their parents'. That nostalgia included making American industry Number One again, which left the companies in a powerful position to define the requirements of success. Workers, on the other hand, nervously hoped that they might at least keep their jobs, while also wondering about the costs of doing so.

It would certainly have been extremely difficult for the UAW to avoid losses in this period. But losses are one thing — workers don't always have the strength to win their demands — and concession bargaining is another. This new direction was defined not by its defeats, but by the refusal to fight, and the rationalization of those defeats as "victories." The UAW had, over the years, suffered a major decline in its ability to act as a social movement; now it was surrendering its most basic economic role as a bargaining agent. A temporary defeat (lower wages) therefore became a long-term change in direction (selling concessions).

No to Giving Up and Giving Back

The Canadian UAW rejected the direction of its parent organization. The context in which the Canadians made their decisions was no doubt more favourable than that facing the Americans. Auto lay-offs were not as severe, the national mood had not yet shifted to the right, and the union was simply not as isolated economically, politically, and socially. Canadian Big Three wages were about twenty-five per cent above the national average, half the gap between American autoworkers and the rest of their community. The Canadian movement was more highly unionized and aggressive. The NDP provided a countervoice that the Americans didn't have. And Canadian nationalism, unlike American nationalism, allowed for much more skepticism over the claims and demands of American-based multinationals.

At the same time, however, the 1981–82 recession was deeper in Canada than in any other major developed country. Canadian autoworkers, like their American counterparts, faced a daily barrage of warnings that the auto industry was now a dying industry which could only continue to exist with fewer jobs that would go to those who worked harder for less. Fighting concessions wasn't easy; workers had seen far too many closures to write off any threats as mere posturing. Brantford, for example, once ranked behind only Toronto and Montreal as a centre of heavy industry. It was quickly being wiped off the industrial map, but workers never stopped fighting. When corporations tried to take advantage of the desperation in the community in the early eighties, Canadian UAW members went on strike at Trailmobile, a trailer manufacturer, for over eight months and at Hussman, which supplied store equipment, for nine months. Concessions were successfully resisted.

At least as important as the corporate threats was the uncertainty of the Canadian UAW's ability to venture in a direction entirely different from that of the Americans. Would the parent tolerate an independent direction? Would it view the Canadian example as reinforcing the opposition to the American leadership? If the American UAW made concessions, could Canadians who worked for American companies reject that direction without risking their jobs? Did the Canadians have the collective bargaining strength to stand up to the auto companies if the Big Three really decided to take them on?

In early 1982, the Canadians made the key decision — the one that launched the eventual breakaway from the Americans. The Canadian UAW chose to break ranks with the Americans and reject an early opening of the agreements with Ford and GM. Under the leadership of Bob White, the union saw the basic danger of concession bargaining: if the union consented to participate, it would collapse from internal conflicts and nullify its role as a social force within the Canadian labour movement and in Canadian society. The risk of fighting for traditional bargaining had to be taken.

This decision wasn't made in an intellectual vacuum, but in the context of the momentum against concessions that was already growing in the union by that time. The fight against concessions had begun during the struggle over wage controls. It continued after controls at places such as Kenworth, the manufacturer of heavy-duty trucks in Montreal, where workers stayed on strike for nine and a half months to reject concessions and make gains. Less successful, but still crucial to sending a message to corporations about the union's determination to fight was the twenty-two month strike and boycott of Blue Cross, the supplier of medical insurance.

The issue of concessions intensified after the concessions to Chrysler, when the independent parts units of the Canadian UAW confronted employers who were "whipsawing": demanding concessions in one unit, arguing in a competing unit that those concessions be matched or surpassed if workers wanted to keep their jobs, then telling the first unit that it was underbid and inviting those workers to start the merry-go-round of concessions again.

The union response was reinforced by educationals, especially in the Paid Education Leave (PEL) Program negotiated at the end of the seventies. At the council, the ideal forum for the exchange of information on the treatment of workers, a more comprehensive strategy was developed. It began with a declaration that the national office, which was the signatory to all UAW agreements in Canada, would not sign any agreements that were opened in mid-term to make concessions. The potential chaos of units opening up their agreements to undercut each other had to be stopped immediately. As a result, local decisions that might have been reached democratically could now be overridden. The justification was the authority of the Canadian Council, a broader democratic forum which took into consideration the negative implications of individual local decisions on all UAW locals in Canada.

Where locals entered into new agreements, as opposed to mid-term reopeners, the union was reluctant to set the precedent of taking away any unit's ratification rights. Thus, the no-concessions policy was enforced in much the same way as in the fight against wage controls: through the distribution of educational material on why making concessions propelled workers into a no-win rat race to the bottom; through community meetings with bargaining committees and stewards; and through of the union's staff, who were responsible for bringing that policy into each set of negotiations and supporting any reluctant committees.

The council also set up a special no-concessions fund, with contributions from all locals, to provide special assistance to any units on strike that were forced to resist concessions. (Over half a million dollars in support was distributed by way of that fund.) One of the early strikes against concessions was an eight-month strike at Rockwell's auto components plant in Milton. The strike was lost, but the message to employers was loud and clear: the

In the U.S., the resentment amongst workers against staff who weren't facing concessions led to a decision to cut staff salaries in the name of solidarity. The Canadian staff were part of the same staff union, but the American logic didn't fit. The Canadians (staff and administration) decided instead to contribute $100 per month to the no-concessions fund (slightly more than what their American counterparts were giving back). This maintained wage parity within the staff union but made the gesture of solidarity a meaningful rather than token one.

union might lose a particular fight, but not before that fight had had a severe impact on the employer. The Rockwell strike made it less necessary

Paid Education Leave

The Canadian UAW Education Centre housed the PEL program, which was first negotiated in 1977 at Rockwell. It was initiated by Education Director Gord Wilson, after a fact-finding trip to Europe and was especially inspired by the educational work done within the Swedish trade union movement. Dan Benedict, an early advocate for PEL within both the North American and international trade union movements, was asked to come on the Canadian staff to develop and implement the program.

The political orientation of the program — its orientation to understanding the economy and addressing broad social change — had roots going back to the forties. The immediate drive to put the new program into place came from the top. Union policy was that no staff rep could take it off the table without authorization from the Canadian director's office. Once negotiated, a committee that includes the local and the education department chooses the students to attend the course. As of 1995, some 5,000 workers had gone through the four-week course. The uniqueness of PEL lies in its combination of the following elements:

1. Ideological Orientation

The PEL program wasn't set up to provide bargaining and contract-administration skills but to contribute the background for using and developing such skills. PEL aims at providing working people with an understanding of capitalism, their place in this system, the role of unions as independent working class organizations, the history of workers and their organizations, and the principles and philosophy of the Canadian UAW. The program's goal is to develop future activists with a commitment to the union and to progressive change.

2. Adult Education

The course includes lectures but is biased towards group discussions in a comfortable atmosphere. PEL provides workers with an opportunity to use and develop their intellectual skills as they discuss the major economic and social issues of the times.

3. Peer Training

The PEL program includes a program administrator and brings in staff, activists, and academics to share their knowledge and experience. But the main teaching load falls to over 100 local union discussion leaders who come from CAW plants and offices and have been trained to lead the learning process.

4. Blocks of Education

The basic program is four weeks, though recently one- and two-week programs were introduced. The shorter programs allow for more specialized courses such as work reorganization, health and safety, competitiveness, workers' compensation, and leadership development for women and people of colour.

5. Residential

While some courses occur off-site, the main courses take place at the CAW Family Education Centre. The advantages of making the courses residential come from workers being at their own place with its rich history and the opportunity to continue the education informally outside of the classroom.

6. Company-Paid

The program's financing is negotiated from the companies, though the program is completely administered by the union. The original contributions per worker were one cent per hour worked (enough to get started) and now range up to three cents per hour.

for other workers to be tested. In general, the no-concessions fight of the council was successful, particularly in its ability to support units in a weaker bargaining position.

Two other kinds of confrontations, dealing with concessions of a different kind, reinforced the confidence and militant mood in the Canadian region: the fight for union security at Fleck Manufacturing, a producer of wire harnesses for the auto industry, and a series of plant take-overs which were part of a larger attempt to deal with the growing number of plant closures. Both events drew national attention because of the issues involved, the response of the authorities, and the fact that they were really political battles led by the direct actions of workers outside of Parliament.

At Fleck, eighty per cent of the workforce voted in 1977 to join the UAW. The plant manager promptly notified the workers that the company had no intention of recognizing the union, and in the spring of 1978, the workers — generally young women, many single mothers, and all low-paid — faced the option of conceding or going on strike. Three days before the nervous workers were to begin picketing, they were called to the lunchroom, where an Ontario Provincial Police (OPP) officer read them the sections of the Criminal Code dealing with the illegality of workers threatening or intimidating anyone; he did not read them their rights to picket peacefully. Eighty of the women went on strike; forty felt threatened and were sufficiently intimidated to stay at work.

> After the strike began,
> Troops were rushed,
> To defend property
> But before the trouble started
> Nobody seems to have bothered
> To defend living standards.
>
> — Frank Scott

If there was ever any doubt about which side the police were on, that doubt quickly disappeared as 500 OPP constables amassed in and around Centralia, the industrial park near London, Ontario, where the plant was located. The policing costs at Fleck were higher than for any other event in Ontario history.

Al Seymour, the UAW service rep at Fleck, found that his office and home phones had been bugged. Presumably believing that the strike might fold if Seymour was kept away, the police arrested him, and three officers drove him the "very long way" to the station to make him fully aware of his vulnerability. When Seymour returned to the picket line, a local magistrate banned him from the county until after the strike was over. The provincial government's unique focus on

Women on picket line at Fleck strike. The strike brought solidarity and support from women in other UAW locals, other unions, other labour centrals, the NDP, and the cultural community. Photo by Schuster- Gindin.

this small plant turned out to have an interesting explanation: the owner was a top official in Premier Bill Davis's office.

The strike lasted for five months. Bus loads of activists from other UAW locals and from other unions came as morale boosters to completely shut-down the plant from time to time. The women's movement mobilized pickets to keep the profile of the strike high. Community artists donated their time to a unique cultural event and show of solidarity across unions. The Fleck strike became a rallying point for the fight over union security, a fight that had been carried on over the past decade with front-line troops who were often immigrant workers and women. The fight had been waged at Artistic Woodworkers and the Canadian Textile and Chemical Union in the early seventies, and at Radio Shack and the Steelworkers shortly before Fleck.

> We didn't strike so much over economic issues as to prove we had the guts to stand up.
>
> — Debra Riley, twenty-four-year-old Fleck worker and single mother of two

The strikers surprised even themselves with their collective strength. As the strike dragged on, the company lost contracts from GM. These factors, together with the support from other UAW locals and the sympathy growing across the province, resulted in a victory for the Fleck women. Soon after, the Conservative government of Ontario legislated union security (the Rand formula).

In the summer of 1980, the increasingly common plant closures became an issue at the Canadian Council, and that forum galvanized a response. As speaker after speaker told stories of lost jobs and destroyed lives, the frustration grew into anger, and the anger, into a search for actions. As Bob White stepped up to the podium to conclude the debate, he looked around the hall and grimly declared: "If it takes occupations of plants to stop this ... then we'll occupy them." On the return trip, the delegates from the Houdaille bumper plant in Oshawa and others who had been told their plant would close separately discussed their options and reached their own conclusions.

In early August, the council delegates appeared before the premier of Ontario and key cabinet members to argue — to no avail — for legislation governing plant closures. The brief had called for expropriation of any plant that didn't justify its decision and deal fairly with its workers. But the next morning, 8 August, 1980, a more effective "presentation" was made to the premier: the Houdaille workers took over the Oshawa plant and renamed it "UAW Industries." Although the take-over was illegal and therefore strike

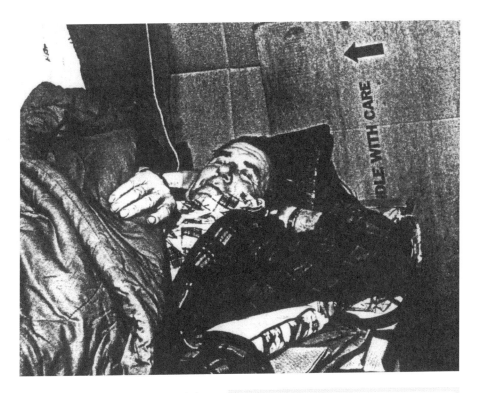

pay should have been out of the question, UAW president Doug Fraser agreed at White's insistence to waive that technicality and provide strike pay for the workers. In the coming weeks,

Worker getting ready for "bed" during Houdaille take-over, August 1980. Courtesy of the CAW collection.

workers took over Beach Appliances in Ottawa, and Bendix and Windsor Bumper in Windsor.

In terms of plants remaining open, only the Windsor Bumper take-over was successful. Often, the experience simply left workers more aware of the limits on their power. Having taken the most radical of steps and seized the owner's property, they were confronted with the question of "What next?" Nobody offered easy answers. Preventing or reversing closures required much broader changes in the economy and in society. However, where workers did act, they made gains: if nothing else, their severance pay and/or pensions were increased. Other workers benefited to the extent that employers watching these events decided, in their own self-interest, to show a bit more sensitivity to workers in the handling of closures. As a result of

Workers scaling fence to take-over Bendix plant in Windsor in 1980 after company announcement of closure. Courtesy of the CAW collection.

these actions and pressures involving other unions, the provincial government introduced modest reforms in 1981. The changes extended worker rights to advance notice of workplace closures and improved their severance payments. Like other social legislation, this policy lagged behind that in Europe but surpassed anything in the United States.

The issue of concessions ultimately centred on the future of the auto majors. Because of the high profile of the Big Three negotiations, those talks would set the pattern and mood for the future direction of the Canadian UAW. If the union had, however, allowed concessions in other places, the fight at the auto majors would have been weakened if not undermined. But the militancy in all sections of the union, especially since the mid-seventies, had reinforced both an understanding of the need to fight back and the confidence that fighting back actually mattered.

The exuberant challenges to the status quo of the sixties had not changed the world, and as the excitement gave way to disillusionment, the corporations began a much longer-lasting and successful counterrevolution. Facing greater competition from Europe and Japan, the economic and political élite emphasized the need to keep prices down in order to remain competitive. This plan translated in the mid-seventies into pressures on workers to accept lower wages, though it would later be extended to tougher working conditions along with the wage restraint.

In the U.S., the labour movement had lost its ability to lead any serious resistance, and as the eighties arrived even the UAW had ceased to be an independent voice challenging corporate morality and corporate actions. The Canadian left did not escape this malaise, yet Canada's labour movement retained a breath of defiance, and the gap between the Canadian and American labour movements grew in terms of both membership numbers and direction. The economic strength of Canadian workers in the seventies — their ability to resist the corporate pressures for concessions — was not, however, matched by any corresponding political strength. The government was thus able to introduce legislated wage controls to accomplish what the private sector did not. And in order to increase the likelihood of those controls being successful, economic policy allowed unemployment, and therefore worker insecurity, to rise.

At the end of the seventies, with the deepening of the recession, the pressures for wage concessions intensified. The leadership of the American UAW accepted the logic of concessions. The Canadian leadership, both leading and reflecting the mood of its members, rejected concession bargaining. For the Canadian section of the UAW, past tensions with the Americans could always be attributed to internal union politics (e.g., Canadian opposition to profit sharing in the late fifties), strong disagreements over a specific but unique problem (United Aircraft in the seventies), or different national circumstances (the contrasting roles of the two governments in responding to Chrysler's possible bankruptcy). But once the issue became the direction of the union's primary activity — bargaining — and that issue pitted the entire Canadian region against the top leadership of the UAW, a change in the relationship between the American and Canadian sections of the UAW became increasingly likely.

PART FOUR: TOWARDS A NEW UNIONISM

In dealing with concessions, the Canadian UAW's goal was to defend its members and maintain the integrity of its organization. But the very refusal to change fundamental principles led it to the most fundamental of changes in its structure: a break with its parent organization (Chapter 8). That change led to further dramatic changes in the regional and sectoral composition of the union (Chapter 9). Along with the volatile economic and social climate of the times, these developments confronted the Canadians with new questions regarding direction and structure (Chapter 10).

Oshawa workers filing in to union meeting to vote on tentative agreement with GM in 1984. The formal steps that led to the Canadian breakaway began shortly after the negotiations. Courtesy of the *Globe and Mail*.

CHAPTER 8

BREAKING AWAY

If Bob White thinks he's going to get a better deal out of those auto companies ... he's crazy ... [the Canadian members] may well get screwed in terms of benefits under the new regime ... the auto companies will now play some real hardball with the Canadians.

— Doug Fraser

It is hard to fight an enemy who has outposts in your head.

— Sally Kempton

We should have at least put up a fight instead of saying "We can't win — we surrender" ... the plant shut down anyway ... we should have done like the Canadians.

— American worker

In the early eighties, when globalization was quickly becoming something-not-to-be-questioned, the Canadian section of the UAW stubbornly embarked on a direction that went against the tide of economic change, against the apparent end of nationalism, and even against its own history (only a decade earlier, it had been the staunchest defender of international unionism). Given the extreme and growing integration of the industry, did the Canadian split amount to anything more than a symbolic move? And where would this new direction ultimately take the new union?

Globalization, Nationalism, and Internationalism

In Canada's case, globalization was hardly new; it essentially meant "continentalism" — further integration into the U.S. economy and, courtesy of American interests, an eventual move towards also bringing Mexico into that relationship. Despite the apparent inevitability of this trend, Canadians put up resistance well into the eighties. Even the federal Liberals had included nationalist elements in their policies during the early eighties (the National Energy Policy and the Foreign Investment Review Agency), and, of course, there was the massive mobilization against free trade in the mid-to late eighties.

In contrast to the popular resistance to globalization and continentalism, a unique favourable consensus had emerged within business. In the past, those in the business world in Canada had always been divided on the issues of free trade and nationalism, depending on whether they were concerned with protecting domestic markets or searching for foreign markets. However, by the eighties, no significant division remained. Big business was united on the free trade issue and small business fell into step behind that leadership. In spite of the feelings of some individual capitalists, not one section of business was part of the anti–free trade alliance. In fact, it was becoming very difficult to define the term *Canadian* as it applied to business.

The Mulroney Tories became the vehicle through which big business defeated nationalist-leaning policies and, by way of the FTA, essentially achieved the constitutionalized economic integration into the United States. But even the Tories recognized the antagonism across the country; in the campaign that preceded the move towards the FTA, they knew enough to keep a safe distance from continentalism.

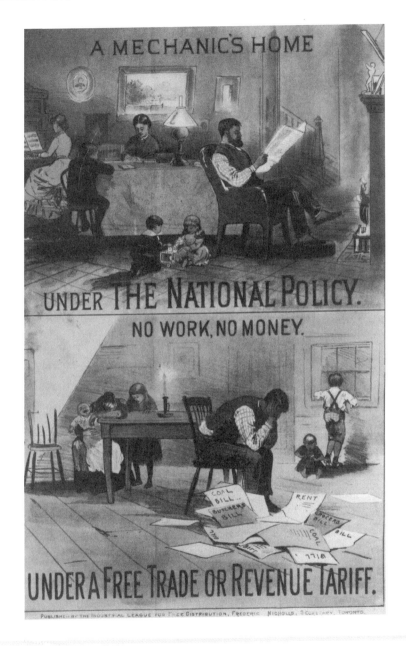

Poster against free trade with the U.S., 1872. Courtesy of National Archives, C-954466.

This popular opposition wasn't based solely on abstract nationalism: it was a result of the fact that the United States, once a model of the good life, no longer held much appeal. Further economic integration with the U.S. might be viewed as unavoidable from the perspective of uncertainty and fear, but it hardly had the power to move people with its promises and vision. The role of autoworkers in the economy placed the union at the centre of the debate on globalization and further integration into the United States; the response of the union placed it at the centre of the oppositional movement.

By the mid-seventies, the integration of the Canadians into the UAW and the American economy seemed complete: wages were virtually equal, the industry was more integrated than any other cross-border industry in the world, and the opposition to this integration had apparently collapsed. But during this period, Canadian workers began to shift the focus of their bargaining from the United States to Canada. Having achieved wage parity with the Americans, Canadians lost interest in catching up with the Americans.

In the past, Canadian UAW members, attempting to steadily improve their living standards, turned first to bargaining and then to national political action. The promise of the good life through collective bargaining was the ultimate lure of ties to the American union. But the situation had changed in two ways. First, as the postwar period of relative security and sharing in steady growth ended, the importance of bargaining seemed to diminish in relation to political events. Recession and restraint shifted union attention towards job policies and industrial strategies, legislated wage controls, labour laws as they affected organizing, and employment standards as they influenced health and safety and plant closures. To deal with such issues required addressing domestic politics; Canadians had to adopt a national perspective. For the Canadian UAW, building new ties with Canadian workers became more important than reinforcing the ties to American labour.

Second, even in bargaining itself — which remains a crucial element even as the significance of the political climate grows — the American leadership role was waylaid. The relative weakness of American labour, compared to the general militancy of the Canadian movement in this period, led to the greater attraction of wage comparisons within Canada over those in the U.S. It was in the process of bargaining, the *raison d'être* of unions, that the issues of Canadian autonomy and union direction came to a head.

The corporations had responded to the intensified competition they faced (and encouraged via free trade and capital mobility) with a new belligerence towards their workers. The companies, with auto in the lead, had made the transformation of collective bargaining relationships a crucial part of their overall strategy. The general disenchantment amongst Canadians with the American model was matched within the Canadian UAW by a growing disillusionment with the American union's response to this attack. The difference in the response of the Canadian UAW to the same corporate assault led to the split inside the UAW.

This conflict between the union and its parent organization reflected national differences, but more important, it stemmed from divergent strategies and notions of the role of unions. The Canadians were challenging the logic of globalization in a way that was both nationalist and concerned with the purpose of nationalism. Had the Canadian UAW even reluctantly adopted the American response, the union would have become just another vehicle for bringing American ideology and directions into Canada. Alternatively, since these differences over direction also existed to some extent within Canada, the UAW would have become a mechanism for reinforcing the weakest tendencies within Canadian labour. Instead, the Canadian UAW was able to retain its leading role in the labour movement and in broader struggles such as the fight against free trade.

The direction of the Canadian UAW seemed, however, to undermine the historic internationalism of progressive unionism. According to internationalists, corporate internationalism was based on competitiveness, while worker internationalism was based on solidarity. This definition was true, yet it skirted key problems. The international labour movement was too diverse to effectively coordinate activities. Each national labour movement was rooted in its distinct stage of development. Each movement faced a different context, and each was separated by cultural and ideological differences. These variations became most obvious in the difficulties encountered by Canada and the United States in their attempts to develop practical cross-border strategies. These problems arose in spite of the countries' relatively similar language and culture.

But more important, international solidarity couldn't work unless each of the labour movements became stronger. New kinds of international solidarity are not compatible with a reality that includes an American labour movement that has been unable to organize its own "South"; a Mexican labour movement in which workers at different auto plants within the same company can't even communicate with each other; and a Canadian movement that can't organize the fastest-growing sectors (private service).

Under these circumstances, if labour wants to challenge the internationalism of the corporations, it must first be strong nationally. However, national strength does not simply mean strong national governments. Such governments legislated wage controls, imposed the FTA, skewed taxes against working people, and forced cut-backs in the social wage on the general population ("for its own good"). Similarly, national strength means more than allegedly strong unions. Unions that are strong enough to sell wage concessions and false partnerships will reinforce rather than challenge the view that there is no alternative.

Rather, national strength requires local and national institutions — unions, community organizations, political parties, and the service and administrative bodies within the various levels of the state — that are accessible to working people, and that are democratic and effective. These institutions must be able to articulate working class needs and fight on behalf of and alongside workers in their struggles. Only on such a *national* base can internationalism be meaningfully achieved.

While the Canadians were breaking away from the international union (which was really an American-based union with a Canadian section) and concentrating on building a strong national union and national movement, the CAW also increased its commitment to internationalism. After the split, the CAW channelled more resources into international education and the enforcement of solidarity, especially through its ties to the South African labour movement, South and Central America, and (later) Mexico. In bargaining, the union negotiated a company-paid Social Justice Fund which financed important international projects. These international ties included some awareness of long-term self-interest but they could not be, and generally were not, justified in terms of developing goals such as "international bargaining" or "joint efforts to affect corpo-

One of the most successful internal educational campaigns undertaken by the union was around the struggles of black workers in South Africa. What made it so effective was its direct link to those workers, the support of the CAW leadership, the focus on taking the educationals to the base by way of local union meetings, and — especially — the role played by a small group of activists inside and outside the union.

rate decisions." They reflected cultural solidarity, and a direct identification with workers in struggle.

The struggles in other countries would be fought on a national basis, and the role of internationalism was both modest and indirect: to attract national and international attention to issues, to provide financial assistance and technical and moral support, and to act nationally to limit the power and ideology of capital. If Canadians and American autoworkers could resist their employers' attempts to speed up the line, Volkswagen workers in Mexico would face less pressure to work at a pace that forced forty-year-olds into involuntary retirement. If Canadians could challenge the logic of competitiveness (rather than try to compete with fellow workers in other countries), then workers in South Africa would feel less isolated when they also resisted that logic. In essence, progressive internationalism can only be built on a strong and progressive nationalism.

Confidence and Independence

Given the pressures of globalization and the dependent relationship that had existed within the union and Canada for so long, how did the Canadian UAW develop the self-confidence to attempt a split from its parent organization?

Unions do not set out explicitly to develop confidence. On the contrary, concrete issues and struggles absorb their time and energy. And while educational campaigns and policies can help, it is the struggles themselves, rather than any prearranged plan, that build collective confidence. Yet building confidence contributes to no less than building the potential of the union to survive attacks and initiate progress. In a sense, the entire history of the Canadian UAW centres on the development of that potential amongst its activists and members.

As Big Three bargaining developed in the early eighties, each step further escalated the stakes and each success seemed to build the Canadian UAW's ability and confidence to act independently. As pointed out earlier, struggles outside the Big Three — against wage controls, with anti-union employers, over plant closures and wage concessions — set the stage for the Canadian UAW's decision in early spring of 1982 to reject the American proposal of opening the Ford and GM collective agreements. In a sense, once the actual decision was made, rejection of the American direction was relatively easy to uphold, since it didn't require the Canadians to go on strike or risk immediate retaliation. The real test was to come when the agreements expired and the alternative was a strike; would the companies let them get away with trying to achieve more than the Americans?

The mood within the labour movement was sombre and even sympathetic; reporters were writing articles on the defeat of labour. An editorial in the *Financial Times* in April, 1980, warned against any economic stimulus. The economic establishment was determined to let the 1979 recession continue as a crucial part of the fight against inflation and to break the resistance of the stubborn labour movement. In the early eighties, unemployment was higher in Canada than in any other developed capitalist country.

And in the auto industry, a report by Ross Perry, *The Future of Canada's Auto Industry*, summarized the prevailing pessimism: "Two recent studies predicted a reduction [in jobs] in the range of 30 and 50 per cent from the peak employment year 1978 to the mid-1980s. This amounts to a loss of between 29,000 and 41,000 direct wage-earning jobs. These forecasts are based on conservative assumptions ..." In this context, unions were wondering if they could resist the concessionary patterns being set in the U.S., especially after the once powerful and still respected American UAW felt compelled to move in that direction.

In the U.S., "what's good for GM is good for the country" carried some weight. Americans hoped that by restoring the once dominant position of their companies, workers could also return to the good old days. In Canada, that kind of endorsement of corporate leadership, especially since GM was a foreign multinational, was not as accepted. Leo Panitch, observing Canada–U.S. cultural differences at the time, noted that in the U.S. the folk hero of the period was Lee Iacocca, a leading capitalist who was demanding concessions from workers, while in Canada the folk hero was Bob White, a trade unionist fighting those very same concessions.

GM was the target in the fall of 1982. As the negotiations began, the new GM president calmly made the same threats that had, in the United States, led to the rally of public support for the company. He declared publicly in September, 1982, that a refusal by the Canadians to fall in line with the Americans could lead to the fullscale closure of facilities and plant relocation. It was, however, one thing to ask workers to "do their part" and another to threaten entire communities with devastation if they didn't comply. Rather than mobilizing public support, the comments sparked a public backlash (in future, GM and other companies laid the groundwork for their demands with slightly more sophistication).

The lay-offs in the industry, especially the scheduled weeks of downtime, were so pervasive during the 1982 negotiations that the union had difficulty finding a strike deadline during which even half the workers would be working. On the dates that would have been the normal deadline at Ford, for example, no assembly plant was scheduled to work. The union took a cautious position: it recognized not only that times were difficult, but also that it faced an environment that differed from the American one (e.g., Canadian inflation was higher). The union had done its homework; it publicly took advantage of GM's vulnerable position as a foreign multinational. It also sent the clear message to the company that it would settle if the company made a reasonable offer, but that it was ready to fight if GM forced it to the wall.

General Motors decided that a war would be too costly and settled without a strike. It succeeded in removing the PPH program from the agreement, though the Canadian agreements retained it slightly longer than those of the Americans. The company did not ask the Canadians to repay the COLA that workers had retained by not reopening, and the Canadians won a small wage increase, over and above COLA. The Canadians breathed a sigh of relief. Their gains were modest, but they had challenged the Big Three collective bargaining system — including both the companies and their own union — and survived.

Unfortunately, the feelings of relief were short-lived. A dispute at Chrysler followed, and the Chrysler workers stated their demands in absolute terms. They had lost $1.15 per hour when the concessions agreement removed COLA. Other catch-up demands could wait; the workers wanted first and foremost to reinstate COLA. Chrysler had offered the American workers a continuation of the agreement with future COLA but without the restoration of the lost COLA and other wage increases. The workers rejected the agreement by a vote of two to one but the union leadership convinced them that a strike would be suicidal. They therefore ended up in limbo, with no agreement and no strike.

In Canada, the company, newspaper editorials, and every consultant on the continent were joined by the international union itself in warning workers that the cupboard was bare. With the added authority of President Doug Fraser's vantage point on Chrysler's board of directors, the UAW was telling the Canadians that their demands were unreasonable. An increase as small as twenty-five cents per hour would push Chrysler into bankruptcy and cause the loss of hundreds of thousands of jobs. If the Canadians demanded more, Chrysler might actually do what GM had only threatened — leave Canada.

The Canadian UAW's analysis concluded that the wage issue had little or nothing to do with Chrysler's survival. The key was economic recovery and Chrysler's ability to return to full-capacity utilization. Nor did it make sense for Chrysler to move out of Canada. Relocation would be extremely costly, and the company could make substantial profits in Canada even at the wages the workers insisted on. Nevertheless, Chrysler did have the power to carry out any decision it made, and the Canadians had no guarantees.

The leadership decided the risk was necessary, and the membership simultaneously made it clear — by way of wildcats, at membership meetings, and through their bargaining committees — that it wouldn't accept any other decision. The strike began on 5 November 1982. During the Chrysler strike, newspaper reporters had been told by their editors to balance the stories by finding breaks in solidarity. But the reporters were themselves surprised at the degree of support for the strike on the picket lines and at the workers' ability to argue against concessions and justify demands. The solidarity of the workers was overwhelming across all the Canadian units.

Chrysler's expectation that pressure on the workers would weaken the union did not come true; in fact community support from other unions, many local businesses, and sections of the church was growing. Nor did the company's hope — that, one way or another, the Canadians would be influenced by their parent organization in Detroit — materialize.

Chrysler's top negotiators arrived from the U.S. The head of finance came. UAW president Doug Fraser came. And Iacocca himself slipped quietly into Toronto to meet with White. After a five-week strike, it was Chrysler

> Despite the hysteria of the times ... sweeping changes have taken place amongst Windsor autoworkers ... during the past few years ... progress was being made [towards] ... increasing demands for greater independence for Canadian trade unions.
> — Cyril Prince, Local 200, March, 1954

Press conference, Chrysler negotiations, 1985, when the Canadians completed their restoration of full parity with GM and Ford. From left to right: Jim O'Neil, Bob Nickerson, Ken Gerrard, Bob White, Buzz Hargrove, Sam Gindin. Courtesy of the CAW collection.

that made the concessions. The company agreed to the opening day economic demands of the workers, and the Canadians even won an acceptable increase for the Americans (seventy-five cents per hour plus future COLA). By 1985, Chrysler was recording the highest profits in its sixty-year history while paying wages that were higher than those it had earlier warned would result in bankruptcy.

The Chrysler strike had "really done it." The Canadians had achieved something that the American union was not only unable to do, but had in fact given up on. They had also shown that they could generate the pressure necessary to force the Americans to come to Canada and negotiate on the basis of Canadian demands. Along the way, they proved that their analysis and intuition were correct, while the experts (including the union leadership in the U.S.) were wrong. The Canadian David had been smarter and tougher than the American Goliath, and even non-union Canadians expressed admiration.

Then came the 1984 bargaining round. General Motors had settled in the U.S. with no real wage increases built into the agreement (the ratification vote was only fifty-seven per cent). The Canadians decided to target GM again. Chrysler had not yet been brought back to pattern (i.e., parity with GM and Ford) so it wasn't an option. Since Ford hadn't yet settled in the U.S., targeting Ford risked entanglement in the American strategy. If, for example, the U.S. went on strike while Canada was already on strike, the Canadians could be left hanging until the Americans had settled. This vulnerability was the last thing the Canadian union needed.

This time, the confrontation dealt with who had ultimate authority over the bargaining program in Canada — the Canadian director or the UAW president. The 1982 GM settlement in Canada had been reached without a strike, and the American leadership had rationalized the differences in terms of higher Canadian inflation and the profit-sharing plans, negotiated by the Americans and rejected by the Canadians. At Chrysler later that year, the Americans disagreed with the timing of the Canadian demands (i.e., immediate restoration of the COLA float) but they couldn't criticize the Canadians' ultimate goal: bringing Chrysler back to parity with GM and Ford. Now, however, the union was involved in pattern bargaining for the entire Canadian auto industry. The Canadians were asserting independence and, by their actions, essentially saying to American workers, who were themselves questioning the leadership of their union, "Hey! You don't have to go down that road!"

It is possible to imagine the two sections of the union simply deciding to follow their own agendas within the same international union. Other unions seemed to have managed this arrangement. However, this plan was not an option given the specific nature of the UAW as an organization, and the lack of consensus within the American section on its own direction. There is no other example in the history of bargaining of a relationship that is as integrated as that between Canada and the U.S. in the Big Three negotiations. In fact, there are very few domestic industries with such integrated bargaining. Workers doing the same job have generally earned the same wage, whether they worked for GM, Ford, or Chrysler and whether they worked in Canada or the United States. In the past, rigid wage parity was a source of strength for the workers on both sides of the border; at a time of strain, it became an inflexibility that the structure couldn't handle.

To be more accurate, the structure *invited* comparisons. It was those comparisons that the American leadership, rather than the union structure, couldn't handle. The American leadership, in its attempt to sell the new direction, was meeting stiff resistance from American workers; the last thing it wanted was a Canadian presence that highlighted this resistance at conventions and intercorporate conferences, and most of all by their bargaining directions and outcomes.

The bargaining with GM Canada was unsuccessful, in part because the American UAW leadership warned GM to limit what it gave to the Canadians. The Canadians went on strike — nervous and very apprehensive about the high stakes, and with the knowledge that the company and the American leadership of their own union were talking to each other. But by this time, the Canadian union had defined its course, and it understood that it had substantial bargaining clout. Although the common perception of globalization was that it represented a shift in power to the corporations, leaving workers relatively defenceless, the Canadians knew better.

The *Globe and Mail* had earlier editorialized that in challenging GM the Canadians were "looking staunchly backward." The *Toronto Star*, for all its apparent identification with Canadian nationalism, showed little interest in it taking this particular form. Their earlier editorial patronizingly brushed the Canadian autoworkers aside, proclaiming "It's hard to see what they hope to achieve by this strike."

Corporations were indeed more powerful, but the internationalization of production also left companies more vulnerable at any particular point in time.

In the past, the corporations usually retained excess capacity to meet sudden increases in demand, and they often had the luxury of double-sourcing: if one plant shut down, another could pick up some of the slack. But as the companies cut overhead to save costs, this flexibility also disappeared. And as they reduced duplication, increased specialization, and moved to just-in-time production, many groups of workers were left with the power to affect a disproportionately wide range of a company's operations. The Canadian strike made this power especially clear, as 50,000 American workers were soon laid off, with more to follow.

The catch was that the companies retained the power to move those crucial parts of their operations, though at some cost, to locations where the workers were under "better control." As a result, the Canadians had both the power to win and, as one worker put it, the power to hang themselves.

The union had to balance its demands, taking corporate warnings of competitive limits with a grain of salt, but also aware that the threats were not just propaganda.

In the long term, that balance could be shifted in the workers' favour only if national and international legislation limited corporate mobility, and if workers' militancy became more generalized on a global basis. International ad hoc militancy — with or without formal international links — would at least leave the corporations nervous about the expense of relocation with the possible rise of militancy at the new site.

The Canadian leadership made it clear that whether or not its strike was approved by the parent organization, it would strike for the right to share in the industry's growth in productivity. The solidarity of the workers was strong, and after a thirteen-day strike, GM conceded annual improvements for each year of the agreement. This increase wasn't labelled the traditional AIF, but was renamed "special Canadian adjustment" (SCA) and added to COLA rather than the base rate; like COLA and the base rate, the SCA was included in calculating overtime, premiums, vacation pay, etc. The reason for this creative introduction of yet another initialism into the agreement was to obscure the visibility of the Canadian gains and limit the antagonism of the American UAW. The workers ratified the agreement by a vote of almost six to one.

The GM strike confirmed the ability of the Canadian UAW to act independently in the most difficult of circumstances. The union had taken on the largest manufacturing company in the world and shown that, in spite of globalization, workers had a measure of power. The workers had confronted their own union and established their own Canadian pattern. The face of the union now wore a giddy smile. That smile mixed pride, surprise at the union's progress, growing self-confidence, and nervousness about the ultimate step of permanently separating from the international union and past dependency.

The Split

Detroit's interference in the Canadian negotiations made future change in the bargaining relationship inevitable. The bargaining successes were obviously crucial in allaying the apprehension that remained, but also critical was the role played by the Canadian director, Bob White.

White had many of the attributes of other leaders: he was clever and bright, articulate, astute in sizing up both people and situations, and he revelled in responsibility and tough decisions. Like all leaders in the UAW, he had been significantly influenced by the social unionism of Walter Reuther. Although originally opposed to Dennis McDermott's appointment as director of the Canadian region, White worked closely with McDermott and credited him with influencing White's own social perspectives.

White's greatest attribute was that he clearly understood who he represented. Electoral politics was very important, but always secondary to the impact of any policy or event on working people and the union. The workers and their union were the foundation of both bargaining and future political strength. His personal ties to the international leadership were painful to break, but he would never let those ties stand in the way of his representing Canadian workers.

Robert White was the first (and only) Canadian labour leader to become a media star; he was a nationalist speaking for the underdog, youthful and open. He respected the media, understood it, and used it, but he never overestimated it or became overly dependent on its judgements. He spoke to the members through the media, and the status the media conferred on White was shared by the membership. Through the news clips of White speaking to and often even on behalf of Canadians, UAW activists and members began to see themselves as leading a fight that extended beyond their interests to a broader national arena. White had not intended to make history by leading a breakaway from the international union. His great contribution as a leader was that when the historic opportunity did arise, he didn't try to escape from it.

White had decided to go to the Canadian Council in early December to garner support for autonomy demands from the international union. (White wanted to ensure that the Canadian bargaining conference would set Canadian goals, and that the control over the right to strike, over access to the strike fund,

Of the union's two living past directors, Dennis McDermott strongly supported the breakaway, while George Burt opposed it.

and over Canadian staff would rest with the Canadian director.) Just before the council meeting, White called a meeting to inform the staff of his intentions and to test the waters. The six-hour session included arguments for and against taking the steps that would very likely lead to the split. The

As Bob White was the first to point out, the role he played in the union was critically dependent on Bob Nickerson and Buzz Hargrove, his two trouble-shooters and assistants. Most unions would have envied having either one of these individuals as their leader. Their differing styles and roots complemented each other. Both brought close ties to the rank-and-file to any discussion and never shied away from challenging, pushing, or restraining White according to their views of the union.

Nickerson, who subsequently became the CAW's first secretary-treasurer, had, as a service rep, played an often unrecognized role in developing local activists. As an assistant, he played a particularly important role within the labour movement in supporting the early struggles of women to break through barriers within the male-dominated union structures.

Hargrove joined the staff in the mid-seventies and immediately became active in the two most pressing issues of the time: organizing the unemployed and fighting worker concessions, including wage controls. Hargrove was in his early thirties and had been on staff for less than three years when White became director. Nevertheless, White acknowledged his potential by choosing him as an assistant.

impressive overall commitment of the staff members to press ahead in spite of any risks to themselves — their paycheques came from Detroit — reinforced White's determination and strengthened the resolution he took to the council. As was happening in the union overall, the struggle over the future of the Canadian UAW had unified the staff and brought out the best in them.

The debate at the council was equally impressive. Some delegates made passionate appeals for international solidarity and historic ties, and a few questioned whether the union could survive on its own. But the delegates had been through enough over the past few years to clearly understand that they had to assert their autonomy. No one really expected Detroit's reaction to lead to anything but a split. The only questions for most delegates were when the split would occur and under what conditions.

When, as expected, the international executive board rejected those conditions, White returned to the council on 11 December 1984. The Canadian union's "parliament" decided that day, virtually unanimously, to establish a new Canadian union. Of 350 delegates, only four voted against the decision. In his own comments to the council, White emphasized that, with the formation of their own union, the Canadians could no longer blame the Americans for any failures. The point of full autonomy was full responsibility.

The new union would obviously need a governing structure between conventions that was broader than its current single elected officer (the direc-

At a demonstration of pensioners at the 1987 Bargaining Convention, one retiree took up White's call for responsibility within Canada with a picket sign reading "YOU CAN'T BLAME BIEBER THIS TIME!" Owen Bieber was the UAW president at the time of the split.

tor). White proposed the formation of a twelve-member national executive board (NEB), which would (in line with caucus sensitivities) be representative of all sections of the union. Eventually, affirmative action positions were included for two women and one person of colour. To limit potential bureaucratization, only three officers would hold full-time positions: the president, the secretary-treasurer, and the Quebec director. Since the remaining officers would retain their current union functions, officers would, in some cases, continue to work on a part-time or full-time basis in the workplace.

Because the two large locals in Quebec themselves could dominate any vote in Quebec and thereby choose one of the NEB members, the overall convention formally elected the Quebec director. In fact, this "safety valve" was never used; the elected Quebec caucus member was rubber-stamped by the delegates in recognition of Quebec's unique status. This procedure was later modified so that Quebec's candidate for the board did not need the ratification of the convention.

The three full-time officers, plus two others, would be elected at the convention. The remaining seven would include those elected as executive officers of the Canadian Council (six), plus the elected president of the Quebec Council. This method allowed for a partial integration of the council and NEB structures but also assured some stability in the case of a radical electoral change in the union. A complete change would have to occur over two elections at least a year apart (i.e., at the convention and the Council meeting).

Within the union, the remaining controversy over the split was as much about the process as about the decision. This controversy was especially heated at the crucial and politically divided Oshawa local (Local 222). Some members argued that the Canadian Council had no constitutional

International Union, United Automobile,
Aerospace & Agricultural Implement
Workers of America (UAW)

ROBERT WHITE
*Director for Canada
and International
Vice-President*

CANADIAN
HEADQUARTERS
205 PLACER COURT
NORTH YORK, WILLOWDALE
ONTARIO M2H 3H9
PHONE (416) 497-4110
TELEX 06-986509

January 10, 1985

To: All Canadian UAW Members

I am taking this opportunity to write to you personally about the recent important developments within our union.

You have no doubt read or heard that on December 1, the Canadian UAW Council, made up of 350 UAW leaders elected from local unions across Canada, endorsed my recommendation that the UAW in Canada seek greater autonomy—or independence—within the International Union. These delegates approved my recommendation because they felt strongly, as I did, that the UAW in Canada must have the freedom to pursue Canadian collective bargaining goals and address the concerns of Canadian UAW members as effectively as possible.

Accordingly, I attended the meeting of the UAW's International Executive Board on December 10 with the aim of trying to obtain more independence for Canada within the International Union. I made what I believe to be the best arguments possible to try to change the structure of the International to make it more representative of Canadian workers. After more than four hours of debate at that meeting, my motion was rejected 24 to 1, with myself casting the single dissenting vote.

During the debate, I had made my position clear: I had been authorized by both the Canadian and Quebec Councils that if the IEB was not willing to allow Canada full autonomy on certain terms, through structural changes, then we should proceed to set up two separate UAW's: one in Canada and one in the U.S., ensuring that each would be financially and structurally sound and have close fraternal ties.

Immediately following the 24 to 1 vote, I made a motion to set up two organizations. A majority of International Executive Board members voted in favour of that motion.

We are now in the process of putting together a committee which will include myself, most likely the President and Secretary-Treasurer of the International Union, and others. We will try to work out the necessary financial arrangements to make sure that a separate UAW in Canada is financially sound. We also have lawyers and various Canadian UAW staff members reviewing all concerns—be they constitutional, legal, or financial—so that this transition is made as smoothly as possible in order that all our members are fully protected. All these procedures will take time. We will keep your local union leadership informed as we go along. They, in turn, will be passing the necessary information on to you.

2

It is impossible for me to deal with all the issues coming out of this new development in this letter. However, let me assure you that this is being done in the best interests of all our members in Canada.

What we are doing, really, is restructuring an organization called the "International Union, UAW," which was joined at the top, where one Canadian sat on a 25-member Executive Board, where our union dues went to Detroit, and where we received in return, certain benefits, including the sharing of a strike fund. We are restructuring that into two organizations, where our union dues will all stay in Canada, where we will have an elected, Canadian executive board, where we will have a strike fund to support our members forced on strike in the same way and in the same amount as we have always done. We expect to retain the same local union structure and dues structure as we have now.

This does not affect jobs. It is not a declaration of war on the companies we work for, on the American workers, or on the U.S. leadership of the International Union. It is taking control of our own decisions, being accountable and responsible, and not passing the blame on to someone else.

I intend to lead this restructuring. It will be done carefully and intelligently. In the end we will have a strong, dynamic, democratic, and financially sound UAW in Canada.

This really is a natural evolution, a growing up of our union. Believe me, in the long run, it will be in the best interests of the UAW members in Canada and the Canadian labour movement. We hope to have some material, with much more detail, distributed in the plants and offices, as soon as possible.

It is important as we go through this change that we do it together, and not allow corporations, politicians, or other outside interests to interfere with our direction.

Thank you for your support in the past, and may 1985 be a successful year for you.

Fraternally yours,

RW:WC:ac
opeiu343

ROBERT WHITE,
UAW director for Canada and
International Vice-President

Bob White's letter to members announcing Canadian Council's decision to form Canadian union.

authority to make such a decision and that, considering the fundamental nature of the decision, the council should have called for a referendum vote. They were right about the council not having the constitutional blessing to make the decision, but a referendum in Canada also held no "constitutional authority." The central issue was not constitutional authority; it was the democratic legitimacy of the split in Canada.

The option of a referendum was discussed in some depth at the national office. The reason for its ultimate rejection was that, while adding little, it created substantial risk. There was no question that the members overwhelmingly supported the split. The staff, local activists, and the delegates elected to council were in regular contact with members and readily confirmed this support, as did the meetings and newspapers of the local unions. Even former UAW president Doug Fraser, who was critical of the Canadians for leaving, laughed when asked about a referendum vote; according to Fraser, "White would easily get eighty-five per cent." The concern about a referendum was less about letting the members decide — they had made their feelings known through other forums — than about creating an opening for others outside the Canadian UAW to intervene, even at the last moment.

The companies had already mentioned that they were rethinking future investments. If the Council announced a vote, the companies could have escalated such warnings in order to influence the debate. The American UAW knew that White had the full support of the leadership. If there was an in-plant vote, however, the UAW could certainly release rumours about a refusal to transfer any monies to the new union, leaving it without a strike fund and reinforcing concerns about staff salaries and services. Since the collective agreements were legally with the parent union, not the Canadian UAW, it could be argued that once the Canadian office led a breakaway, that office was no longer the bargaining agent for any of the units in Canada.

On 12 December 1984, the Detroit Free Press carried the headline, "UAW Rift May Cause Canada to Lose Jobs."

An elected union official in Local 222, the largest local in the union, actually raised this issue with the Ontario Labour Relations Board to give the government an excuse to step in and challenge the council decision. If the Oshawa local had subsequently decided to stay in the international organization, the resolution to split might have quickly unravelled. Other GM units would not have wanted to be separated from Oshawa, and other

Big Three workers would be worried about bargaining without GM. As it turned out, while the membership meetings eventually held in Oshawa were rambunctious, workers still voted overwhelmingly to support the council decision.

Once the Canadian Council made its decision and exhibited the solidarity that would discourage the companies, the government, or the UAW from trying to intimidate Canadian workers, it asked each local to hold meetings to ratify the decision. Any local that chose to reject the decision and form a new union could stay with the international union. At the meeting of Local 251 in Wallaceburg, fifty-eight per cent of the membership of about 1500 decided to stay with the UAW.

> The argument made by the Local 251 president was that the local was satisfied with the current relationship to the UAW and that the only interference it had seen in its internal affairs had been the attempt by the Canadian staff rep to prevent the local from making concessions. In 1987, that president was defeated and became assistant personnel manager at Eaton-Yale.

Over the nine months following the council decision, financial and legal matters were settled. The UAW agreed to transfer $36 million to the Canadians; this amount was less than their fair share but it was sufficient to equip the new union with an adequate strike fund and some cash for administrative purposes. At the founding convention in early September, 1985, the Canadian UAW formally established the new union, and in the summer of 1986, the union was renamed the Canadian Auto Workers.

A Culture of Resistance

The massive disinvestments in auto and the dissolution of the Autopact predicted by the experts in the event of a Canadian split didn't materialize. Yet economic restructuring both within the workplace and through plant closures was taking its toll. The new Mulroney government had made it clear — after the election, of course — that it would shift power to the corporations by way of a greater reliance on markets and competitiveness. The test of any policy or activity would be whether or not it increased Canada's competitiveness in business terms.

(Top) The original CAW Education Centre in Port Elgin, Ontario in the mid-1950s. (Bottom) The new CAW Education Centre. Courtesy of the CAW collection.

In the mid-eighties, the CAW suffered casualties in terms of plant closures, especially in the auto parts sector, and any gains that were made were generally limited and vulnerable to future changes. But the union continued to fight back. This stubborn resistance was central to the CAW's survival and strength as a social force in the country. One measure of the strength of the new union was that, after the split, it did not withdraw into a shell to consolidate, rebuild, and establish some breathing room. Its activism at all levels increased with barely a missed beat. Expectations were raised,

Detroit's valuable services were more than adequately replaced, and rather than having to cope with the loss of financial subsidies from the UAW, the CAW found itself with additional resources for its own priorities. The split didn't drain or divert the CAW; it energized the union.

The attitude of the new union was that it could and should participate in all relevant struggles. It supported other workers on strike, made organizing even more of a priority, invested a sizable portion of its strike fund in modernizing and expanding the education centre, assisted locals in developing their own newspapers, introduced innovations in bargaining, and played a vital national role in the crucial debate over free trade and the future of the country.

The first act of the new union involved a group of young women who had, with the support of the CLC and its affiliates, taken on one of the most powerful institutions in the country — the Canadian Bank of Commerce. Along with other unions, the Canadian UAW contributed money for strike pay, and it also provided staff. The minute the formation of the CAW was officially declared, the bank workers marched into the convention in Toronto.

After giving the workers a boisterous feet-stomping ovation, the CAW delegates followed the strikers, many single mothers and immigrant women, out of the hotel and down Bay Street to the bank's headquarters. For the CAW, this support indicated recognition of the changing nature of the workforce and made a statement about solidarity with low-paid workers.

The union's first two financial decisions were also significant. They involved organizing and education; that is, expanding the union's membership base and deepening its commitment. The Canadian section of the union had, since the sixties, led all regions within the UAW in organizing. With its new independence, it decided to hire ten additional organiz-

Frustrated with the bank's refusal to negotiate with the workers, the women, along with their bargaining rep, Jim O'Neil of the Canadian UAW, made the decision to sit-in and stay-in at their workplace. For women who had never been on a strike before and who were responsible for child care and supper, this was a wrenching and tense period. Security was already tight in the bank, but someone found an unguarded fire door and let O'Neil in to help maintain the worker's confidence as they began their thirty-six-hour sit-in.

ers for a year to protect existing standards in the union and accelerate the recruitment of new workers. The decision was in part related to the opportunities created by the wave of media attention surrounding the split. The CAW had been receiving increasing numbers of calls from groups of workers attracted by both the union's well-publicized successes and the fact that it was becoming Canadian (which, to these workers, meant that decisions were made in Canada, not in a foreign country, and that money collected in Canada stayed in the country).

The decision regarding education was much more costly and risky. It involved the rebuilding and expansion of the union's education centre in Port Elgin. That expenditure reflected the priority the union placed on education and was indicative of the permanence of the CAW. It announced that the union was here to stay and that it was building for the future. This education centre belonged to the workers. At Port Elgin, workers exchanged information about the latest management strategies in the workplace, tried to get a handle on the deficit, and learned about a history they had previously been denied — their own. It was a place where they studied the role of workers in the scheme of things. Port Elgin was also the home of the CAW's unique Family Education Program. Run in the summer as two weeks of vacation and education for the families of CAW members, the program symbolized the union's commitment to integrating the family and union culture. And, as the home of the Canadian Council, Port Elgin was the place where activists renewed contacts with old friends and later met in crowded rooms to share rumours and complaints or out-yell each other in debates. Paintings, photographs, and posters reflected everyday lives and paid tribute to past struggles. At Port Elgin, working people were more than "just workers."

In collective bargaining, the union consolidated its separation from the U.S. and tried to restore the notion that bargaining was not about corporate demands (concessions) but about workers' demands (sharing in progress, improving the workplace). The union lobbied for legislated changes, and when Parliament wavered under corporate pressure, as it did with indexed pensions and advanced lay-off notice in Ontario, the union confronted it in bargaining — both to win gains and to demonstrate that the change in legislation was in fact practical. And with its new control over its finances, the CAW was able to provide financial support for the struggles of other unions when they came for help: woodworkers on the West Coast, telephone workers in Newfoundland, food-processing workers in Alberta, public sector workers in Ottawa.

The "culture of resistance" that had developed in the union was rooted in a historical legacy and recent involvement in struggles. The role of education was to reinforce and consolidate that culture ("education" also included films, pamphlets, union newspapers, music, and even writing classes that encouraged workers to resist the dominant culture and tell their own stories). As a culture that permeated the union, it did not depend on or wait for leadership from "the top." Local activists and members proved themselves quite capable of leading on their own. The best example of this autonomy was in aerospace, where the local leadership at de Havilland Aircraft and then McDonnell-Douglas took on the issue of health and safety and led the largest collective refusals Canada had ever seen.

When Mulroney announced his intention to move towards the FTA with the United States in 1986, the CAW was there in opposition with its credibility and organizational/financial clout. Leadership meetings and forums were held in every community with a CAW base across the country. Bob White, as leader of the CAW, was generally viewed as a central leader and spokesperson for the anti–free trade coalition. Over one million pamphlets were distributed in the plants, to homes, at schools, and in malls. Full-page ads appeared in newspapers across the country when opposition to the agreement was flagging and in need of revitalization. And CAW activists across the country brought the issue into the plants and worked with others to introduce more Canadians to politics by way of the anti-FTA fight.

In spite of the subsequent close defeat, the fight against free trade proved the potential of the Canadian labour movement and highlighted its importance as a relevant and democratic social force. Without the intervention of the labour movement, the crucial debate over the future direction of the country would have been a brief and hardly noticeable interruption in Canadian life. In the past, the economic and political élite of the country had always been divided on free trade. Now, however, business was united in its favour; the media, with a few exceptions, endorsed that support; and opposition from the NDP had no fire. Canadian labour, along with its resource-poor but commitment-rich coalition partners, forced a national discussion which, at least for a brief moment, had the establishment nervously making accommodating promises.

After the 1988 federal election, Bob White of the CAW and Leo Gerrard of the steelworkers' union each wrote scathing public criticisms of the NDP's belated and tepid handling of the free trade issue. The tone of the criticisms didn't suggest any break with support for the party, but it high-

Meeting inside plant at de Havilland after work stoppage over health and safety.
Courtesy of the CAW collection.

The modern health and safety movement emerged in the mid-sixties, when the
workers placed the issue of working conditions on the agenda. From the beginning
and into the nineties, that health and safety movement was influenced by the rising
consciousness of public health and the environment, and by outside activists.

In the early seventies, wildcats by miners in Northern Ontario, members of the
Steelworkers union, forced a Royal Commission on Health and Safety, and the
Saskatchewan NDP government introduced legislation patterned on earlier legislation
in Sweden that was unique to North America. That legislation emphasized both a
greater role for the state in policing health and safety and the empowerment of workers
who could themselves force the issue. That empowerment included the establishment
of health and safety committees, the right to information, protection against reprisal
and above all, the right to refuse work that might endanger workers. The
Saskatchewan legislation became the model for progressive reform on the continent.

In Ontario, worker militancy over the issue surprised trade union leaders. The
NDP made it a central issue, and this forced legislative changes and significant
increases in government budgets dealing with workers' health. In the mid-eighties,
there was another round of worker pressure and militancy over the issue. In 1987
and 1988, workers at de Havilland and McDonnell-Douglas staged the largest
work refusals that had ever occurred for health and safety, shutting down
production and making major gains in cleaning up the workplace, training and
educating the workforce, and monitoring the health of workers.

lighted an emerging change in labour's attitude to the party.

The labour movement seemed to be rebelling against past notions that the NDP had all the political savvy and labour's role was to provide the bodies and money. The

Labour Day march against the proposed Free Trade Agreement, September 1987. Courtesy of the CAW collection.

movement was asserting that it had fully understood the significance and potential of the free trade issue while the party caucus had not; that it had broadened the notion of politics and mobilized public opinion in a way that the party had not; and that even in terms of narrow electoral strategies, it was right and the party was wrong. While these events were encouraging in terms of labour's development, they reflected the NDP's inability to deal with the new economic times. That failure would reveal itself even more painfully in the 1990s. The comment made by Charlotte Yates in *From Plant to Politics* on the relationship between the CCF/NDP and the UAW/CAW in the early eighties seemed to be confirmed: "The party moved away from its social democratic principles towards a more conservative political image at the same time that the UAW was becoming more politically militant in

What was and remains an issue, was the style and orientation of the NDP campaign ... this reflected a deeper problem: a feeling of disillusionment and drift which threatens to reduce active commitment to passive support ... "Is our party becoming a pale imitation of the other parties? Can we still count on it to stand up for us?"

— CAW brief presented by Bob White to NDP task force, March, 1989

its own action ... As had happened so many times in the past, the UAW and the NDP were marching to the beat of two different drummers."

The UAW made its breakthrough in Oshawa in 1937, after a fifteen-day strike against GM. That strike was dragged out and given national significance by the interference of the premier of Ontario. In 1984, another strike at GM of similar duration was catapulted into national prominence by an external player. This time, the interference came from the source that had inspired the Canadians to establish their own branch of the UAW in the thirties, but whose own spirit had since been sapped — the American UAW. The internal UAW conflict that was the inevitable result led to the formation of a new Canadian union. The breakthrough of 1937 had developed into the breakaway of 1984.

This event had a current context and immediate causes, but it cannot be fully understood without reaching back to the past. Two issues have dominated much of this book: how the Canadian section of the UAW managed to avert the decline of the UAW, and how the Canadian union members developed the confidence and maturity to leave home when the outside world was more threatening than ever. The autoworkers where not the first to break away from an American-based union. Other unions in telecommunications, paper, and chemical had made this move in the seventies. What gave the split of the Canadian UAW such importance was not only the union's prominence in Canada, but its past role as a leading defender of international unionism and the issues and timing surrounding the break with the Americans.

The Canadian move to independence was a statement about coming of age that contrasted with the country's own increasing economic dependence on the United States. The split was therefore also one step in the building of a Canadian working class. The significance of this step is not that Canadians are inherently superior, but that the struggle to improve workers' lives and communities can only be won if it is fought on the basis of a national project linked to a national labour movement. History isn't made in the abstract, but in specific spaces with specific cultural, economic, administrative, and political histories.

The years just before and after the split were probably the most exciting in the history of the Canadian UAW. This excitement had less to do with good times (old problems persisted and new ones arrived) than with the union remaining a place where it was still possible to fight for, and hang on to, alternative ideals. The issue the union now faced was whether, in these most difficult of times, it could maintain that twin sense of resistance and possibilities.

CAW MERGERS

UNION	MEMBERS AT DATE OF MERGE	EFFECTIVE DATE
Canadian Association of Communication and Allied Workers (CACAW)	1,200	February 17, 1995
Canadian Association of Smelter and Allied Workers (CASAW)	2,000	June 2, 1994
Canadian Brotherhood of Railway, Trasport and General Workers (CBRT&GW)	33,437	June 1, 1994
Owen Sound Glass Workers (Local 248)	300	November 22, 1993
Canadian Union of Mine, Mill and Smelter Workers	1,600	August 20, 1993
United Electrical, Radio and Machine Workers of Canada (UE)	9,000	November 30, 1992
Canadian Textile and Chemical Union (CTCU)	700	June 1, 1992
Canadian Association of Industrial Mechanical and Allied Workers (CAIMAW)	6,500	January 1, 1992
TCU-Airline Division	3,500	May 24, 1990
The Brotherhood Railway Carmen of Canada	8,000	May 29, 1990
Great Lakes Fishermen and Allied Workers Union (CSAWU)	400	March 23, 1989
Canadian Seafood and Allied Workers Union (CSAWU)	3,000	May 30, 1989
Fishermen, Food and Allied Workers Union (FFAW)	24,000	November 7, 1988
Canadian Glass Workers Union	800	November 10, 1987
Canadian Association of Passenger Agents (CAPA)	800	January 1, 1987
Canadian Air Line Employees' Association (CALEA)	4,100	July 1, 1985

gh/opeiu343

CHAPTER 9

THE MORE THINGS CHANGE, THE MORE THEY ... CHANGE AGAIN

Won't Canadian business lobby to reduce spending on social and other programs? NOT AT ALL
— Business ads during FTA election

Everybody knows the boat is leaking.
Everybody knows the captain lied....
Everybody knows the plague is coming.
Everybody knows it's moving fast.
Everybody knows ...
— Leonard Cohen

Our union is based on certain principles that we refuse to change and directions and structures that we must change to preserve and win those principles.
— CAW 1994 Convention Document

The formation of the CAW in the mid-eighties coincided with the election of Brian Mulroney and the Conservatives into office. The Tory victory symbolized the capture of the national agenda by big business in a way not seen since the early years of the depression. The Tories laid the foundation for a revolution which, ten years later, the Liberals cynically brought into full force. The social programs and gains that were fought for years ago and that were fundamental to a sense of citizenship in Canada were being diminished and demolished.

Although Canadian governments had focused primarily on fighting inflation since the mid-seventies, inflation continued to rise through the eighties. The government was planning to introduce the Goods and Services Tax (GST) in the early nineties, but this tax would directly raise prices, and result in even higher inflation if workers successfully raised their wages to compensate for the tax hike. At the same time, the freedom of corporations to relocate plants and invest money had been increased because of both international developments and domestic policy decisions. This combination of factors reinforced the government's determination to focus on restraining inflation. Concerned about competitiveness and capital outflows, but reluctant to strengthen controls over investment and finance, the government tightened the screws on the economy even further by way of higher interest rates.

This move not only destroyed jobs and denied people a chance to participate in productive work — in the name, strangely enough, of strengthening the economy — but it also set the stage for the later debt crisis. Slow growth and high unemployment resulted in lower government revenues and higher social costs. The subsequent budgetary deficit would be financed by money borrowed at higher interest rates. The growing deficit became the basis for another attack on public sector wages and social services. Taxpayers rebelled against further taxation because the unfairness of the tax system wasn't addressed and because the added revenue was going to pay interest and therefore represented no improvement in services. As a consequence, services faced the knife — and the cuts would be deep enough to change the nature of Canadian society.

During this radical restructuring of the economy, politics, mood, and nature of Canadian society, the CAW was undergoing its own internal transformation.

Mergers: Developing a New Membership Base

In the decade after the split, the CAW's membership increased by fifty per cent to almost 200,000. In contrast, membership in the UAW over this same ten-year period fell by one-third. By 1995, the number of UAW members was half of that in 1979, just before concession bargaining began.

The increase in the membership of the CAW is, however, misleading: it doesn't accurately reflect the union's experiences. It hides the losses and pain of the closures and downsizing that occurred, and it understates the even larger increases in the number of new members. As a result of the accelerated restructuring of the economy, plant closures had become common even in so-called good times. The deep recession at the end of the eighties and into the early nineties was, however, particularly destructive. Between 1985 and 1995, CAW members suffered through 250 closures, which affected about 28,000 workers.

In addition, thousands of jobs were lost through the everyday growth in productivity because of new technology, because companies were allegedly working smarter, or, as was often the case, because of a combination of the new technology, lean production, and plain old-fashioned speed-up (In fact, corporate policy had never dismissed speed-up as an option.) Roughly 10,000 to 15,000 workers, primarily in large auto and aerospace plants but also in telecommunications and the airline sector, lost jobs through so-called downsizing.

> Local 195, the amalgamated local in Windsor, has lost well over 100 plants since its charter in the thirties, and the heaviest losses occurred in the past decade. Yet in spite of the grim reality that corporations can and do carry out their threats to close workplaces, the local — to its credit and to the credit of the CAW staff involved with it — has maintained the union policy of fighting concessions.

These losses would have cut the union's size by over one-third to under 80,000. But an aggressive organizing campaign offset much of this major loss. Workers clearly wanted to join unions, and the CAW's economic restructuring had also included new plants and therefore potential members. The added resources invested in organizing resulted in the recruitment of almost 450 units representing about 43,000 new members in this ten-year period (50,000 if the government-imposed vote amongst a number of rail unions, won by the CAW, is included). This growth compensated for the

Mock cemetery and grim reaper with gravestones citing plant closures, set up at May 15 rally in Ottawa. Photograph by Brenda Stoddart.

other losses. While the above factors essentially cancelled each other out in terms of numbers, the primary surge in membership came from almost twenty mergers that added about 73,000 dues-paying members to the CAW. The total number of such members originally exceeded 100,000, but some of these groups, especially those connected to the fisheries, suffered catastrophic job losses in the early nineties.

The mergers were rooted in the history and structure of the labour movement in Canada. In the private sector, the trade union movement had generally grown up as a branch plant of the American movement. As unions broke away to form their own Canadian structures, they found that they were too small to survive on their own. A union structure and diversity that might have worked in the larger economy of the U.S. was impractical and too fragmented in Canada. The corporate aggressiveness and the tough economic times highlighted this weakness. Many unions, including some that still belonged to American international unions, therefore welcomed admission into a larger union.

Common industrial employers or sectors were only one factor involved in the restructuring of the labour movement. Sector-wide mergers had a strong logic, yet other factors turned out to be more significant: union histories, ideology, attitudes to interna-

Bridgnath Theodore working on axle line at Scarborough, GM's van plant which closed in 1993. Photograph by Gayle Hurmuses.

tional unions, government-mandated reductions in the number of unions, and bureaucratic concerns over staff and leadership positions.

Past conflicts over raids, competition over bargaining strategies, and failed attempts to cooperate left a bitter legacy between certain unions who seemed to be logical partners. A unit that had just broken away from an international union to become Canadian would not merge with another international. Even Canadian sections of internationals that wanted to merge their Canadian operations would generally be blocked until the Americans approved the merger. Ideological compatibility turned out to be an important factor not just because of the legacy of labour's own cold war, but because the trade union movement was in fact in the midst of a debate about alternative directions. Some unions were on the same wavelength in

Reservations agents at Air Canada, 1982. Courtesy of the CAW Collection.

responding to the new challenges; others were not.

The CAW was an attractive potential partner to many sectors because of its high profile, strong servicing reputation, independence from the Americans, and stance on concessions and fighting the corporate agenda. The first of the mergers, which occurred in the summer of 1985, was with the Canadian Airline and Employees Association, a small but active and progressive union representing passenger and reservation agents. The association had rejected mergers with other unions in the same sector because of past conflicts and differences. Its vote to join the Canadian UAW came just before the formal founding of the CAW. A group of workers in comparable positions at Canadian Airlines also joined the

Passenger agents were originally predominantly men, and the view was that women were not suited to the work.

— Craig Chouinard

CAW, though only after a great deal of internal resistance.

Checking the trains. Photo by CAW member George Haber.

The largest of the mergers occurred in 1994. The Canadian Brotherhood of Railway Transport and General Workers (CBRT), which began as an industrial union in the rail industry three decades before industrial unionism made its breakthrough in manufacturing, merged with the CAW. When the Canadian UAW was first being organized in the thirties, the CBRT (then the CBRE) ranked as one of the largest unions in the country. It also preceded the CAW in becoming a general union across the country, having moved from representing only railworkers to also speaking for workers in hotels and hospitals, truck drivers, garage mechanics, ferry workers, and workers on the Great Lakes. The CBRT's rail members, along with the CAW's earlier merger with the Carmen (which represented workers who maintained the interior of trains) and the government-mandated vote to streamline the number of unions in rail, left the CAW as the dominant union in rail.

Although the first bargaining round in rail under the CAW banner ended, as past rounds normally did, with back-to-work legislation, the union nevertheless showed that the mergers did create the possibility of developing new and more effective strategies. In bringing together seven of the rail unions, the CAW acted as a catalyst to replace much of the past distrust and tensions with collective confidence and discipline. Unity was possible.

Furthermore, sections of railworkers had, almost a decade ago, argued against the traditional strategy of a shut-down, which usually accomplished nothing more than bringing in the government. Now, as part of the CAW, they advocated focusing on one company in order to increase pressure on that company as work was shifted to its competition (the strategy developed in auto). And, by leaving some rail lines running rather than shutting down the entire national system, this tactic would weaken the rationale for government intervention. The union also experimented with very modest job actions — and even rumours of actions — to see if they chased business to other companies.

> The *Globe and Mail*, 29 August 1987:
>
> *The next time we'll be looking at different things, like having a strike on only one railway and letting the other operate, or a work-to-rule.*
>
> — Gary Fane, Brotherhood of Airline and Railway Clerks
>
> *A railway strike does not have to be an all-or-nothing proposition. If we do battle, it will not be to be defeated, or have someone rescue you. We have to put maximum pressure on the railways and minimum pressure on the public.*
>
> — Abe Rosner, Council of Railway Shopcraft Unions

The streamlining of the economy, just like the streamlining of auto production, clearly left the companies extremely vulnerable to creative tactics. The issue that remained was to convince the rail unions outside the CAW that, from a unified base, such strategies were worthwhile.

Other large mergers brought in groups with a left-nationalist ideology. Some, such as the United Electrical Workers and Mine Mill, which had been expelled from the CLC during labour's cold war but survived, continued to play a significant role on their own. UE was eventually accepted back in; Mine Mill was not. Others had been part of a separate labour central, the CCU (Confederation of Canadian Unions), which was established in the late sixties to fight the international unions and work towards building democratic and independent Canadian unions. In spite of their relatively small size, these unions had led a number of important strikes in the West and in Ontario and were able to place crucial nationalist issues on the agenda. However, the formation of the CAW and external economic pressures put into question the need for, and ongoing viability of, remaining isolated from the rest of the labour movement. A number of the CCU unions, the largest of which was the Canadian Association of Industrial, Mechanical, and Allied Workers (CAIMAW), eventually joined the CAW and brought with them a strong western base with members in industrial plants, in mines, and in the private service sector (particularly hotels and restaurants).

In the early debates about how aggressive the CAW should be in pursuing mergers, Buzz Hargrove, then one of White's Assistants, argued that the potential growth in the union's existing sectors was low, while the risk of decline was high. In addition to continuing to organize in these traditional sectors, the union must therefore also be diversified. Furthermore, there was some responsibility on the part of the union to welcome any groups it could help. As long as the viability of the CAW wasn't being endangered, such an expansion of the union was, he argued, one vital aspect of social unionism. The diversification would give the union a national base of like-minded groups, allowing it to continue to play a leading role in determining the ideology and direction of the Canadian labour movement.

Mergers with airline groups and the broadly diversified CBRT raised the total number of women in the union to over 40,000. This reinforced the demand for leadership schools for women, and strengthened the base for more effective women's networks across the country. The rail mergers almost doubled the number of skilled trades in the union to over 35,000, strengthening their potential lobbying effectiveness nationally and provincially. The merger with the Canadian Textile and Chemical Union led to the innovative establishment of a storefront office in downtown Toronto, allowing the union to work with, and build ties to, the neighbouring immigrant communities.

The most controversial of the mergers involved the Fishermen, Food, and Allied Workers (FFAW) of Newfoundland. The FFAW was "more than just a union." It was a powerful presence in Newfoundland's communities and in the politics of the province. In the early seventies, the leaders had,

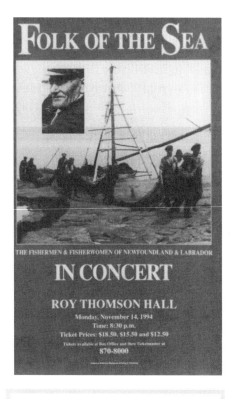

FFAW brings songs and music of
Newfoundland to Toronto,
November 14, 1994.

Fisherman on the Great Lakes
(Marine division, Local 444).
Courtesy of the CAW collection.

remarkably, forged a union that united workers in diverse circumstances: independent fishermen who owned their own boats, trawler workers on company boats who shared in the catch, and fish plant workers on shore. After a series of militant strikes, the group merged with the Packinghouse Workers, an industrial union. A subsequent merger with the Retail Workers resulted in the creation of a new organization, the United Food and Commercial Workers (UFCW).

When the Newfoundland workers realized that their union neither reflected their values nor provided the services they needed and that these problems couldn't be solved through internal democratic procedures, they decided to split from the UFCW. But would the UFCW accept the separation peacefully or try to destroy them? The FFAW leadership concluded that leaving the UFCW necessitated simultaneously joining another union. The CAW was the obvious choice because of its principles and because few unions would risk the consequent hostility of the internationals.

> *This is not a legal battle, it's a political struggle. The workers want a union that represents a value system, and if some people have differences with that, they can go to hell.*
>
> — Richard Cashin, FFAW, responding at CAW Council to UFCW raiding charges

White and the CAW leadership understood the possible implications of allowing the Newfoundland workers to join the union: a bitter and costly fight with the UFCW, attacks from the international unions that saw this move as opening the door for other groups considering going Canadian, and the financial costs of taking on a union with low dues and high costs. From the perspective of direct gains for the CAW, the merger offered little. Nevertheless, the NEB and the union voted in favour of merging. Workers were not the property of any union. If committed unionists and determined workers wanted to join a different organization, and they could not realistically do so because there was no way to express and carry out a democratic decision, then the CAW had a responsibility to support them.

The legal and organizational battles with the UFCW cost the CAW a very substantial sum of money. The merger shook up the labour movement and seemed to put the issue of workers' democratic rights inside their unions on the agenda. However, the lack of consensus within labour assured that this issue of internal union democracy was never satisfactorily resolved.

From Non-American to Canadian

With their breakaway, the Canadians were no longer part of an American union. It was not the split, however, that made the union truly Canadian. It was the mergers, which nationalized the union by involving all regions of the country and no longer limiting unionization to central Canada. The mergers transformed the union into a microcosm of the entire Canadian economy, not just of the heavy manufacturing sector.

The CAW was now building cars, planes, trains, buses, subway cars, and the accompanying components. It was digging salt, nickel, and coal out of the ground, refining aluminum, and pulling fish out of the sea. Members of the CAW were shipping resources by rail and truck, transporting people by plane, truck, and bus. They were manufacturing telecommunications equipment and servicing the equipment to facilitate national and international communication. They worked in hotels and casinos, served food in restaurants, and cared for patients in nursing homes.

The crucial change wasn't just the diversification of the union into a number of sectors and regions, but its central role in so many parts of the economy across the country. The CAW had become the largest union in a wide range of manufacturing sectors, the dominant union in transportation services and the fisheries, and an increasingly important union in mining and the hospitality sector.

In 1984, ninety per cent of the CAW membership was contained in a few centres in southern Ontario and in the Montreal area. Those Ontario centres were Windsor, St. Catharines, London-Woodstock, Chatham, Cambridge-Kitchener-Brantford, and the Toronto-Oshawa-Oakville-Brampton area. With the mergers, the CAW became the largest private sector union not just in Ontario, but also in Newfoundland, Nova Scotia, New Brunswick, and Prince Edward Island, and had a major presence in Quebec, British Columbia, Alberta, and Manitoba.

Although the mergers certainly added new and difficult challenges, they were also a source of strength and vitality. The mergers brought unions with their own rich histories, activists with talent and experience, and the energy of new members. In addition, they encouraged the development of a broader working class consciousness on the part of the past and future CAW members. CAW activists, having heard a report on the fisheries at the council, read the newspaper differently and paid more attention to what was happening to working people in Newfoundland. Students in the PEL program, listening to a passenger agent explain the impact of lean production on her work, realized that work reorganization was in fact part of something bigger and that service workers were really workers.

Particularly important was the contribution of the mergers to the momentum of the union. A union characterized by growth is more likely to feel confident about the possibilities of moving ahead. The 1993 Big Three negotiations were an example of the influence of that general mood on a union. The union entered that round of bargaining at a time when the labour movement felt weak and uncertain and wage increases in Canada were at the lowest levels ever recorded. This set of negotiations was the CAW's first Big Three bar-

gaining round since both top officers of the union had left (White to the CLC, Nickerson to active retirement). Yet the union and its new leader, Buzz Hargrove, went in demanding and expecting to win not just COLA, but additional wage increases, more paid time off, large pension hikes including increases for the 23,000 Big Three workers in retirement,

Larry Bauer, Local 444 president and head of Chrysler bargaining team during 1993 negotiations. When he died suddenly of a heart attack in May 1994, the Windsor Star *honoured him in an editorial that said: "His heart couldn't keep up with his soul."* Courtesy of the CAW Local 444 collection.

improvements to income security, and significant gains on social issues.

It was a brash, but ultimately successful position for Hargrove and the bargaining committees to take. That success stemmed from many factors, but the readiness of the workers to fight for their issues was the most important. One factor that should not be ignored, however, is that without the momentum of the mergers and with a falling membership, the leadership and membership might have been defensive, cautious, and relieved to take a

241

Although workers are now producing more than ever, real wages (wages after adjustment for inflation) have grown more slowly than they did in the thirties and at a small fraction of the growth in other decades.

Real Wages:	Growth per Decade
1920s:	12.1%
1930s:	10.3%
1940s:	34.4%
1950s:	42.5%
1960s:	36.8%
AVG, above:	27.2%
1970s:	8.5%
1980s:	2.0%

(The trend of the 1990s is running at or below the 1980s.)

Source: *Perspectives on Labour and Income*, Statistics Canada, Vol. 5, No. 2.

safer and less ambitious road.

Although there were many benefits, the changes inside and outside the union necessarily raised new problems or highlighted old ones. They raised interrelated issues about union finances, the administration of an increasingly complex organization, and the development of a common identity to keep the union together.

The CAW always had certain crucial financial and administrative advantages. Its members were generally concentrated in a narrow region of the country, in a few highly unionized industries, in larger plants, with full-time positions, and with relatively high wages. This concentration in itself provided the national union with a strong revenue base and relatively low operating costs.

Union policy reinforced these strengths by negotiating, wherever possible, full-time elected company-paid reps in the larger units, and by encouraging smaller units to amalgamate into larger locals. The union's commitment to leadership training supported the development of this local activist base of stewards and full-time officials. Locals in Canada were large, even relative to the United States: in the mid-eighties, the average CAW local had about fifty per cent more members than the average UAW local.

That local structure strengthened the democracy, effectiveness, and finances of the union. The existence of strong and independent locals reinforced the accountability of the national office. It also meant that council and executive board discussions and debates weren't just abstract posturing but reflected a serious local mandate. If locals weren't in favour, decisions couldn't be carried out. If they were, policy could lead directly to action.

The ability of the locals to manage their own affairs meant that a qualified pool of potential staff and leaders was more readily developed, and that the ratio of staff to members was low compared to other unions.

These factors allowed a relatively small but well-qualified staff to serve the members. Although the staff was highly paid relative to other unions, this cost was offset by the higher dues (since the general members were also relatively higher paid), and the need for a smaller staff. The overall financial structure built on this base was sound.

The original principle of staff salaries was that they match the weekly pay of a Big Three skilled worker with eight hours overtime per week (forty-eight hours for fifty-two hours of pay).

By the eighties, however, the economic restructuring had begun to undermine some of these advantages. There was a rash of plant closings. Plants were moved to rural areas and new plants were set up in non-union areas. And as a matter of corporate policy, the new plants that replaced old plants were generally smaller. As a result, organizing was both more essential and more expensive. Furthermore, the ongoing cost of serving new, inexperienced, and often smaller units was high while their dues — given the pressure to keep wages low in this period and the difficulty in raising them quickly to a standard pay level — were relatively low. And although the union had always spent substantial amounts on broader political activities, the increasing importance of nonbargaining issues like free trade in the lives of its members led to increasing expenditures on political campaigns.

In each of the five years ending in 1991, the union reported a deficit in its general funds. This period included high expenses for organizing and the costly merger with the FFAW, but the majority of mergers actually came later. (Two-thirds of the workers who joined the CAW by way of mergers came after 1991.) The total deficit over the period exceeded $27 million. The subsequent mergers added to these cost pressures, since it became more expensive to serve a membership base that was increasingly spread across the country and in a wide range of sectors.

The safety valve for the union in this period was the strength of its strike fund. That fund was structured to subsidize an eight-week strike at its largest unit, GM. But the changes in GM's operations had left such a standard irrelevant; only a complete war with GM could lead to that long a strike, and in such a war, the size of the strike fund would not be decisive. The union was therefore able to draw on the strike fund to cover its deficits over this period, without running out of monies for strike pay.

Nevertheless, depleting the strike fund was not a long-term solution. The union leadership at the Big Three was justifiably anxious that the strike fund not be drained. The existence of a large strike fund was still important to the membership and as a message to the companies. The CAW leadership therefore tested the council on an increase in the dues structure, from the current two hours per month to 2.5 hours per month. The mood was not receptive. The economy was in a tailspin, and workers' wages were stagnant. More significant, resistance was building against new taxation (the GST had just been introduced), and an increase in the dues check-off sounded uncomfortably like a new tax.

Between the council meeting and the 1991 convention, the union distributed more information on the changing times and the needs of the union, and lobbied activists. At the convention, members overwhelmingly approved an increase of twenty minutes (rather than the original half hour) in the dues structure. Although there was some nervousness about a backlash in the workplace once this increase hit the paycheques, none occurred. Explanatory pamphlets were distributed to all the locals, and the local leadership explained the necessity of the increase. The change in dues was soon old news.

The new dues structure allowed the union to move closer towards balancing its budget. But the initial costs of bringing in other new groups of workers, full-scale unions in their own right, were high. There were adjustment costs in dealing with their staff, nationwide educational campaigns to explain the structures and processes of the union, and the internal politics and subsequent delay in moving small units towards amalgamation into more viable locals. In offsetting these costs, the union could not impose another dues increase. The solution lay in more careful and systematic management of the operations of the increasingly complex union.

This issue of *management* was, however, not just a financial question: it raised difficult questions about the structure and nature of the union: To what extent can a union decentralize to allow for local initiative and provide services, while resisting regionalism and the loss of a coherent national direction? How can a union maintain the strength to respond to its powerful enemies, but also allow for the membership input and control that is even more fundamental to mobilizing for struggles? How can the organization introduce new rules and more formal structures while avoiding any hint of bureaucratization? How do leaders whose strength and credibility have always stemmed from their focus on direct bargaining even think of standing back and becoming managers? How does that leadership stay in contact with the larger and more dispersed staff and maintain staff morale?

Militant Loyalty

The most important internal issue the CAW faced, and which encompassed the management issue, was recreating the magnetic force that brought and kept the union together; the CAW had to create what Walter Reuther long ago called militant loyalty to the union and its cause. Amongst the challenges and potential problems of this issue were changes in the composition of the workforce, the relationship to the rest of the labour movement, and the crisis in left politics.

Within major auto companies, the limited expansions over this period had aged the workforce. In the mid-seventies, the average Big Three worker was in his or her early thirties; by the end of the eighties this worker was approaching the mid-forties. This aging was particularly evident amongst staff and activists, and it raised the question of the ability of the union to renew itself through the future commitment and energy of young people. In the late nineties, when those who entered the auto plants during the boom years of the mid-sixties will look to retirement, the issue will

> ... [the union] is still in the process of formation. It is a young union, not yet set organizationally or administratively, that must keep itself flexible and on its toes to meet constantly new and changing problems. We need organization and adaptation, rather than routine administration and regimentation.
>
> — Walter Reuther, July, 1937

become the union's integration of their replacements. Will the new generation of workers, with generally higher education levels and having grown up in relatively conservative times, be alienated from the union or will they lead a new rebellion against corporate Canada?

The changing face of the union raised the question of integrating groups of workers with different experiences and union cultures into one organization. Over and above the mergers, economic restructuring was reducing the traditional white-male base of the union, while new hires and newly organized units added greater numbers of women, recent immigrants, and people of colour. This diversification demanded increased sensitivity to ensure that the union truly represented all members and their needs. Developing leadership from these groups was especially crucial. This was not just as a matter of equal opportunity, but a matter of ensuring that the daily life of all CAW activists includes interaction with members from all parts of the union. And the union would benefit from developing and using all the potential and talent that existed in the workforce.

The union addressed these issues in bargaining, in educationals, through films, and in its structures. Though difficult, the issues seemed manageable. A growing constituency was demanding changes and the leadership was committed to responding. The union had to decide how fast changes could be made, whether the resources applied were reasonable or needed to be increased, and what the best approach might be. Harder to manage, and therefore more dangerous, was the possibility of the union being overwhelmed by changes outside the union. Such changes had infected and weakened other unions and other labour movements.

Just as new circumstances and the issue of direction had caused the split from the international UAW, similar debates about direction now caused tensions within the Canadian labour movement. The isolation of the CAW amongst the private sector unions was primarily caused by the threat the CAW's successes posed to the existence of international unionism in Canada. But it was also related to the nature of unionism, as some unions began to accept the need for a less adversarial approach.

The CAW certainly made compromises; it didn't have the power to avoid them. As long as American society remained on the right, the achievements of Canada and Canadian labour would remain limited. In the midst of the euphoria after the split from the Americans, Phil Bennett, the head of the GM Master Bargaining Committee and a strong supporter of the breakaway, asked the sobering question: "How long can we continue to go in a different direction than the Americans?"

The Canadians had put this nagging question aside to form the CAW. They couldn't ignore it, but neither could they wait for American labour to revive itself. They could only continue their own struggle, insisting that unions remain independent working class organizations and arguing that, with corporations more aggressive than ever before, the last thing unions should adopt is the illusion of false partnerships. From 1975 to 1988, the Canadian labour movement faced this danger, and it survived relatively well compared to other labour movements. The CAW had even emerged stronger. But in the subsequent years, an effective response to this threat became much more difficult.

In the earlier period, the issues and responses were much clearer. The union was confronted with a steady series of chal-

Percentage of Workforce Unionized in Major Countries, 1975–88

	1975	1988	CHANGE
Canada	34%	35%	+ 1%
Germany	37%	34%	- 3%
U.S.	23%	16%	- 6%
U.K.	48%	42%	- 6%
Japan	34%	27%	- 7%
Italy	47%	40%	- 7%
France	23%	12%	- 11%

Source: Bamber and Lansbury, *International and Comparative Industrial Relations*

lenges to traditional unionism and saying "NO!" was an effective solution: NO to wage controls in the mid-seventies; NO to concessions at the end of the seventies; NO to the opening of agreements in the early eighties; NO to the new direction of the American leadership; and NO to free trade with the United States. Such a response was not easy. It took courage because it resulted in difficult changes to long-standing structures and attitudes within the union. But it provided the union and workers with a ready response, if not complete answers.

The union was also much more homogeneous at that time. In recent years, it has become more diversified, and it is still in the process of accommodating the internal changes. Moreover, the Canadian labour movement itself was more unified in the earlier period. There was still a general consensus within labour that concession bargaining and false partnerships damaged, rather than helped, working people. The fights of the autoworkers were the fights of the labour movement, even if there were tensions over jurisdiction and over which unions were the informal leaders of the Canadian labour movement.

Before, the union had positioned itself as the underdog challenging American multinationals and the American UAW to protect past gains and Canadian sovereignty. Now, as globalization seemed to push nationalism aside, and with the CAW being the largest private sector union in the coun try, that nationalist underdog role had ebbed.

The passage of time became the most crucial factor. In the early seventies, members of the corporate and political élite were beginning their attempt to change people's economic and social expectations, and people resisted. But over time, those expectations did change. The strategy of outright refusal, effective for a period of time, was becoming increasingly difficult to sustain. Some unions acceded to "the end of adversarialism," prompting the media to challenge the CAW on why it too wasn't changing.

The change in the national mood inevitably also affected many CAW members. Many workers, tired of banging their heads against corporate/government walls gave up on social change and turned inward. ("I'll work overtime to make up for the tuition increases for my kids"; "reduce my taxes, and I'll take care of my own pensions.") Some exhausted activists found their confidence wavering and cynicism invading their thoughts. When hope falters, the pressures of daily life increase the incidence of burn-out, and a paralyzing demoralization threatens to take over. After swimming so long against the tide, the swimmer gets tired.

All of this seemed to be directly related to the union experiencing, in 1994, its first staff strike. Regardless of the immediate events, personalities, and bargaining issues that led to the strike, the changes in the organization and in society were having an impact on the staff's view of itself. The move to independence had been accompanied by the formation of an elected executive board, and that necessarily shifted some of the effective power in the union away from the staff and towards the board. The sheer size and complexity of the organization limited past informal contacts; the staff had, for example, doubled since the split. In addition, some staff were starting to suffer from the same let-down that other activists faced: exhaustion from years of struggles over increasingly limited gains; the perception that everything — their life, their work, their assumptions — had become more complicated; an uncomfortable uncertainty about where the labour movement and their own union were heading; and a questioning of whether things would or could get better.

The election of the Ontario NDP in September, 1990, seemed to be the tonic that the labour movement so desperately needed. The significance of the NDP victory — over and above the fact that it had never before happened in the province — was that Ontario is the industrial heartland of Canada, with an economy equal in size to those of major countries such as Sweden. Starting the nineties with a victory symbolized a rejection of the corporate agenda that had dominated the eighties. For workers, it meant that, after years of struggling against the corporations, governments, and the institutions of the state, they might actually have some friends in high places to support their struggles and needs.

The Crisis in Social Democracy

Soon, however, many workers were wondering which groups in society had won the election and which had lost. Long-standing promises such as public auto insurance were not only postponed but discarded and discredited. The deficit in Ontario was a problem that couldn't be wished away, but rather than changing how deficits, and therefore politics, were discussed in Canada, the NDP began, as journalist Tom Walkom put it, "talking Tory." The NDP used the deficit to pressure its allies into line, rather than to clarify and expose the underlying democratic questions: Why do financial institutions have so much power? How can we democratize economic power so that bankers are not determining social policy? If the crisis is so dangerous, why aren't we discussing the responsibility of the rich in contributing to solutions?

As part of its deficit response, the NDP introduced the cynically misnamed "social contract," which took away the most fundamental union right — the right to bargain — from public sector workers. That single policy reinforced the denigration of public sector workers, legitimized future attacks on unions, added to divisions within labour, and effectively severed the NDP's ties with its most important potential base.

Some workers rejected the NDP for the "wrong" reasons. The NDP's introduction of some long-sought progressive changes like employment equity no doubt resulted in a backlash amongst many working people. But that backlash was rooted in the fact that these issues were not placed in the broader context of working class struggles. The party's overall language and direction did not clearly identify it as fighting on behalf of working people. And its backtracking had disarmed the party's past supporters in the workplaces; they no longer played a role in explaining the purpose of positive changes and defending the party against unfair criticism. Even amongst those who would still vote for the party given the lack of choices, most would do so without the enthusiasm that is so critical to the success of parties who don't have the luxury of big money behind them.

The gains the NDP government had made — and it had taken a number of important steps, including legislation reducing the barriers to union representation, and the barriers facing women and visible minorities in the labour market — were undermined. In other provinces, NDP governments appeared to be more durable, but only where the absence of a centrist Liberal party allowed the NDP itself to fill that role.

As the NDP developed its strategy, one perspective that it lacked was the "old" socialist idea of a party that defined its role as moulding the working class into an effective political force. That perspective emphasized developing the understanding of working people and building vehicles for collective intervention in all aspects of their lives. It aimed at overcoming fragmentation of the working class by encouraging their collective confidence in building a better world. But at this crucial time in history, with the right vulnerable in terms of its inability to deliver and with working people desperate for leadership, social democracy had no answers, and the NDP wore that failure. The tragic impact of the Ontario NDP government's reign was, unfortunately, to further destroy hope and to demoralize, divide, and ultimately demobilize rather than activate working people.

That the NDP had limited answers was not simply an Ontarian or Canadian matter; it was part of a more general, international crisis in social democracy. As corporate power increased, social democratic parties followed the swing to the right, hoping that moderation might increase their chances of election. However, even if the socialist ideal of a planned and democratic economy was forgotten, and even if social democrats simply wanted to maintain the welfare state that capitalism itself had earlier accepted, such goals could no longer be maintained in a nonradical way. Globalization and international finance would undermine even modest goals if the power of capital was not addressed. As John Crotty summarized it in an essay in *Creating a New World Economy*:

> The bottom line is this: Capital mobility gives the wealthy classes around the globe veto power over the economic policies and priorities of every nation. No progressive, democratically controlled system of economic regulation can function effectively if it does not break that veto power through the imposition of capital controls.

Although some CAW activists did work for the NDP in the 1995 Ontario election and although, as individuals, many decided they had no alternative but to cast their ballots for the NDP, the union as an institution

Workers take over the Caterpillar plant after company announces take-over and refuses to negotiate, April 1991. Courtesy of the CAW collection.

could not endorse the party's role in government by endorsing them in the election. The CAW would, of course, participate in the process to revive the NDP, but it was clear that the immediate support and solutions the union needed would not come from the party.

The union would have to draw on its own strengths. It would have to reach into the historical legacy and culture of struggle that had led working people to build the UAW and then the CAW. It would have to rely on: the momentum from the split and the new legacies the merged sections brought to the union; the conscious leadership decision to keep expectations high and demands aggressive; and the structures that provided forums for ongoing collective discussions and development of responses. Those structures included the Canadian and Quebec Councils, the strong locals and the locally rooted executive board, the extended education and training for activists, and a tightly knit staff.

The mergers truly transformed the CAW. For every person who was a member a short ten years ago when the union was formed, there were two current members who didn't directly experience the split. The number of members outside of auto had tripled. Members who worked in auto plants used to outnumber others by almost three to one; now, they were a minority, though they still comprised by far the largest and most influential single group in the CAW. Previously, less than ten per cent of the union members were outside of Ontario; now, well over one-third came from outside that province. Of the original twelve-person executive board elected after the split (including the union's top three full-time officers) none remained.

When the union celebrated its tenth year, it was therefore remarkably different from the organization that nervously left the UAW. While the union looked for quiet periods to deal with its internal changes, dangerous external changes were accelerating. The mid- to late eighties, the period just after the formation of the CAW, when Canadian labour led the challenge to corporate Canada's FTA, once seemed like the peak of labour's mobilization. But events since then warned of the steep decline on the other side of that perilous peak. The union would, in confronting these most threatening times, have to creatively rethink what a new unionism, which preserved the basic insights of the old, might look like.

CAW at CLC demonstration for jobs, Ottawa, May 15, 1993. The bottom photo shows an aerial view of the demonstration. Courtesy of the CAW collection.

CHAPTER 10

BUILDING IS EVERYTHING

*A strike is a peculiar time in a working person's life ...
workers rarely confide in one another about what's
really going on with them ... But walking the picket line
side by side, having coffee together in the trailer, freed of
the necessity of chasing a production piece on the
assembly line all day, they form friendships and become
philosophers.*
— Bob White

*We are building a labour movement not to patch up the
old world so you starve less often and less severely; we
are building the kind of labour movement that will
remake the world ...*
— Walter Reuther

... we've lost ...
No. We just haven't won yet.
— Rick Salutin

THE CAW: BIRTH AND TRANSFORMATION OF A UNION

As the CAW approached the end of its first decade as an independent union, it faced the most threatening period since its birth as part of the UAW in the thirties. The steady increase in corporate power had intensified pressures on workers in the workplace and, by way of governments, dismantled progress made over more than half a century. Now the establishment was beckoning workers and unions to accept that there was no alternative and that it was time to give up.

The reality of the "no alternative" argument is, however, that workers have no alternative but to resist and fight. Acceptance of the right-wing arguments simply invites further demands to give up more. Acceptance would also mean that workers' organizations would quickly wither. The choice, as American socialist Eugene Debs once said, is agitation or stagnation. It's this latter concern, of letting the union stagnate and therefore losing it as a vehicle for resistance and change, that is the most threatening. As a consequence, the trade union issue of the times is to consider struggles from the perspective of their impact on building both the union and the capacity of workers for future struggles. Building is everything.

Building Blocks

In the spring of 1994, the CAW established a task force to determine the state of the membership and to obtain its input into the direction of the union. The results were presented to the fall constitutional convention, along with a discussion paper which asked if the union was "just getting bigger and more diverse" or whether there was "a logic to where [it was] heading — a logic that could be built on."

Interest in the task force was extremely high. People appreciated the executive board coming into their communities to listen, and they did not hesitate to make strong criticisms or put forth ideas. Criticisms generally had a positive spirit ("this is my union, I'm proud of it, but some things need changing"). An overriding issue, in the task force meetings and at union gatherings, was that the mergers and diversification seemed to be moving the union away from the traditional model of industrial unionism. Was this direction good or bad? Did this shift happen by design or accident? Should it be halted, accelerated, or modified?

The rapid and complex change, along with the danger of creeping demoralization, gave an urgency to such questions: activists and members needed a clear sense of direction to keep going. But no one — in Canada or elsewhere — had complete answers to the problems working people were now facing. The best that could be said was that some of the necessary building blocks of any effective response were being assembled, and others had been placed on the agenda of the executive board and at other union forums. The

The CAW task force consisted of two teams that travelled to CAW communities to hear what activists/members had to say. Each team consisted of three NEB members and a rank-and-file member. Senior board members Cheryl Kryzaniwsky (Local 2213, airlines) and Frank McAnally (Local 200, Ford Windsor) each headed up one of the teams. The presentations took any form people were comfortable with, and even the local preparations for the meetings were very creative (e.g., a mini-conference to decide the focus of any presentation; a lottery amongst the membership so the task force wouldn't just get expected activists). The task force members insisted on not just presenting the report to the president, but making recommendations based on what they had heard. The response of the union to every recommendation would be reported and updated at future meetings of the CAW Council.

development of appropriate structures, policies, directions, and ideas required experimentation, widespread input, and involvement from all levels of the union as it struggled for change. That difficult process of rediscovery constitutes no less than working people "making history."

As the CAW addressed its future, the following issues were critical.

Back to the Workplace

When industrial unionism first emerged, its base was in the workplace. The union would be built in the workplace, and it would live or die there. Once unionism was established, companies paid to retain their authority at the point of production. The companies consented (under pressure, of course) to wage and benefit increases in exchange for limiting workers' access to management rights. But increased international competition and squeezed profit margins pushed the companies to regain even the limited rights they had earlier surrendered. With unions weakened by high unemployment and job insecurity, the companies were even more aggressive. This aggression often

McDonnell-Douglas worker descending into wing. Courtesy of Jim Littleton.

included a corporate smile and invitations to a new partnership. But the less subtle threat of denying new investment and taking away jobs was always there.

The CAW's response was not to reject all workplace changes but to reject the notion of partnership and the false equality it implied. Workplace change required negotiation between two groups — management and labour — that had some overlapping interests but also clear conflicts. The first priority of the union was therefore to put forth an independent workers' agenda on workplace change to provide the focus for mobilization and bargaining, and it was essential that this agenda was backed up with adequate resources.

In 1993, the union created a department for work organization, a structure unique amongst unions on this continent. The department produced educational programs, pamphlets, and films on the nature of the changes the companies were introducing, and possible worker responses. It developed a cadre of rank-and-file trainers who could lead local discussions and educationals. In addition, the department conducted research on the impact of the current changes and advised local leadership in negotiating workplace change with manage-ment. And it linked that research to broader issues of health and safety, the ergonomics of workplace design, work schedules and hours, and training programs geared to developing the capacities and needs of workers.

The successes of the union were uneven and in many ways limited, but the fact that the union was confronting the issue was significant. It left workers with a

At CAMI, a GM-Suzuki joint venture, the union had direct experience with the Japanese production system. The CAMI workers, in their first complete bargaining round, went on strike for parity with GM and to change certain aspects of how production was organized. That strike, the first in any major Japanese-style plant, was rooted first and foremost in the reactions of the workers at CAMI. But it also reflected the broader CAW context in which the CAMI workers and leadership lived. That environment, passed on through staff, educationals, policies, and conferences, expressed an ideology, demands, and culture that supported challenging the "new" systems of work organization.

clearer understanding of management strategies and greater confidence in fighting to limit the attack on their working conditions. And the union emerged stronger for it.

Time to Control Our Time

The organization of work includes control over the organization of time. In its early days, the union created its base workplace by workplace. However, control over work-time was the issue that historically united workers *across* those workplaces and was therefore so crucial to making it into a movement.

Although current work-time concerns range from part-time workers demanding more time to other workers wanting more flexible schedules to deal with family responsibilities, the primary issue in the earlier days of the labour movement was how much of the workday — and therefore their lives — the workers surrendered to the bosses. Twelve-hour days left little time for relaxation and family or little energy for workers to develop themselves by reading and learning or to engage in politics. For this reason, Karl Marx supported the ten-hour day as a crucial reform in the mid-1800s. May Day, celebrated internationally as labour's day (though only in isolated communi-ties in North America) emerged out of the struggle at the end of the last century for reduced work-time. And the nine-hour movement in Canada, led by the skilled trades, was a historic period in the development of the Canadian working class because of its role in uniting workers across communities and regions.

When the UAW was formed, the dream of reduced work-time was sufficiently important to be included in its first constitution. In the first agreements, negotiated lay-off procedures included, as a measure of solidarity, the sharing of existing work before lay-offs occurred. At GM, there was even a ban on overtime if any probationary workers were still on lay-off. The war brought steady overtime, but once the war was winding down, the Canadian UAW lobbied for standardizing the forty-hour week and ending overtime in order to create job openings for returning veterans. By itself, this solidarity with unemployed workers implied a significant decrease in take-home pay at a time when prices were expected to rise rapidly. The union's solution was to mobilize workers for a major wage offensive to make up for the controls on wages during the war.

In the postwar period, autoworkers made major gains in holidays and vacation time. But overtime returned. From the late fifties through the seventies, there were repeated wildcats over compulsory overtime. The Canadian UAW lobbied for at least voluntary overtime ("Ask me. Don't tell me"), and the union unsuccessfully extended the long 1970 GM strike simply to fight for what workers allegedly won in the forties and fifties: the right to work no longer than forty hours per week.

By the eighties, however, the growing economic insecurity and the increased level of dependence on overtime income virtually eliminated overtime as a rank-and-file issue in the Big Three auto plants. Even the in-plant representatives, historically the leaders in fighting compulsory overtime, were neutralized — in part because many reps were themselves dependent on overtime pay. The Big Three contracts stipulated that, as long as even a few workers in any department worked overtime and therefore needed representation, their rep received credit for overtime. Many stewards were therefore getting credit for at least twice the amount of overtime of an average worker.

At the same time, the companies favoured overtime because it gave them more flexibility and because it allowed them to hire fewer workers and therefore save on benefit costs. As governments cut back on social programs such as unemployment insurance and coverage for health and drug plans, the union ensured that the negotiated plans compensated for the differences.

These rapidly rising benefit costs reinforced the companies' determination to maintain overtime rather than increase the work-force and therefore add more benefits to their costs.

The danger of sustained overtime is that it is a conservatizing force. Overtime becomes an individual solution for a social problem. Confronted with cutbacks in education or future public pensions, and cynical about politics, workers don't join the fight against the erosion of these past commitments or consider direct action, such as taking over government offices in protest. Instead, they turn to overtime. And solidarity is replaced by resentment at the fact that they must pay taxes to support others who aren't "willing" to work as hard as they do. When autoworkers protect themselves in these ways, they isolate themselves.

In Oshawa, 15,000 people lined up for applications in response to a rumour *of job openings at GM. Job openings were few, and decent union jobs even fewer, but this didn't prevent the alleged unwillingness of people to work from becoming a major issue in the 1995 Ontario election.* Courtesy of the Toronto Star.

When the private solutions they seek eventually fail, it may be too late to rebuild links with others and fight for alternatives that might succeed.

A calculation made by CAW research concluded that if each hour of overtime worked had to be offset by an hour of time off, and if legislated standards provided each worker with the right to one paid week of education/training, roughly half of a million full-time job openings would be created. Whether or not the actual number is lower, the potential for job opportunities through the redistribution of work-time is great.

In the 1993 bargaining round, with Chrysler considering a third shift in the Windsor mini-van plant and wanting to switch to ten-hour days to implement it, the union insisted that workers share in the benefits of the greater utilization of equipment through jobs and more paid time off. The outcome was a breakthrough in the eight-hour day; the new schedules would include eight hours pay for 7.5 hours of work. Although overtime would still occur on weekends, the new schedules implied some decrease in overtime. This decrease raised resistance, especially from the skilled trades. But to its credit, the local leadership went ahead with the change, and though some criticism persists, it is now generally accepted. The new shift, the shorter day, and an additional compulsory vacation week created 1,300 new job openings in the Windsor community. At Ford, the negotiating committee added the principle of all vacation time being compulsory. Some workers had become accustomed to working through their vacations and therefore doubling their pay for those periods.

In spite of such moves, popular support for fighting overtime in the auto majors does not presently exist. The first step may be to fight for voluntary overtime, which the companies will fiercely resist, given the need for a minimum workforce to schedule overtime shifts. Another possibility is that, having become accommodated to the longer hours, Big Three workers will refocus on improving the working conditions they face for that extended time. Or perhaps, the leadership role in the struggle over hours of work will shift to other sections of the union.

Workers at Griffin Canada went on strike yesterday in a dispute based partly on an issue [overtime] that caused a high profile battle in the 70's.

— *Winnipeg Free Press*, 2 April 1995
Griffin workers won the right to voluntary overtime when the company schedules full workshifts on the weekend.

Inherent to the issue of hours of work and overtime is the potential for both weakening and, as the past has shown, rejuvenating the union and the labour movement.

From Sectoral Bargaining to Jobs

Industrial unionism was based on the workplace, but its bargaining strategy focused on a sectoral approach. The emphasis was on preventing workers in one workplace from competing with and undercutting workers in another. Such sectorwide bargaining over wages and benefits remains a crucial underpinning of union strategy, but workers are becoming increasingly concerned not only with the price of their labour but with job security.

The problem is that unions can't directly provide jobs. (One important exception is the ability of unions to create job openings through the reduction of each individual's work-time.) Moreover, a focus on job creation usually gets translated into the need to strengthen the companies so they will retain or expand jobs. This strategy is often only a stone's throw away from weakening the workers and introducing concession bargaining.

At its 1994 convention, the CAW responded to this strategy by arguing that any overall job strategy would have to be sectoral rather than company based. And it suggested the policy question: what institutions and regulations will ensure that Canada strengthens its productive capacity in a particular sector? For example, in auto assembly, the union fought for strengthening content legislation; in aerospace, the union argued that the government should use its purchasing power as a buyer of planes or its direct ownership to guarantee an integrated industry; and in rail, the essential factor was a national transportation policy. In other sectors, the focus might be coordinated training: in auto parts, an industrywide training program is underway. In certain communities, the key might be research centres grouping selected firms to develop products that would replace imports while keeping the expertise in the community. Or it might be conversion centres that shift the equipment and skills in facilities that are or will be closed to providing products and services crucial to environmental concerns: the Brampton area CAW locals have been leading the fight to build a "Green Work" alliance to mobilize such initiatives.

Since none of these strategies could be introduced solely by the union — they involved lobbying governments and negotiating with management —

[The difference in the sectoral approach to jobs is that it] rejects the competitive game in favour of taking advantage of the levers we have as a relatively rich society — our resource base, our individual (consumer) and collective (government) purchasing power. Such approaches move us away from concessions towards democratically set rules and regulations on corporate behaviour. They shift the focus from individual companies to the structure of overall sectors ... [and] from how to strengthen companies (who have no commitment to stay) to strengthening the productive capacity of our communities.

— 1993 CAW Bargaining Conference

the union would have to analyze these sectors, develop credible policies, fight for them through lobbies or on sectoral committees consisting of both labour and management, and above all mobilize public support for this direction. The CAW therefore hired an economist to prepare a series of sectoral profiles that could be developed by local leaders and activists working, with the staff and research department, through newly created sectoral councils.

This course of action would not automatically or immediately solve the complex problem of jobs and job insecurity. But, by expanding the scope of industrial unionism and sectoral bargaining to include sectoral job strategies, the union was creating resources and structures that would educate and train its activists, while establishing an agenda that could be fought for. The union was working towards providing that crucial sense of direction.

Diversification: A Union Not a Federation

Diversification has been crucial not only to avoid the decline of the union, but also to growth. Diversification also brought to the union the relative stability of support from more than one sector, and the energy and momentum of the new sectors. A potential problem arose as to whether, in the spirit of solidarity, the CAW was diversifying without focus, overextending its capacities, and merging with units to which it had little to offer. The union held internal debates over this issue, and while it reached no consensus, it seemed to be heading towards a balanced resolution.

The more fundamental issue focused on whether the union's goal of establishing itself in a number of specific, though different sectors, was lead-

ing towards the union becoming essentially a labour central of various unions operating in their own sectors with little control, cohesion, or solidarity. The *last* thing the CAW wanted was to become such a federation.

Workers discussing issues at CAW education camp in Port Elgin.
Courtesy of the CAW Collection.

Industrial unionism had emphasized bringing all workers in a sector under one umbrella and isolating one company to win an industry pattern. As the CAW diversified, it tried to spread that basic orientation to key sectors outside of industry such as the private service sector. The key to preventing the union from becoming a federation of relatively autonomous sections was affirming the collective bargaining role of the union's central office. The union's strong service departments — especially the pension and benefits department — played a vital role in this regard. But the union couldn't retain that focus without the involvement of the political leadership of the union. This reinforced the president's direct involvement in major negotiating rounds.

This heavy dependence on the president was not, however, sustainable in the long term: the demands on the union were simply becoming too heavy and complex. Others in top leadership positions would have to develop the confidence and authority to take over more of those duties. Furthermore, while the national office's bargaining role would establish its authority, developing a strong sense of unity throughout the organization would have to include broader steps, such as building a common overall ideology and greater interaction at the base between formerly different groups.

To some extent, the need to develop a common ideology was alleviated by the fact that the diversification in the union wasn't random; in general, the groups that joined the CAW came because they understood and supported CAW positions, and its direction. Nevertheless, the CAW was itself searching for an effective ideology for the times.

The issue of the base was addressed by emphasizing the need to keep moving smaller units into amalgamated locals in each community. This flow would assemble diverse groups within one structure, giving each group greater collective capacity. Amalgamation would also create and develop workers' common experiences in spite of the range of their different sectors and histories. Units in a particular local who shared interests with units in other communities could cooperate through national councils — as GM workers, for example, now do.

With such strategies, the hazard of over-diversifying could be overcome. Diversification could therefore strengthen the union and spread, rather than undermine, the basic strengths of industrial unionism.

From Social Unionism to Movement Unionism

The UAW (and then the CAW) always rejected business unionism — a unionism that limited itself to the price its members got for their labour. In contrast, the union espoused social unionism — a unionism that considered workers as more than just sellers of labour, that was sensitive to broader concerns, and that contributed to those in need in the community and internationally. This philosophy was reflected in a wide range of activities at the local level that ranged from sports and music camps for kids to shelters for battered women, health clinics, and child care established for union members but open to the general public. A particularly ambitious and successful program involved the development of co-op housing, which started in Windsor, but spread to UAW-CAW communities across the country.

Demonstration of men supporting end to violence against women and children, 1992. Bob White is in the centre and on his right is Frank McAnally, president of the CAW council. Photo by Rod Dennis.

A more powerful version of social unionism, which could more appropriately be called movement unionism, existed in the early days of the union. The distinction is not one of degree or commitment but of orientation. In the early days, when workers were struggling to form their organization, the community wasn't so much the needy recipient of union support as it was a necessary resource for the union in surviving and winning broader battles. The union needed the community. And the union's activities extended beyond a particular progressive position; they were directed at mobilizing and building. That mobilization was, in the minds of many activists, more than a matter of achieving certain reforms; it included the hope of more profound change in the nature of society with the workers themselves playing the leading role. "Talkin' union" was then also "talkin' movement."

The threats to social influence facing today's unions can only be overcome by drawing on that earlier experience of movement unionism, when workers surmounted even greater odds to build the union. Learning from that experience would mean, as Panitch and Swartz write, "opening the way for unions to become, as far as possible, centres of working class life and culture." It means making the union into a vehicle through which its members can not only address their bargaining demands but actively lead the fight for everything that affects working people in their communities and the country. Movement unionism includes the shape of bargaining demands, the scope of union activities, the approach to issues of change, and above all, that sense of commitment to a larger movement that might suffer defeats, but can't be destroyed.

The union has only recently begun discussing the issue in these terms, but concrete initiatives have emerged at various levels. In bargaining, the emphasis on reduced work-time was directly linked to creating job openings for others in the community. The union has been exploring the establishment of local committees, which could include spouses and teenagers, to address the experiences of working class kids in the school system. In April, 1995, a CAW conference in Windsor for young people interested in the environment led to the students' establishment of local environmental committes in their schools. In addition, over 5,000 students have completed the PEL program; these graduates have a background in movement unionism and offer immense potential for activism as the union expands its local activities.

Most recently, in response to the February, 1995, Liberal budget, which marked a fundamental turning point in all of Canada's social programs, the

CAW posters.

union set up locally based Action Groups. The initial purpose was to establish permanent structures to facilitate the distribution of information and analysis in the workplace, thereby strengthening the union's ties to its members. That base, linking CAW activists and locals in the area, could then be expanded into a wider community challenge to the power of Canadian and international financiers to undermine meaningful democracy in our society.

> It doesn't bother anyone very
> much that politics be democratic
> so long as the economy is not.
>
> — Eduardo Galeano

There is a parallel between social unionism and the trade union's past approach to politics. Social unionism emphasized the importance of electoral politics but the politics that emerged was in reality contracted out. Unions contributed bodies and money while party professionals determined the direction and strategy. The trade union movement needs electoral politics, but the cynicism of union members is not unfounded. Relative to the enormous task at hand — challenging corporate power — the politics being offered is meek and narrow. The strength of the CCF/NDP, when it was first formed, lay in the excitement it created as a movement (linked, not by accident, to labour as a movement). Electoral politics will only move people again if it is part of a broader notion of politics; if, as a document prepared for the UAW's 1994 convention stated:

> ... [it goes] beyond being just an electoral machine and becomes an integral part of a movement-building agenda that extends into every workplace and community... that takes on the competitive agenda and that agenda's narrow focus on what society is about ... and works towards developing ... the ideological perspective and alternative vision that can move and unite people ...

Democracy and Change

These building blocks of change in the union — strengthening the workplace presence of the union, creating structures that address workers' influence on the issue of jobs, managing the union's diversification, developing movement unionism — provide the foundation for a democratic union.

They will help to build a union that is stubbornly independent and oppositional to the status quo while also being creative, inclusive, and open to self-
examination.

Trade unionism and democracy share a special relationship — one that is
often glossed over. Unions are democratic at the core, in the sense that their
existence challenges the uni-
lateral and undemocratic
power that corporations
wield in the workplace. And
once established, unions are
a force for countering the
power of private business in
society as a whole. Imagine,
for example, the limited
debate there would have
been over the crucial issues of free trade and cutbacks in social services
without the oppositional base of unions.

> It is the search for fundamental human
> freedom and the extension of certain types of
> social solidarity within and beyond the
> marketplace that have rendered [unions] the
> vehicle for social change.
>
> — Gregor Murray

The goals of unions are rooted in democracy. But those goals aren't
achievable unless the internal life of the union is itself democratic enough
to mobilize its only resource: the will and collective actions of its members.
Unions are voluntary organizations. Workers vote to join a union, and the
ability of the trade union leadership to force workers to follow the line is
limited. That leadership can't fire or discipline workers; on the contrary, it
needs their consent and active support. So while leadership is always important, it draws its strength from workers' feeling that the union is truly theirs:
that is, that the union reflects and fights for their needs.

In good times, this active involvement of the members might seem less
obvious. Workers might view their union as an insurance agent to whom
they pay a premium in exchange for certain benefits. A comfortable union
bureaucracy could make deals with companies that apathetic workers
accept. But good times are never permanent and in bad times, when the
corporations tear up old deals, a union with such a limited vision of itself
would be incapable of mounting an effective response.

Three particular issues form the core of the CAW's internal democracy.
First, all members are equal. Second, the union places a high priority on
increasing the number and furthering the development of the activists who
take the responsibility of running the union's daily operations. Third, the
union must balance the internal democratic process with effectiveness in

271

Dennis McDermott, member of Joint Labour Committee to Combat Racial Intolerance in front of committee display c. 1950. Courtesy of Kalmen Kaplansky and National Archives, PA-139582.

democratizing corporate power in the workplace and in society.

No member should face discriminatory barriers to participation; the union must, as industrial unionism emphasized from its earliest days, be inclusive. Removing such barriers is a matter of addressing a fundamental union right, drawing on the potential talent and commitment of the membership and demonstrating to minority workers that the union welcomes them. In this regard, it is significant that, in his first address as CAW president, Hargrove chose to focus on fighting the issue of racism and sexism not just outside the union, but within it as well.

Nine of the twenty-one staff members hired since the 1992 convention were women and/or workers of colour; this initiative was part of the union's attempt to correct for obvious underrepresentation on staff. While the proportion of women and people of colour amongst the union membership had risen dramatically (as was particularly evident to those who watched the

CAW demonstrators marching up Parliament Hill in the 1993 CLC demonstration for jobs), they were not yet represented in the leadership face of the union. Programs were therefore established to develop the confidence and skills of this group and remove participation barriers. Child care has become stan-

There is no issue more pressing for our union than the recognition and rights of visible minorities, and the problems of racism and sexism in our communities, in our workplaces and in our local unions and national union.

— Buzz Hargrove, CAW Special Convention, 27 June 1992

dard at all CAW functions. When the Big Three negotiations in 1993 left a healthy strike fund, the executive board voted to divert a portion of future strike fund contributions to a unionwide educational program on human rights. That program would start with the education of local leadership, stewards, and other activists.

The regional nature of Canada, and now the union, has added another dimension to the issue of equal access. Sensitivity to regional concerns is fundamental, yet the union doesn't want to risk regional fragmentation. For example, at 600 delegates, the Canadian Council was becoming so diverse and large that some leaders suggested breaking it up into regional councils. But this idea was overwhelmingly rejected by delegates both within and outside Ontario. Delegates reaffirmed the importance of maintaining the Canadian Council and keeping it in Port Elgin. They supported the expansion of the education centre in Port Elgin so it could accommodate the expanded council, continuing transportation subsidies to representatives from distant locals, and supplementing the council with other structures and measures. (the expansion in Port Elgin has, however, been postponed until the union's financial situation improves).

The supplementary steps included establishing regional conferences (e.g., there is now an annual western regional conference); decentralizing certain educational programs (e.g., basic courses such as Workers' Compensation Benefits (WCB), which depend on provincial legislation); and extending the sectoral councils. In most cases, the sectoral councils actually united the union around nationwide, as opposed to regional, concerns (e.g., the aerospace council brings together workers from Halifax, Montreal, Toronto, and Winnipeg). In other cases, the structure of the union and the nature of the membership meant that the new councils were essentially regional (e.g., the hospital council in Nova Scotia).

While equality of access to participation is a principle and a goal, the degree of actual participation in the union varies widely. Only a relatively small minority of workers can be called activists; i.e., workers involved in the daily decisions and administration of the union. This dependence on a relatively small cadre was true even in the early days of the union. The expansion of union democracy necessitates increasing the number of such activists, developing their commitment and capabilities, and reinforcing their role as essentially "organizers of the organized" — that is, as building the membership and introducing more workers to union life.

The strengthening of the activist base and the expansion of the number

Participation of Former Members

The union has also tried to extend the principle of participation to include laid-off members and retirees. The success in keeping permanently laid-off members involved has been very limited and isolated to a few locals (e.g., McDonnell-Douglas). The link to the union's retirees has been much more successful.

One reason for the success with retirees is that, in major agreements, the union continues to negotiate pension improvements over and above indexing (some unions bargain special lump sum improvements but very few negotiate additions to the basic pension benefit). The second element of the successful mobilizing of retirees is that they remain structurally linked to the union by way of their participation in elections for local officers and convention delegates (they cannot, however, vote for in-plant representations or on tentative agreements). The retirees are therefore an important political force in some locals. Furthermore, the national office of the union provides them with staff assistance in organizing themselves into effective local chapters with their own dues provisions.

These retirees now number close to 25,000. Given their experience, organizing skills, time, and access to some resources, the retirees have made an important contribution to community and national campaigns around issues such as medicare and public pensions, and individual retirees have also moved into leadership positions of other national organizations of retirees. Since the peak hiring in auto was in the mid- to late sixties, the ranks of the retirees will grow significantly over the next decade, increasing their potential role.

of potential activists — workers with a growing interest in the union — would result in more effective checks and balances to the power of both the local and top leadership of the union. (Bureaucratization can occur at both

Buzz Hargrove in discussion with workers. Courtesy of the CAW collection.

levels.) These two goals are also vital simply because the number of demands on the existing activists is disproportionately high. Building that cadre of activists and activists-to-be is achieved by expanding educational opportunities, by establishing the widest range of forums and conferences, and, above all, by maintaining the union's constant involvement in campaigns and struggles. Activism creates activists.

For the CAW in the nineties, additional activists were coming from the PEL program and the leadership schools for women and people of colour, from the new unions that had merged with the CAW, and from the attempts to launch a broader attack against the financial institutions that had, essentially, taken control over Canada's social programs and services.

Democracy is about process but also about results. Democratic procedures won't carry much weight if they are ineffective in the achievement of goals. For unions, that effectiveness is shaped by the power and resources of the companies and state institutions that workers confront. The union must

Democracy and Consensus

Some union decisions are made through direct democracy, such as a vote to strike and the ratification or rejection of a collective agreement. Many others are delegated to elected representatives. At CAW constitutional conventions, the highest decision-making body of the union, decisions are formally made by the votes of the delegates. But controversial votes at this level (and at the bargaining convention) have been rare because of the attempt to establish some consensus on potentially divisive issues before the convention.

This only works, in democratic terms, because of the depth of other union structures that can debate the issues on the way to a consensus. Controversial issues can, for example, be raised — without resolution but only to get a sense of where people are — at regular meetings of the Canadian Council or through regional and sectoral conferences. In addition, preparatory meetings are held before the convention to discuss policy papers and resolutions and the local delegates and staff brought in for such meetings are chosen to ensure representation from all sections of the union. (Such meetings now include some eighty people of which about one-third are staff.)

Though the number of speakers from the floor is high at the convention and criticism is not unusual, conventions have involved less of a fight over policy and direction than an endorsement of those preconvention decisions, and a cultural event. As a cultural event, the convention celebrates the struggles and achievements of the union, establishes contacts, builds unity, and motivates participants to continue the fight.

Democracy is not supplied by a constitution. Nor can it be reduced to a mechanism for keeping leaders in line (as relevant as that need is). Union democracy is primarily about workers making changes: changing themselves, changing their immediate world, and laying the basis for eventually changing the larger world. Union democracy is built by workers in their struggles to build the union, which acts as their line of defence and base for progress. Democracy is therefore not separate from struggles, nor is it static; it must constantly be redefined, recreated, and reinvented.

therefore be sufficiently centralized to balance the centralized power of the other side, yet decentralized enough to permit local initiative and mobilization. The risk is that centralization will reach an overwhelming level and that the union will consequently become bureaucratized.

In the earlier years of the union, the existence of an organized left was one check on over-centralization. It brought particular activists together around specific issues and demands and challenged the top leadership of the union. This raised the level of debate throughout the union and often pushed the CAW in more militant directions. The left-right conflict at times degenerated into destructive factional fights; however, at least in Canada, the survival of that left opposition into the seventies strengthened the union. Its absence places an even greater responsibility on the activists in the union and on the role of the union's democratic structures.

From the Past to the Future: It Depends

During the twenties, when unions were floundering and corporate power and social inequality were growing — a time with some parallels to today — few would have predicted the explosion of industrial unionism. When the depression first hit and unemployment climbed, the prospects for a union breakthrough seemed to slip even further. Yet the persistence of the few and the growing anger of the many lead to a movement of protest and reform, out of which industrial unionism grew and spread its roots.

The UAW emerged in the United States during the "worst of times." Its spread to Canada wasn't based on formal or institutional internationalism, but on the powerful example of internation-al action. American workers held sit-downs, and Canadians were inspired by the new possibilities of unionism. But even with this

> So thanks old friend for the songs and the stories
> Of all that we've been and all we might be
> And the next time the going gets tough
> I'll remember you stood here long before me
>
> — Tom Juravich, "A World to Win"

exciting breakthrough, union membership dwindled as the economy began to decline again and corporate intimidation increased. Unions remained fragile until the relative shortage of labour during the war and the stability and prosperity of the postwar years provided a chance for working people to consolidate and make steady material gains.

Ironically, the "best of times" included the seeds of the problems that would eventually undermine the American union. The weakening of the locals and the destruction of the left opposition removed both safeguards against union bureaucratization and a source of future dynamism. In the sixties, the resulting American union couldn't tap into the energy of the new movements. By the end of the seventies, the American UAW had lost the confidence and spirit to fight concessions.

The Canadians were "the same but different." They faced a different economic and political context as they moved hesitantly towards the American model, and they didn't get to the full basics of that model until the end of the fifties. By then the sixties were near and, unlike the Americans, the Canadians had retained a legacy that could be rejuvenated to become a part of the social rebellion. When the corporations demanded concessions in the late seventies and into the eighties, the Canadian UAW resisted.

The differences that had emerged between the American and Canadian UAW were rooted in a combination of factors: economically, in the delayed growth of Canada's manufacturing base; politically, in the later development in Canada of supportive labour legislation and the consequent longer struggle for union recognition; internally, in the persistence of a strong left based in strong locals; structurally, in the uniqueness of the Canadian Council; and culturally, in the differing role of nationalism in the two countries. American nationalism was the nationalism of the dominant power in the world, and it tended to tie the union to establishment goals. Canadian nationalism, particularly in the later years, was a response to that American domination. It was an expression of opposition to American-based companies and a rejection of the American vision of the good life.

In the early seventies, the capitalist economies adopted a radical shift in direction, particularly in North America. The postwar period of steady growth was over, and a transition began towards lowering the expectations of workers while strengthening the flexibility and power of corporations. The conflict over the best response to the new situation faced by workers, particularly in bargaining, led to the split of the Canadian union from its parent organization. The split was not easy. Like other national institutions, the Canadian section had long been dependent on the Americans for leadership and support. But the move to independence was tied to a new confidence and maturity; once the Canadians were on their own, they soared. Although the economic and political environment was increasingly hostile and many of the fights were defensive, the CAW experienced the most exciting and exhilarating period in its history.

Yet that culture of resistance could not, without other changes, continue indefinitely. Workplace closures, high unemployment, hostile governments that attacked established social programs, friendly governments that caused bitter disappointments, and divisions between unions searching for new directions took their toll. Mergers with other unions and an impressive degree of organizing gave the CAW some much-needed momentum, but by the early nineties, the crisis that was demoralizing and affecting the left internationally was also highlighting the vulnerability of the CAW.

The split that had given birth to the CAW, and unified the membership and leadership around building the new union, was also the source of new divisions within Canadian labour. The example and profile of the CAW challenged the direction of other private sector unions, and left many of their leaders uncomfortable. Bob White had, even before the split, raised the issue of uniting autoworkers, steelworkers, electrical workers into a Canadian Metalworkers Federation. But the timing was wrong: relationships were to grow worse, and besides, other Canadian unions would have to wait for their American parents to act first.

These divisions over the role of unions in the context of the new corporate aggressiveness also played themselves out in the relationship with the NDP. It was hardly surprising that, having severed its historical ties with its own union over the issue of concessions, the CAW would have trouble living with a social democratic government that used the power of the state to break collective agreements and enforce concessions on public sector workers.

These divisions were not just external. The issue of the relationship with the NDP also created internal tensions; relations between some of the staff and the national office remained somewhat strained after the staff strike; and more open disagreements surfaced within the union over social issues such as employment equity and gun control. But the one issue around which the union remained united, and which continued to be the key to building the union, was the issue that created the CAW in 1985: the determination to resist concessions and to maintain the independence of the union as a voice and structure through which to defend working people.

Like other unions, today's CAW faces the most threatening attacks in its history. The Canadian labour movement has maintained itself better than most movements around the world, but as the status of the American labour movement and especially of the UAW reveals, there is no basis for assuming the continued success of even the strongest unions. And for the CAW, as President Buzz Hargrove has emphasized, the issue is not only whether the union can survive, but also whether it can continue to play a crucial leadership role within Canadian labour and Canadian society.

STATEMENT OF PRINCIPLES

WORKING PEOPLE NEED UNIONS

We formed our union because we could not depend on employers to provide us with dignity, a measure of security, and a rising standard of living. And, over the years, we did make impressive gains. But our objectives remain far from fulfilled, and, with even our past gains under attack, WE NEED UNIONS TODAY AS MUCH AS WE EVER DID.

DEMOCRATIC UNIONISM

Unions are voluntary organizations. We can only be effective if the membership knows the union truly belongs to them. This means a union which reflects the goals of its membership, allows the members full participation, and encourages workers to develop their own skills and understanding.

Internal democracy also means we view each other as EQUALS. Racial discrimination or sexual harassment violate our principles, undermine our solidarity and erode our strength. We not only oppose such responses but will actively work to overcome them.

UNIONS AND A DEMOCRATIC SOCIETY

In our society, private corporations control the workplace and set the framework for all employees. By way of this economic power, they influence the laws, policies, and ideas of society. Unions are central to our society being democratic because:

Unions bring a measure of democracy to the place of work,
which is so central to people's lives.

Unions act as a partial counterweight to corporate power and
the corporate agenda in society more generally.

SOCIAL UNIONISM

Our collective bargaining strength is based on our internal organization and mobilization, but it is also influenced by the more general climate around us: laws, policies, the economy, and social attitudes. Furthermore, our lives extend beyond collective bargaining and the workplace and we must concern ourselves with issues like housing, taxation, education, medical services, the environment, the international economy.

Social unionism means unionism which is rooted in the workplace but understands the IMPORTANCE OF PARTICIPATING IN, AND INFLUENCING, THE GENERAL DIRECTION OF SOCIETY.

BUILDING TOMORROW

Unions were born out of struggles to change the status quo. Our successes extended progress beyond unions themselves, and our struggles became part of a SOCIAL MOVEMENT for a more humane society here and for peace and justice internationally. These struggles were first steps towards developing the confidence that change is possible and that our vision of society is NOT JUST A DREAM.

*We are proud of the leadership role we have played, aware of the
difficulties continued progressive change will face, and committed
to building the social solidarity that can take on this challenge.*

National Automobile, Aerospace and Agricultural Implement Workers Union of Canada, (CAW-Canada)

At the same time, the CAW is on the verge of a generational change. The UAW emerged out of a generation living through the Great Depression and the war. In the sixties, a new generation flooded the auto plants and produced today's leadership and activists in the traditional CAW sectors. It must now prepare to pass the union on to the next generation — one that has not experienced postwar prosperity but instead grew up in an age of permanent insecurity that weakened the will to protest and the drive to reform.

We can hope that members of the next generation will simply say "We won't take it anymore"; that they are fed up with an economic system that produces so much more with so much less, yet constantly degrades their lives. We can hope that they will look around at the growing polarization of wealth and power, and at the international financiers that now determine the availability of jobs and what we can and cannot do, and ask: "What happened to democracy?" We can hope that they will reject the continual demand that Canadians must be more productive when their own skills and the skills of their friends are unused and unwanted. And we can hope that this generation demands "a common sense that makes sense."

But that next generation, like our generation, will rely on what the previous generation built and left, what it has passed on. That previous generation, in this case, is us; the issue becomes what *we* will now leave behind.

The labour movement and the CAW today face one of those historical moments when the only answer to questions about the future is: "It depends." People and their organizations make their own history. They don't, of course, make history without constraints, nor do they make it from scratch. The CAW confronts this challenge with an impressive cadre of activists, staff, and leadership. It is rich with opportunities for participation and equipped to accommodate the ongoing development of the union. It has a legacy going back to the thirties that was renewed with great excitement a short decade ago when the CAW was born. That legacy tells the inspiring story of working people's efforts to constantly stretch the limits they faced, expand their options, learn from defeats, and build on successes.

In the nineties, the challenge is to translate all the uncertainties into a wide-ranging debate in the CAW to develop the self-confidence that asks not if the union can do it, but how. And the development of that confidence will rest, above all, on the commitment of activists, staff, and leadership at all levels to take the individual and collective responsibility for building the capacities, and leading the struggles, that will shape the future.

Suggested Readings

What follows are some of the books and articles that I either found particularly useful or think would be of interest to anyone wanting to dig further.

A. Canadian Labour History, General

Craig Heron, *The Canadian Labour Movement: A Short History* (Toronto: James Lorimer & Co., 1989)

Bryan D. Palmer, *Working-Class Experience: The Rise and Reconstitution of Canadian Labour, 1800–1980* (Toronto: Butterworths & Co., 1992)

Stuart Jamieson, *Industrial Relations in Canada* (Toronto: Macmillan Canada, 1973)

Leo Panitch and Donald Swartz, *The Assault on Trade Union Freedoms: From Wage Controls to Social Contract* (Toronto: Garamond Press, 1993)

Craig Heron's book provides an excellent and very readable overview of Canadian labour history. Palmer's path-breaking book, which challenges conventional approaches to history, is more difficult to work through. It emphasizes the daily life of working people as opposed to the more common emphasis on their unions and is particularly thorough on skilled workers in the last half of the 1800s. Jamieson's short book seems to focus on the institutions of bargaining and legislation but is in fact much richer. The Panitch-Swartz book analyzes the specific conditions that led to past gains for Canadian labour and the limits of those gains as conditions changed. It is especially strong in its analysis and discussion of labour's relationship to the state and the NDP.

B. American Labour History, General

Kim Moody, *An Injury to All: The Decline of American Unionism* (London: Verso, 1988)

Mike Davis, *Prisoners of the American Dream: Politics and Economy in the History of the US Working Class* (London: Verso, 1986)

Moody's book attempts to shed light on how the American labour movement declined into business unionism — a question certainly relevant to the Canadian labour movement in its present vulnerable phase. Davis also addresses the failure of American labour and the left to put forth an alternative politics. His book is more theoretical and though brilliant, is a relatively difficult read for those less familiar with left debates.

C. UAW Canada, General

Charlotte Yates, *From Plant to Politics: The Autoworkers Union in Postwar Canada* (Philadelphia: Temple University Press, 1993)

Pamela Sugiman, *Labour's Dilemma: The Gender Politics of Auto Workers in Canada, 1937–1979* (Toronto: University of Toronto Press, 1994)

Bob White, *Hard Bargains: My Life on the Line* (Toronto: McClelland & Stewart, 1987)

Education committees of the CSN and CEQ, *The History of the Labour Movement in Quebec* (Montreal: Black Rose Books, 1987)

Dan Benedict: *forthcoming history of the CAW*

Yates' book addresses the interaction of internal conflicts and external politics that shaped the Canadian autoworkers in the postwar period. In fact, it ranges far beyond the union's definition of politics and political mobilization, and is an important contribution to the history of the CAW. Sugiman's book is a history of women workers within the Canadian autoworkers. It tries to come to grips with the contradictions and dilemmas faced by women fighting for equality within a progressive, but male-dominated, union. White's book is the personal and inside account of the life of a leader who was so central to the union, with a special focus on the period leading to the formation of the CAW. The history of Quebec places workers' struggles and politics in a broad historical and social context. It was written for worker activists and is available in both French and English. Benedict's avidly awaited comprehensive history of the CAW should be out shortly.

D. UAW U.S., General

Michael Goldfield, "Worker Insurgency, Radical Organization, and New Deal Labor Organization," *American Political Science Review*, December, 1989

Sidney Fine, *Sitdown, the General Motors Strike of 1936–37* (Ann Arbor: University of Michigan Press, 1969)

Victor Reuther, *The Brothers Reuther and the Story of the UAW* (Boston: Houghton Mifflin Company, 1976)

Nelson Lichtenstein: *forthcoming biography of Walter Reuther*

Goldfield's article describes the radical social climate in the early thirties, out of which the CIO later arose. Fine's is the classic book on the famous sit-down strikes, scholarly in its analysis and details. Reuther's book is an inside account of the UAW and the family that played such a prominent role in its development. Unfortunately it was written in 1976, before Reuther broke with the UAW adminstration, so it does not include that story. There have been dozens of biographies of Walter Reuther, but the forthcoming one by Lichtenstein, who has done some of the most interesting research on the role of the UAW in the workplace, should be especially interesting.

E. Specific Periods and Local Histories, UAW Canada

Autoworkers before the breakthroughs in 1936 and 1937

John Manley, "Communists and Autoworkers: The struggle for Industrial Unionism in the Canadian Automobile Industry," 1925–36, in *Labour/Le Travail*, Spring, 1986

The breakthrough in Oshawa in 1937

Irving Abella, "Oshawa 1937," in Irving Abella (ed.), *On Strike* (Toronto: James Lorimer & Company, 1975)

Factionalism in the late thirties

Dan Benedict, "Good-Bye to Homer Martin," in *Labour/Le Travail*, 1992.

The Ford Blockade of 1945 that won the Rand Formula

David Moulton, "Ford Windsor 1945," in Irving Abella (ed.), *On Strike* (Toronto: James Lorimer & Company, 1975)

Mary E. Baruth-Walsh and G. Mark Walsh, *Strike! 99 Days on the Line*, (Penumbra Press, 1995)

The cold war within Canadian labour

Irving Abella, *Nationalism, Communism, and Canadian Labour: The CIO, the Communist Party, and the Canadian Congress of Labour, 1935–1956* (Toronto: University of Toronto Press, 1973)

The split from the UAW

John Holmes and A. Rusonik, *The Break-up of an International Labour Union: Uneven Development in the North American Auto Industry and the Schism in the UAW* (Industrial Relations Centre, Queen's University, 1990)

Sam Gindin, "Breaking Away: The Formation of the Canadian Auto Workers" in *Studies in Political Economy*, Summer, 1989

Specific local histories

David Fraser, *Years of Struggle: A History of Local 200 of the UAW at Ford of Canada, Windsor Ontario, 1941–55* (Thesis, University of Western Ontario, 1982)

Michel Pratt, *La Greve de la United Aircraft* (Quebec: Les Presses de l'Universite du Québec, 1980)

Elizabeth Kelly, *Our Expectations, a History of Brantford's Labour Movement* (CAW Local 397, Brantford, 1987)

Stephen Herzenberg, *Towards a Cooperative Commonwealth? Labour and Restructuring in the U.S. and Canadian Auto Industries*, unpublished PhD. dissertation, Department of Economics, Massachusetts Institute of Technology, May 1991. [Case study of Budd Automotive]

David Sobel and the CAW Local 303 Heritage Committee, *You Can't Bring Back Yesterday, A History of CAW Local 303* (CAW Local 303, 1993)

[Histories of Chrysler Local 444 in Windsor and Airline Local 2213 are forthcoming]

F. Introduction to the New Sections in the CAW

Julie Guard, *The "Woman Question" in Canadian Unionism: Women in the UE, 1930s to 1960s* (unpublished PhD. dissertation, Department of Education, University of Toronto, 1994)

Gordon Inglis, *More Than Just a Union, The Story of the NFFAWU* (St John's: Jesperson Press, 1985)

John B. Lang, *A Lion in a Den of Daniels: A History of the International Union of Mine Mill and Smelter Workers in Sudbury, Ontario 1942–1962* (MA Thesis, University of Guelph, 1970)

Mike Smolski and John Smaller, *The History of the International Union of Mine, Mill, and Smelter Workers in Canada* (Ottawa: Steel Rail Publishing, 1985)

Don Taylor, *All For the Cause: An Illustrated History of the CBRT & GW* (Ottawa: Mutual Press, 1989)

Patricia G. Atherton, *CAIMAW: Portrait of a Canadian Union* (MSc. Thesis, UBC, 1981).

James L. Turk, "Surviving the Cold War: A Study of the United Electrical Workers in Canada," in *Canadian Oral History Association Journal*, Volume 4, Number 2, 1980.

G. Selected List of Locals that Have Printed Historical Overviews in Magazine or Pamphlet Form to Commemorate Their Anniversaries

CAW-Canada Local 27, 40th Anniversary: *Local 27 CAW London 1950–1990* (London: CAW Local 27, 1990)

CAW-Canada Local 89, *Local 89 50th Anniversary: 1942–1992* (Amherstburg: CAW Local 89, 1992)

CAW-Canada Local 112, 50th Anniversary: *CAW Local 112* (Downsview, Ontario: CAW Local 112, 1992)

CAW-Canada Local 112 Women's Committee, Lynne Salmon and Sherry Hillman, *The Women of CAW Local 112: Past to Present — History* (Downsview: CAW Local 112, 1993)

CAW-Canada Local 195, 50th Anniversary: *Canadian CAW Local 195 Windsor 1936–1986*, (Windsor: CAW Local 95, 1986)

CAW-Canada Local 199, *CAW Canada Local 199 50th Anniversary: 50 Years of Service to our Members and the Community, December 13, 1986*, (St. Catharines: CAW-Canada Local 199, 1986)

CAW-Canada Local 1524, *25th Anniversary 1993: CAW-Canada Local 1524 Kitchener*, (Kitchener: CAW Local 1524, 1993)

CAW Local 1967, *Local 1967 CAW: 25th Anniversary*, (Toronto: CAW Local 1967, 1992)

UAW Local 28 and W. Devine, *The First Thirty Years: A History of UAW Amalgamated Local 28 1947–1977* (Toronto, UAW Local 28, 1977)

UAW Local 195, *UAW Local 195 Windsor Anniversary: 30 Years of Progress 1936–1966*, (Windsor, UAW Local 195, 1966)

UAW Local 222, *Forty years of Progress: UAW Local 222 Oshawa*, (Oshawa: UAW Local 222, 1977)

UAW Local 240, *Local 240 TOP UAW: 40th Anniversary 1942–1983*, (Windsor: UAW Local 240, 1982)

UAW Local 1520 and Marilyn E. Wilkinson, *UAW Local 1520: A History of the UAW at the St. Thomas Assembly Plant 1968–1984* (St. Thomas: UAW Local 1520, 1984)

Permissions

Every effort has been made to trace the copyright ownership of all documents and illustrations reprinted or reproduced in this book. We regret any errors and will be pleased to make any necessary corrections in future editions.

Grateful acknowledgement is made to the following people or organizations

LEONARD COHEN, "Everybody Knows."
RON DICKSON, "All that shines in the dark is not necessarily charitable" "Making parts," and "Ratification." Reprinted by permission of Ron Dickson.

REDD EVANS & JOHN JACOB LOEB, "Rosie the Riveter." © 1942 by Paramount Music Corporation. Copyright renewed in 1969 and assigned to Paramount Music Corporation. All rights reserved. Reprinted by permission of Paramount Music Corporation.

JOE GLAZER, "Too Old to Work." © Reprinted by permission of Joe Glazer.

INDUSTRIAL WORKERS OF THE WORLD, "Auto-Workers: Join the One Big Union." Reproduced by the permission of the Archives of Labor and Urban affairs, Wayne State University.

TOM JURAVICH, "A World to Win." Reprinted by permission of Tom Juravich.

CARL SANDBURG, "I am the People, the Mob." in Chicago Poems by Carl Sandburg, copyright 1916 by permission of Holt, Rinehart and Winston, Inc and renewed 1944 by Carl Sandburg, reprinted by permission of Harcourt Brace & Company.

FRANK SCOTT, "Social Notes." From The Collected Poems of F.R. Scott by F.R. Scott. Used by permission of the Canadian Publishers, McClelland & Stewart, Toronto. Reprinted by permission of McClelland & Stewart, Toronto.

MAURICE SUGAR, "Sit Down."